The ANIME Companion

WHAT'S
JAPANESE
IN
JAPANESE
ANIMATION?

The ANIME Companion

GILLES POITRAS

Stone Bridge Press • *Berkeley, California*

PUBLISHED BY

Stone Bridge Press, P. O. Box 8208, Berkeley, CA 94707

tel 510-524-8732 • sbp@stonebridge.com • www.stonebridge.com

Text © 1999 Gilles Poitras.

Line drawings by L.K. Grant, Kokoro Grafix.

Cover art and "Companion" face designs by Lea Hernandez.
© 1999 Lea Hernandez.

Cover design, icons, and text layout by L.J.C. Shimoda.

Credits and copyright notices for animation images used in this book
accompany their respective images throughout the text.

Printed in the United States of America.

10   9   8   7   6   5   4   3   2   1
2005 2004 2003 2002 2001 2000 1999

LIBRARY OF CONGRESS CATALOGING-IN-PUBLICATION DATA
Poitras, Gilles.
    The anime companion: what's Japanese in Japanese animation? / Gilles
Poitras.
    p. cm.
    Includes bibliographical references.
    ISBN 1-880656-32-9
    1. Animated films—Japan—Themes, motives. I. Title.
    NC1766.J3 P65 1998
    791.43'3—ddc21
                                                          98-44487
                                                             CIP

CONTENTS

THIS AIN'T NO SPEED RACER!

Do you consider yourself, or do others consider you, an otaku?

If so this book is for you.

Are you an anime fan that has begun to wonder about the little Japanese cultural details that show up again and again in the shows you watch?

If so this book is for you.

Are you a fan of Japanese cinema?

If so this book may be for you.

Are you merely curious as to what this is all about?

If so this book may be for you.

Are you afraid of anything that is different and unusual?

If so put this book down and get a best-seller instead.

Ever since the late 19th century there have been attempts to expose the West to many aspects of Japanese culture such as theater, architecture, gardens, the tea ceremony, calligraphy, print arts, and more. These have had some success but have tended to convey a view of Japan as a refined and artistic culture—and also as rather formal and even boring. Then anime and manga made their way across the seas, and many who had tired of the higher arts, or had no interest in them anyway, discovered Japan in a different light. What was intended as popular entertainment for domestic consumption became a worldwide phenomenon. Because of anime and manga more and more non-Japanese are being exposed to a culture with which they have been only vaguely familiar, and they are starting to ask questions about what they see.

This book is an attempt to identify some of the Japanese things, people, and places you may run across while watching anime or reading manga.

I admit that this book contains certain limitations in its selections.

First, I have limited my research to only a few hundred of the ever-growing number of videos available in English translation in the United States.

Second, all anime examples I provide, with the exception of *My Neighbor Totoro*, are subtitled anime. This is because I don't like re-dubs, and because in many cases I needed to listen to the original dialogue to understand what certain items were. I hope these limitations are not a source of frustration for fans outside the U. S. who do not have access to many of these titles and that my book will still be of some use to them.

It is my desire that this book be a useful source of information about Japan for its readers. The next time someone comments on your enjoying "kids' stuff" or "those nasty cartoons," just dazzle them with a few facts about Japan and get back to enjoying yourself. But don't forget the importance of exposing others to anime and manga. As I heard a panelist at Anime America in 1995 say, "Anime is a disease and the only cure is to expose others to it so we have more people to talk to about it."

DEDICATION

This book is dedicated in thanks to Takahashi Rumiko, whose work and the anime adapted from it continue to make us laugh, wonder, and cheer her characters on, even when we feel like hitting some of them on the head for being such idiots.

After all, the real reason we are into this stuff is simply that we like it.

For those new to anime I must emphasize that anime is not to be confused with cartoons. Anime uses animation to tell stories and entertain, but it does so in ways that have barely been touched on in Western animation. While the U.S. continues to pump out cartoons with gag stories, musicals with cute animals, animated sitcoms, and testosterone-laced TV fare, the Japanese have been using anime to cover every literary and cinematic genre imaginable in a highly competitive market that encourages new story ideas and the creative reworking of older ideas and themes. My young nephews tell me they like anime because it often really has a story, one that continues to unfold with each episode, if the anime is a series, rather than just being a group of separate stories with the same characters. They also like it that villains can be understandable, complex persons and that heroes can make mistakes and show weaknesses.

Now not all anime is like this, but good stories and good characters are an important part of the anime mix; they are why there are anime fans. The audience for anime, in fact, is much broader than that for cartoons. It would be interesting to trace the evolution of anime relative to the age of its intended audiences in Japan. After all, at one time anime was for little kiddies. It has slowly evolved into the sophisticated forms we see today.

HOW TO USE THIS BOOK

This book can be used just like an encyclopedia to find Japanese cultural details in anime (and some manga). All the entries appear alphabetically. the entries are primarily in the form of the *Japanese* words most likely to be encountered in anime, since the English translations of these words in subtitled or dubbed versions are often not consistent. For convenience, a brief translation or explanation of the term in English appears next to some entries, but where the translation is complicated or unnecessary (as in the case of a place name, for example), no explanation appears.

Words in **boldface** type at first mention within an entry indicate cross-references to other entries.

After the main entries is a reverse look-up (that is, English to Japanese) list of entries for finding Japanese entries if you only know the English word or concept (many entries are cross-referenced by more than one English word).

On page 2, just before the entries begin, is a list of entries by icon categories, useful if you are interested in finding particular types of examples in anime and manga.

Romanization

The method used here for romanizing, that is, transcribing character-based Japanese words into letters of the English alphabet is based on the standard Hepburn romanization system, with the following major exception: the letter n is used before consonants b, m, and p (other English publications often use an m here instead). Macrons, or "long signs" ($\bar{o}$, $\bar{u}$, etc.), are used to indicate extended vowels on Japanese words, but the usage here is inconsistent when it comes to anime and manga titles and character names. This is because I've tried to follow the spellings used in the Japanese export versions, and the various publishers and production companies do not consistently apply macrons to the words that need them (in fact, they generally leave them out). Macrons are also not used on familiar Japanese place names (Tokyo, Osaka, Honshu, etc.) unless the names are part of an "official" Japanese name (for example, Tōkyō Daigaku, but Tokyo University). Some titles and character names, again following the practices of the export versions, appear here in nonstandard romanization, such as Ryuunosuke instead of Ryūnosuke. Personal names follow Japanese usage, that is, the family name is given first, as in "Takahashi Rumiko."

Problems with Titles

Examples from anime and manga are given at the end of each entry with as much identifying information as is needed for readers to find the original source if they are so inclined. All titles of anime and manga cited in this book are from the U.S. English-language releases; releases in other parts of the English-speaking world may in some cases be titled differently.

In all cases I have tried to use the exact title.

There are a few exceptions, such as *Patlabor*, which some tapes give as *Mobile Police Patlabor* and some as *Patlabor Mobile Police*. I have simply used *Patlabor*, which is a common way of referring to this series.

Repackaging sometimes causes titling confusion, since what originally came out on three tapes may be newly released as a single tape. I have tried to keep the title citations detailed enough so that you can know what scene appears on which tape. Episode numbers are given where possible, and OVAs (Original Video Animations) are usually referred to by title or number so that you can find the specific reference regardless of whether you have an earlier version or a rerelease. Examples of repackaged anime include the following:

> The *Tenchi Muyo!* first OVA series mostly came out as one OVA per tape originally and later as two per tape.
>
> *Gunsmith Cats* came out as three tapes subtitled and one tape redubbed.
>
> *Giant Robo* was six tapes redubbed and three subtitled.

The Case of Ranma

Probably the most confusing repackaging situation involves the *Ranma 1/2* tape titles for the early OVA and TV tapes. The redubbed versions of these had two episodes per tape, and the subtitled versions had three episodes per tape. For this reason there are some citations in this book with entries in the form of "*Ranma 1/2* (TV sub tp. 3, dub tp. 5, ep. 9)"; this means that episode 9 is on tape 3 of the subtitled release and on tape 5 of the redubbed release.

For the OVA tapes this gets even more complex in that the first two subtitled tapes contain the same material as the first three redubbed tapes.

Perhaps the following chart will make it simpler:

OVA TITLE	ON THE RE-DUBBED TAPE TITLED	ON THE SUBTITLED TAPE TITLED
Shampoo's Sudden Switch! The Curse of the Contrary Jewel	*Ranma 1/2 Desperately Seeking Shampoo*	*Ranma 1/2 Collectors Edition: The OAVs 1*
Tendo Family Christmas Scramble	*Ranma 1/2 Desperately Seeking Shampoo*	*Ranma 1/2 Collectors Edition: The OAVs 1*
Akane vs. Ranma! I'll Be The One to Inherit Mother's Recipes	*Ranma 1/2 Like Water For Ranma*	*Ranma 1/2 Collectors Edition: The OAVs 1*
Stormy Weather Comes to School! Growing up With Miss Hinako	*Ranma 1/2 Like Water For Ranma*	*Ranma 1/2 Collectors Edition: The OAVs 2*
The One to Carry On, Part 1	*Ranma 1/2 Akane and Her Sisters*	*Ranma 1/2 Collectors Edition: The OAVs 2*
The One to Carry On, Part 2	*Ranma 1/2 Akane and Her Sisters*	*Ranma 1/2 Collectors Edition: The OAVs 2*

The above chart applies only to the first six OVAs (what the company calls OAVs); subsequent OVAs had the same titles for both the redubbed and subtitled tapes.

Numbered vs. Unnumbered Tapes

Another area of confusion involves numbered and unnumbered tapes. When a citation provides a tape or episode number it means you will find that number written on the box or on an insert. Some series do not provide numbers, so in these cases the citation provides the full box title. The *Maison Ikkoku* tapes, for example, form a series, but they do not have the tape numbers written clearly on the box. It gets even more confusing with *Blue Seed,* which has the tape number on the first six boxes but not on the remaining seven boxes. Fortunately, in the case of both *Maison Ikkoku* and *Blue Seed* the product numbers are sequential and end in the tape number, so with a little bit of work you can figure out if you are holding tape 4 or 7.

Clear as mud?

This may help:

The subtitled *Maison Ikkoku: Ronin Blues* has the product number VVMIS-002, and *Maison Ikkoku: Kyoko + Soichiro* has V-MIS011, and from this it is easy to figure out which one is tape 2 and which is tape 11 in the series.

I have used a similar method when citing manga volumes. For example, because the *Ranma 1/2* manga uses volume numbers I cite those numbers in the reference, but I cite the unnumbered *Urusei Yatsura* manga by the full title of each volume.

On the whole, the tape citations I provide are intended to be as clear as possible to aid you in locating what I am referring to. If you cannot understand, the fault is mine not yours.

FOR THE LATEST ANIME COMPANION NEWS …
No book like this can be complete, and for this reason I maintain a supplement on the World Wide Web with corrections and additions to existing entries as well as new entries. The Web pages also contain notes for each of the entries in this book detailing the secondary reference sources I used to track down information on aspects of Japanese culture. The Anime Companion Web Supplement can be accessed at **http://www.sirius.com/~cowpunk/.**

Obtaining Anime and Manga

The anime and manga cited in this book are for the most part available from U.S. publishers and distributors. As licensing deals tend to change over time, it's generally impossible to keep track of which publisher or distributor is responsible for which title, and for that reason such information has not been included in this book. Searching on the Internet or asking dealers is probably the best way to find what you're looking for, and most well-stocked video stores or comic shops can order specific titles for you. You can also try ordering directly from publishers or distributors, or through one of the many mail order companies that advertise in anime magazines.

For ordering information check the web pages of the various companies on the Internet. A handy list of anime and manga companies, as well as anime publications, is available on the Anime Web Turnpike at **http://www.anipike.com/.**

ACKNOWLEDGMENTS

I would like to thank:

Fred Schodt, who for nine months hounded, I mean encouraged, me to write this book.

Janice, who put up with my spending so much time working on this.

Shon Hernandez, who continues to be an inspiration for otaku everywhere.

Ross TenEyck, Dave Pyun, and Ron Spillman for helping me track down some original words in the Japanese editions of manga.

All of my Bay Area buddies, especially:

Michael Duffy, whose title suggestion evolved into *The Anime Companion* and who said, "At last acknowledgment comes to me."

Suizi Lin, past CAA president and the first person to call me an otaku (she probably has no idea how honored I was).

All of the folks at Cal-Animage Alpha, who have for years kept this U.C. Berkeley alum exposed to new anime at their showings.

Charles Gousha, fellow BMUG member and otaku.

Hugo at Paradigm, for regularly handing me anime in exchange for green papers from my wallet.

Rory and the gang at Comic Relief and the folks at Dr. Comics and Mr. Games, for their excellent selections of manga and anime-related goods.

Movie Image, for having such a great selection of anime for me to rent from.

Sam at Brewed Awakening for fixing my morning espressos and letting me use one of his tables as a work area.

Finally, thanks to Lori Grant for her line drawings, to Lea Hernandez for the wonderful drawing of the original anime "Companion," to Linda Shimoda for her lettering and layouts, to Kazuko Matsuzaki in Tokyo for tracking down permissions, and to all the companies, artists, and their representatives for generously allowing me to reproduce selections from their work.

GILLES POITRAS
Oakland, California

ICONS AND ABBREVIATIONS

The following icons are used to indicate general subject categories:

	Building/Structure/Landmark		History/Society
	Clothing		Home
	Culture		Nature
	Entertainment/Game		People
	Food and Drink		Religion/Mythology/Belief
	General		Sport/Activity
	Geographical Feature/Location		Weaponry/War

The following icons are used to indicate anime/manga reference categories:

A   examples seen in anime

M   examples seen in manga

AM   examples seen in both anime and manga

The following abbreviations are used in the examples sections:

anim. seq.	animation sequence	p., pp.	page, pages
chapt.	chapter	pt.	part
ep.	episode	st.	story
ff	this page and following pages	tp.	tape
OVA	Original Video Animation (sometimes seen as **OAV**)	vol.	volume

AIDORU ("IDOL" SINGER)

"Idol" or pop singers are not unique to Japan; every modern country has its clean-cut prefabricated stars known for their short careers. In Japan highly competitive management companies maneuver to get their latest singers in the spotlight for as long as they can before the next act comes along. In anime, idol singers struggle for success or deal with the results of it; they sing in unlikely concert locations, even in outer space, and some are not even human, like the virtual idol Sharon Apple in *Macross Plus*.

 The most famous idol singer in anime is Minmei from the original *Macross* series; her voice actress, Iijima Mari, continued on to a successful singing career. • The award for most unlikely concert setting must go to idol singer Amy Lean, whose concert at Cape Kennedy is interrupted in *Moldiver* (OVA 2). • In *Kimagure Orange Road* (OVA 3, ep. 1) we get to see a rare portrayal of a male idol singer. • The award for best anime portrayal of idol singers has to go to the group Cham in *Perfect Blue*.

AGING POPULATION

Japan has one of the fastest aging populations in the world. The percentage of the population over the age of 65 reached 13.5% in 1993. The birthrate in Japan was 1.5 children per family in 1992; since the Japanese have the longest life expectancy in the world the percentage of aged will continue to increase, as will problems regarding the care of the elderly.

 Roujin Z centers around the unexpected consequences of an experiment dealing with the problem of care of the elderly.

AINU

The indigenous people of northern Japan, often referred to as Caucasian. The Ainu are actually related to many of the different peoples of Siberia. Until the late 19th century the Ainu continued to live in northern **Honshu** and southern Kamchatka and were a hunting-gathering culture living in small villages where game was plentiful. Today the Ainu are found mainly in **Hokkaido** and nearby islands; commercial fishing and crop cultivation are major sources of income. Increased intermarriage with the Japanese after WWII has left very few pure-blood Ainu.

 In *Dagger of Kamui* Jiro spends some time with the Ainu in search of clues regarding his father's past. The credits for this anime include an expert in "Ainu Customs and Morals Research."

AICHI KEN

Aichi Prefecture. Located in central **Honshu**, its capital is Nagoya. Aichi is a major industrial area in Japan. The territories of the old provinces of Mikawa and Owari make up Aichi Prefecture.

 That Labor Police teams will be established in Aichi Ken, **Miyagi Ken,** and **Chiba Ken** is mentioned by Nagumo Shinobu in her lecture in *Patlabor 2*. • In *Blue Seed* (tp. 2, ep. 4) Azusa Matsudaira is from Aichi.

RANTS

Many of the sidebars in this book consist of me blowing off steam and griping about various matters. I consider this my right and, more importantly, duty as a fan. Anyone who has been around the anime and manga fan scene for more than a few days knows that fans and otaku are often highly opinionated and outspoken. This is an established tradition in fandom: when we see something we don't like we say so! When we disagree with what someone else has said we say so!

So I have added some of my comments. Agree or disagree; better yet, post your replies in **rec.arts.anime. misc** and everyone can join in.

AJISAI (JAPANESE HYDRANGEA)

 A shrub with thick, dark green, ovate leaves that have serrated edges. The flowers are small, ball-shaped clusters that bloom in summer. The colors of the flowers depend on the acidity of the soil. The earliest literary references to ajisai are in **Man'yōshū**, an 8th-century collection of poems.

△ In *Urusei Yatsura* (TV tp. 8, ep. 30, st. 53) we see hydrangea after Ataru's true self speaks in class.

• We see hydrangea in the rain in *Blue Seed* (tp. 5, Omake Theater), Kyoko admires some ajisai in *Maison Ikkoku: Soichiro's Shadow* (ep. 1), and some are seen as Akane walks home in *Ranma 1/2* (TV sub tp. 3, dub tp. 5, ep. 9).

AKA-CHŌCHIN (RED LANTERN)

 Large red paper lanterns (**chōchin**) hung outside eating and drinking establishments as advertisements.

△ An aka-chōchin is seen attached to the **yatai** in *Neon Genesis Evangelion* (tp. 6, ep. 12). One is outside the tavern in *Tenchi Universe* (tp. 4, ep. 12, st. 1), *Botchan*, and *Student Days.*

AKAGAWA JIRŌ

 A best-selling novelist who was born in Fukuoka Prefecture in 1949. His first novel, *Ghost Train* (Yūrei Ressha), was published in 1976. He is best known for his humorous mysteries.

△ Akagawa Jirō is the author of the stories *Incident in the Bedroom Suburb* (Hometown no Jikenbō) and *Voice from Heaven* (Ten kara no Koe), which are available in anime versions.

AKASHI

 A city in southern Hyōgo Prefecture in western **Honshu**, located on the Inland Sea west of Kobe. During the **Edo period** Akashi was a castle town on the San'yōdō highway.

△ Akashi is mentioned in *Ghost Story* and in *Urusei Yatsura* (TV tp. 15, ep. 55, st. 78).

Ⓜ The bombing of Akashi in WWII is depicted in *Adolf: 1945 and All That Remains* (p. 40).

AKA TO SHIRO (RED AND WHITE)

 Red and white are decorative colors used together on happy occasions. For example, a person opening a business will probably receive red and white floral decorations, and red and white cords (**mizuhiki**) will be attached to gift envelopes.

△ Notice the red and white cords on Pretty Sammy's baton in *Tenchi Muyo! Mihoshi Special* and in *Pretty Sammy*; the red and white cord holding the cover on the wedding photo in *Here Is Greenwood* (tp. 2, ep. 3); and the red and white curtains of the circus in *Urusei Yatsura* (TV tp. 15, ep. 55, st. 78).

AKIHABARA

 Located in northeastern Chiyoda Ward in Tokyo, this neighborhood is famous for its electronics shops. The area was originally a neighborhood around the Akiba Shrine, and after WWII a black market thrived in a group of buildings that had not been destroyed in the bombing. After the black market was closed down by the authorities, dealers of radio parts continued to operate in the area. Over time more shops opened and more goods were brought in. Nowadays hundreds of shops with bright signs offering discounts and hard-to-find items do a busy trade. The neighborhood is well connected to the rest of Tokyo by several train and subway lines.

◪ The major action in *Pretty Sammy 2* takes place around Akihabara (unless you think the mother's routines are the best part).

AKUSHU SURU (SHAKING HANDS)

 Bowing is still the major form of greeting in Japan, but the Western custom of shaking hands is catching on in some circles. Men are more likely to shake hands than women, probably because they are more likely to interact with foreigners as part of their work.

◪ In *You're Under Arrest* Miyuki shakes Natsumi's hand when they are introduced. • In *Oh My Goddess!* Megumi shakes Belldandy's hand; in this case one of the women is Japanese and the other one is a foreigner, so the two of them shaking hands is not as unusual.

AKUTAGAWA RYŪNOSUKE

 1892–1927. A writer known best in the West for his short stories, Akutagawa Ryūnosuke also wrote poetry and essays. His works are known for their depiction of the darker side of humanity. The most famous collection of his stories is *Kappa*, a satire in which **kappa** demons play the major role. Eight years after Akutagawa's suicide in 1927, the Akutagawa Prize

(**Akutagawa Shō**) was founded to honor outstanding works of new writers.

◪ Akutagawa is the author of the story "Hōkyōnin no Shi," which is available as an anime entitled *The Martyr*.

AKUTAGAWA SHŌ

 A prize given twice a year since 1935 to little-known writers to encourage new talent. It was established in memory of the important writer **Akutagawa Ryūnosuke**.

◪ Momotaro claims, a little anachronistically, to have won the Akutagawa Prize in *Urusei Yatsura* (TV tp. 3, ep. 11, sts. 21–22).

AMADO (RAIN DOORS)

 Sliding coverings for windows, glass doors, or **engawa** (verandas), used during storms and to secure a home at night. Traditionally amado were made of wood, but today metal ones are common. When used on engawa the doors are often slid along tracks one after the other to completely enclose the area. Such protection for a building is very useful against not only regular storms

Amado slide easily into place next to each other to protect the **engawa**.

but the **taifū** that hit Japan every year. In anime and manga the amado are usually not seen, but the **tobukuro** that they are stored in is often visible.

 Tenchi is securing the amado along the engawa as a defense against the "space pirate" in *Tenchi Universe* (tp. 1, ep. 1), and we get an excellent view of the father sliding the amado in *My Neighbor Totoro*.

AMATERASU ŌMIKAMI

 The **kami** of the sun, her name translates as "Great Divinity Illuminating Heaven." She is the main female deity of **Shintō**. She is the ruler of the **Takamagahara**. Because of the rudeness of her younger brother, **Susanoo no Mikoto** she once hid herself in a cave, plunging the world into darkness. The other kami lured her out by having a party at which one of the female kami, Ame no Uzume no Mikoto, danced and stripped. The other kami laughed at this sight. When Amaterasu peeked out of the cave to see what was going on she was confronted with a mirror that reflected her face. A strong kami pulled her out, then sealed the entry so she could not go back in. Amaterasu dispatched her grandson, Ninigi no Mikoto, to rule Japan, and his great-grandson was Jinmu, the first emperor.

 The legend of Amaterasu retreating to the cave is alluded to in *Maison Ikkoku: Welcome to Maison Ikkoku* (ep. 1; vol. 1, p. 22).

ANMITSU

 A sweet dish made of gelatinlike *kanten* and other ingredients with syrup. Served cold, it is nevertheless eaten year round.

 In *Urusei Yatsura* Ten asks some girls if they like anmitsu or **shiruko** (OVA "Catch the Heart"); it is clearly seen in the OVA "Electric Household Guard."

AOYAMA

A section of Tokyo in northwestern Minato Ward. In the **Edo period** this area was the site of temples, shrines, and samurai residences. Today Aoyama is, along with the nearby Shibuya and **Harajuku** areas, a major entertainment and shopping area for young people. Aoyama Street is well known for its fashion houses, restaurants, and shops. Aoyama is also the location of the first municipal cemetery in Japan, **Aoyama Reien**.

 Haneda asks Yoko which is the better choice for dinner—Aoyama or Harajuku—in *801 TTS Airbats* (pt. 2).

AOYAMA REIEN

A cemetery in Tokyo. Aoyama Reien was opened in 1872 as the first municipally operated cemetery in Japan. The location is also noted for its cherry blossoms (**sakura**).

 There is a mention of Aoyama Reien in *Mai the Psychic Girl: Perfect Collection* (vol. 3, p. 56).

ASAGAO (MORNING GLORY)

 The Japanese were the first to cultivate the morning glory as an ornamental. Originally it was brought from China in the 9th century as a medicinal plant due to the laxative properties of its seeds. During the **Edo period** it became a very common ornamental flower. Most varieties grown in gardens have large flowers and usually are a bluish purple.

 Morning glories are seen in an opening scene in *Ranma 1/2* (TV sub tp. 6, dub tp. 8, ep. 16), in the rain in *Blue Seed* (tp. 5, Omake Theater), in Otomi's yard in *Sanshiro the Judoist* (pt. 3), and in the flashback in *Rupan III: The Fuma Conspiracy*.

 Morning glories are seen in *Maison Ikkoku* (vol. 6, p. 137).

ASAKUSA

A district in the eastern part of Taitō Ward, Tokyo. This area has retained much of its **Edo period** charm and draws many sightseers. Asakusa was originally built as an entertainment and business district. The famous Yoshiwara red light district was just north of here.

Early in *Mermaid Forest* we see a bit of 1930s Asakusa. In *Ranma 1/2* (TV sub tp. 3, dub tp. 4, ep. 7), this is also one of the places Ryoga went on his way to meet Ranma when they were school mates.

ASAKUSA JINJA

 A shrine dedicated to the memory of the three men who were involved in the establishment of the temple **Sensōji**. Two of the men were fishermen, Hinokuma Hamanari and Hinokuma Takenari, who, in 628, found a statue of the **bosatsu** Kannon in the river Sumidagawa. The third man was the village headman, Haji no Nakatomo, who built the temple. The shrine is the site of many festivals and is also known for the Nakamise, an arcade of shops that starts inside **Kaminarimon** gate.

 We see Momiji and Kome go to Asakusa Jinja in *Blue Seed* (tp. 2, ep. 4).

ASAMAYAMA (MT. ASAMA)

 An active volcano in central **Honshu** on the border of Gunma and Nagano prefectures. In 1783 it erupted and produced large lava flows on its northern slope. The eastern slope has a volcano observation station run by Tokyo University.

 An encounter with an angel takes place at the Mt. Asama Earthquake Research Lab in *Neon Genesis Evangelion* (Genesis 0:5, ep. 10).

Ⓜ The eruption of Mt.Asama in 1783 and some of its aftereffects are mentioned in the Takahashi Rumiko story "Time Warp Trouble" (*Rumic World Trilogy*, vol. 1, p. 46).

ASO-SAN (MT. ASO)

 This volcano in central **Kyushu** has one of the largest caldera in the world, with a circumference of 176 miles.

 Ryoga and a confused old woman travel to this volcano in *Ranma 1/2* (TV sub tp. 3, dub tp. 5, ep. 9).

A VISIT TO A HOME

You enter the house and stand in the **genkan**, where you carefully remove your shoes and step into slippers. A short trip down the hall and you may be looking out on the garden. If it is summer, you are standing on an open **engawa**, perhaps a hanging **fūrin** catches a breeze and rings softly. If it is winter, glazed **amado** keep the cold out while allowing you to enjoy the view. You then step into a room and sit on a **zabuton** at a **chabudai**, or if it's winter at a **kotatsu**, and enjoy a hot cup of **cha** and some **senbei** to snack on. You see **noren** in a doorway and know that the kitchen is there. You ask where the *otearai* (or less formally, the **benjo**) is, and before you enter you change to special slippers used only for that room. As you are going to stay the night, your hosts direct you to the **furo**, which is not in the same place as the toilet, and being proper hosts allow you to use it first. After a comfortable soak you are shown your **tatami**-lined room, where you remove your house slippers before entering. The **futon** have already been laid out for you and you get ready for a good night's sleep. As your head touches the **makura** you are already thinking of the traditional **chōshoku** you will enjoy in the morning.

ATAMI

 A city in Shizuoka Prefecture known for its gentle weather, hot springs, and mountains. Atami has been a resort town since the 8th century. Today the town is part of the Fuji-Hakone-Izu National Park and is on the Tōkaidō Line of the **Shinkansen** train, making it an easily accessible and popular resort.

 Atami is mentioned by Ryoko as a place for her and Tenchi to go to in *Tenchi Universe* (TV tp. 4, ep. 13). • The former Atami region is mentioned as the projected landing spot for an attacking angel in *Neon Genesis Evangelion* (tp. 6, ep. 11).

ATENA (ADDRESS)

 Finding an address in Japan can be quite a problem, since streets are generally not given names and buildings sometimes don't have numbers. Instead, lots may have names and do have numbers. Since lots are numbered in the order of registration, the numbering sequence may be irregular, with lots in different parts of the district having, for example, the consecutive numbers 36 and 37. Usually you ask a local for directions, or the police in the neighborhood **kōban**. People often draw maps to their homes to help visitors find them.

Ⓐ Ten gives maps to Ataru's home in *Urusei Yatsura* (TV tp. 1, ep. 3, st. 2)—not a good thing for Ataru of course. • Belldandy gives complex directions in *Oh My Goddess!* (OVA 1).

Ⓜ Lum is given a map to Ran's in *Return of Lum: Sweet Revenge* (pp. 171–72).

AWA ODORI

 A variation of the Bon Dance (**Bon Odori**) performed in and near the city of Tokushima, in what was once Awa Province. The Bon Dance is also known as the Fool's Dance, Ahō Odori, from a line in a song: "You're a fool whether you dance or not, so you might as well dance."

Ⓐ We see a Fool's Dance parody of the Awa Odori in the **Heian period** capital of **Kyoto** in *Urusei Yatsura* (TV tp. 3, ep. 11, sts. 21–22).

AZABU JŪBAN

 Azabu #10, in Minato Ward near the **Roppongi** district, is a residential area known for its traditional shopping streets. In the **Edo period** this was the location of many samurai homes. Today it is the location of many well-to-do homes and embassies. It is also the location of Azabu Jūban Hot Spring, a natural source in the middle of Tokyo.

Ⓐ The Azabu #10 Hot Spring is mentioned by Goto in *Patlabor: New Files* (tp. 4, ep. 12).

BAKEMONO (MONSTER)

 Monsters, goblins, apparitions, or any of several kinds of kinds of supernatural beings. Also called *yōkai*. However, these do not include ghosts (**yūrei**), which usually appear in human form. Bakemono can appear in various non-human forms including sound, wind, and fire. There are over 500 types of bakemono listed in some books; these include **tengu**, **bakeneko**, and **kappa**.

Ⓐ Ayeka often calls Ryoko a bakemono in *Tenchi Muyo!* • The word *yōkai* is translated as "goblin" in *Urusei Yatsura* (TV tp. 9, ep. 34, st. 57).

BAKENEKO (MONSTER CAT)

 While a **bakemono** is a monster or demon, a bakeneko is a monstrous or demonic cat. There are many folk tales and stories in Japan about bakeneko. Some stories include the cat taking a human form, almost always that of a woman, and cats eating children.

Ⓐ Bakeneko possession of people is seen in *Hakkenden* (tp. 5, ep. 9) and *Urusei Yatsura* (TV tp. 12, ep. 43. st. 66). • A cat *aragami* is in *Blue Seed: Fate and Destiny* (ep. 19).

Ⓜ Godai plays the role of a cat demon, or at least he's made up to look like one, in *Maison Ikkoku* (vol. 6, p. 5).

BAKIN

 1767–1848. The author (full name Takizawa Bakin) of the massive 106-volume literary work *Nansō Satomi Hakkenden* (Satomi and the Eight Dogs). This novel took Bakin

28 years to complete. By the time he was done he was blind, and he had lost his wife and his son. The last parts of the novel were dictated to his daughter-in-law. Bakin was of a low-ranking samurai background, but he gave up his status to become a writer of chapbooks and essays. Samurai themes of loyalty, filial piety, and family honor as well as Confucian (**Jukyō**) and Buddhist philosophy play a large role in several of his works.

▲ *Nansō Satomi Hakkenden* was animated under the title *Hakkenden*.

BAKU (DREAM EATER)

 A legendary critter that eats bad dreams. You can ask for its assistance by writing its name or drawing its picture on a piece of paper that you place under your pillow before going to bed. The legend of the baku came to Japan from China, and there have been some attempts to link its appearance with the tapir, which is found on the Malay Peninsula and in India.

▲ Takahashi Rumiko's vision of this dream eater, in a tapir-like form, can be seen in *Urusei Yatsura* (TV tp. 6, ep. 21, st. 42). • Baku also shows up in *Urusei Yatsura: Beautiful Dreamer* with a different form. • A portrayal of Baku, also called Ra-en, as a dangerous entity is seen in *Vampire Princess Miyu* (tp. 1, ep.1).

Ⓜ See *Return of Lum Urusei Yatsura* (p. 147).

BANZAI

 Originally the term *banzai* ("long life") was used to show respect for the emperor. The custom of raising both hands and yelling "Banzai!" dates from the **Meiji period** in celebration of the new constitution. Today shouting "Banzai!" three times while raising both hands is used to express joy for a person or achievement.

▲ "Banzai!" is shouted by Mink and her friends in *Dragon Half* at the end of the tournament, and Godai says it in *Maison Ikkoku: Ronin Blues* (ep. 2). • We also hear "Banzai!" in *Urusei Yatsura* (TV tp. 4, ep. 16, st. 32), *Project A-Ko*, and *Theater of Life*.

Ⓜ We see the "Banzai!" gesture in *Rumic Theater* (p. 161) and *Barefoot Gen* (p. 89).

BENJO (TOILET)

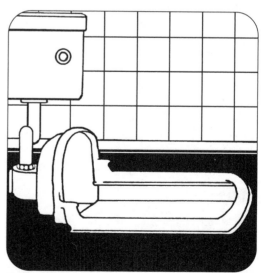 The Japanese toilet, which you have to squat over to use (unless of course you are a man or boy urinating) seems very inconvenient to Westerners. But the Japanese see their "squatter" as more sanitary, since the body does not have to come in contact with the toilet. One end of the toilet has a hood, which you face as you squat. Many public facilities have both Japanese- and Western-style toilets, although it is not unusual for these same places to not have toilet paper or hand towels. Japanese often carry tissues for wiping and a **hankachi** for drying their hands. Since stalls have doors that go all the way to the floor (remember you squat on traditional toilets), you must knock to see if the stall is occupied. The person inside will not speak but will knock in response. In private homes and inns (**ryokan**) are slippers by the door that you use only in the toilet. Toilets and the bath are not in the same room. Flush toilets are common in cities, but many country homes still use pit toilets, where many children believe filthy demons reside.

*Going to Japan? Need a **benjo**? Better be prepared for this!*

The custom of knocking on the stall door is seen in *Urusei Yatsura* (TV tp. 10, ep. 37, st. 60) and in *Return of Lum: Lum in the Sun* (pp. 112–13).

🅰 A good view of a traditional toilet appears when Mihoshi looks for Kiyone in *Tenchi Muyo in Love*.

Ⓜ A squat toilet is seen in *Sanctuary* (vol. 5, p. 128).

BENKEI

Also known as Musashibō Benkei. A legendary warrior monk, Benkei is said to have been very strong and highly skilled in martial arts. He liked to challenge samurai in **Kyoto** to a fight and always beat them. But when Benkei met and challenged the young Ushiwakamaru (**Minamoto no Yoshitsune**) on a bridge he met his match and was defeated. Benkei then became Yoshitsune's loyal follower and died in his defense.

🅰 The famous battle on a bridge between Benkei and Ushiwakamaru is depicted, in a slightly weird manner, in *Urusei Yatsura* (TV tp. 3, ep. 12, st. 24).

BENTEN

Originally the goddess of the river, in time she became the guardian deity of wisdom, the pursuit of knowledge, and the arts. Later Benten was celebrated as the goddess of money. Benten is one of the Seven Lucky Gods (**Shichifuku-jin**).

Ⓜ In *Lum Urusei Yatsura: Perfect Collection* (p. 163) we see one of Takahashi Rumiko's visions of Benten. • Another portrayal by Takahashi Rumiko is in the story "Golden Gods of Poverty" (*Rumic World Trilogy*, vol. 2, p. 15).

BENTŌ (BOX LUNCH FOR ONE PERSON)

Originally bentō were eaten by travelers and outdoor laborers. Bentō now come in many forms, including bentō sold at theaters and railway stations (**ekiben**), elaborate picnic bentō, bentō carried to work by commuters, and, most often seen in anime, bentō box lunches prepared by mothers for their children at school. Since the 1970s shops specializing in bentō have opened, many of them national franchises.

🅰 We see bentō eaten in farm fields in *Grave of the Wild Chrysanthemum*. • Bentō school lunch boxes are often seen in *Urusei Yatsura* (TV tp. 1, ep. 2, st. 2). • Bentō are sold at the hot springs in *El-Hazard* ("Second Night"). • In *You're Under Arrest* (OVA 4) we see Natsumi at the temple eating from a bentō box. • Perhaps the deadliest bentō seen in anime are those prepared by C-Ko in *Project A-Ko*.

Ⓜ Bentō are served to department store night workers in *Maison Ikkoku* (vol. 4, p. 45).

BĪRU (BEER)

Beer is very popular in Japan. Two of the major brewers, Asahi and Sapporo, have agreed to use the same bottle design to make it easier and more economical to reuse bottles from either company. Kirin, however, uses its own style bottles with the company name on them. Sapporo was founded in 1876 and is a major beer exporter. Asahi was incorporated in 1949 and produces wine and soft drinks as well as beer. Kirin, which also produces soft drinks and food, was incorporated in 1907; in 1954 Kirin became Japan's largest producer of beer. All three companies are headquartered in Tokyo.

🅰 In the first *Ranma 1/2* TV episode the fathers have some beer together. • Ryuichi drinks beer after

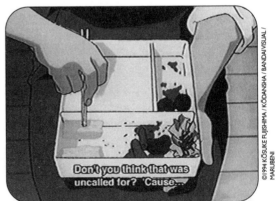

Natsumi in You're Under Arrest *reaches for the omelet in her* **bentō**.

Kirin, Sapporo, and Asahi: Three of the most popular brands of **beer** in Japan.

work in *Incident in the Bedroom Suburb* and *Voice from Heaven*. • A rather angry Shoko orders beer at a stand in *Hyperdoll* (Act 2). • In bars the proper way for waitresses to serve beer is to place it on the table with the label facing the customer, which is what Akemi does in *Maison Ikkoku: Playing Doubles* (ep. 1). • Kirin brand beer cans are visible in *Sanctuary*. • Yebisu brand beer in a can is drunk in *Here Is Greenwood* (tp. 2, ep. 4) and *Neon Genesis Evangelion* (Genesis 0:1, ep. 2).

 We see a beer vending machine on the street in *One Pound Gospel* (vol. 1, p. 28). The star on the label of the can is a logo of the Sapporo brewery and is also seen on a bottle on p. 40. • Godai and some fellow **rōnin** go out drinking beer (Sapporo) in *Maison Ikkoku* (vol. 2, p. 104). We also see a rooftop beer hall (vol. 3, p. 104) with lanterns that have the Sapporo star on them. • In *Mai the Psychic Girl: Perfect Collection* (vol. 1, p. 287) we see a case of beer being consumed by the students.

BISHAMON

 One of the Seven Lucky Gods (**Shichifuku-jin**). Bishamon is portrayed armed and in armor. He is one of the Guardians of Buddha and must protect the Buddhist virtues and teachings against evil.

 The Shichifuku-jin show up in the Takahashi Rumiko story "Golden Gods of Poverty" (*Rumic World Trilogy*, vol. 2, p. 14).

BIWA

 A plucked musical instrument with four or five strings derived from the Chinese *pi-pa*, which was introduced into Japan in the 8th century. **Benten** is often portrayed playing the biwa. Originally this was a solo instrument but later came to be used as part of an orchestra. A famous literary work that is often recited with biwa accompaniment is **Heike Monogatari**.

 We hear and see biwa music in *Ghost Story*.

BIWA HŌSHI ("LUTE PRIEST")

 Biwa hōshi were blind performers who were not actually priests but shaved their heads and wore the Buddhist robes of traveling priests. They often traveled and earned their income by reciting vocal literature to the accompaniment of **biwa** music. Their occupation may have had its origin in China and India, where blind Buddhist lay-priest entertainers were known to exist.

 A blind biwa player is the major character in *Ghost Story*.

Houchi in GHOST STORY plays the **biwa**.

ADULT ANIME, MATURE ANIME

I'm not talking *hentai* ("perversion") here. One of the problems with American English is that the best terms for describing anime, manga, and movies that are too complex for children to easily understand have been appropriated by the porn industry. Face it: *Hakkenden, Wings of Honneamise, Ghost in the Shell, Grave of the Fireflies, Maison Ikkoku,* and *Otaku no Video* are not kiddie stuff. But calling them "adult" or for "mature viewers" suggests there is lots of sexual activity. The reality is that these would more likely bore or challenge kids than corrupt them. In fact I think all parents should seriously consider watching *Grave of the Fireflies* with their kids as an opportunity to discuss what war and its effects on civilians is like. But we are still left with a lack of vocabulary for describing this kind of anime. Perhaps we should take a clue from Viz Communications' subtitle of their magazine *Pulp*: "Manga for Grownups." Or you can just get your friends in front of the tube and hit the play button and let them decide for themselves.

BOKKEN (WOODEN SWORD)

 Bokken are shaped like real swords but made of hard wood. While these are primarily for practice they can be effective in real combat. **Miyamoto Musashi** is said to have defeated several opponents with a bokken.

🅰 When Kuno first appears in *Ranma 1/2* (TV tp. 1, ep. 2) he is carrying a bokken. • Tobimaro's trainer carries bokken in *Urusei Yatsura* (TV tp. 18, ep. 70, "Sensational Debut of Mizunokouji Ton!"). • Bokken are often used by Tenchi's grandfather in the *Tenchi Universe* series, and in one case he also uses a short, knife-sized, wooden blade (ep. 9).

🅼 A bad-girl version of Lum carries a bokken in *Return of Lum: Feudal Furor* (p. 122), and Toge is beaten with a bokken by the police in *Adolf: An Exile in Japan* (vol. 2, p. 70).

BON

 An annual Buddhist festival honoring the spirits of one's ancestors; it takes place July 13–15 or in some locales on August 13–15. Bon is also called Obon or Urabon. Families welcome the visiting spirits with special fires and a spirit altar set up in front of the **butsudan** (Buddhist family altar). During this time many people return to their home towns to celebrate the festival with their families, and many shops close or reduce their hours. Families also visit gravesites to make offerings, and Buddhist priests visit homes to chant sutras for the dead. The reason for the two dates is that Bon is to be observed between the 13th and 15th days of the 7th month; in the Gregorian (Western) calendar this is July, but in the old lunar calendar still observed by many farmers the date falls in August. At the end of the festival, special send-off fires called **okuribi** are lit for the visiting spirits; sometimes this takes the form of lanterns set afloat down a stream or on the ocean.

🅰 In *Moldiver* (OVA 5) one can see the Daimonji **okuribi** fire on Mt. Nyoigatake that forms the Chinese character *dai* ("large"). • Probably *Tenchi the Movie 2: The Daughter of Darkness* has the largest number of Bon references of any anime. We see Tenchi praying at the family gravestone after cleaning it, and Ayeka and Sasami preparing flower arrangements for the spirit altar on which we see a memorial tablet, flowers, candles, and vegetable "horses" with stick legs. Later Tenchi and his father pray at a small fire they have lit in front of the house to welcome the spirits, and a vegetarian meal is served in front of the altar.

🅼 Godai in *Maison Ikkoku* (vol. 3, p. 118) gets a let-

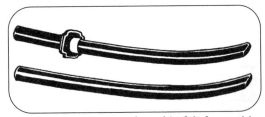

*Bokken of the type commonly used in **dōjō** for practicing swordplay and fighting.*

ter from his mother stating that since he is not likely to come home for the Bon Festival they are sending him a **yukata** made by his grandmother.

BON ODORI

 Bon dances. These are performed at the beginning of the **Bon** Festival to welcome the spirits of the ancestors and at the end as a farewell dance. This kind of dancing originated in the **Heian** and **Kamakura** periods. Every city and hamlet in Japan celebrates the Bon Festival, with large numbers of people dancing about wearing **yukata** in the warm summer weather. The dancing is sometimes done in large open spaces around a temporary stage or **yagura**.

A We see a dance and yagura in a flashback scene in *Urusei Yatsura* (TV tp. 10, ep. 37, st. 60).

M In *Maison Ikkoku* we see people dancing around a yagura at the Bon Festival (vol. 3, p. 124).

BONSAI

Bonsai are trees or plants potted in such a manner as to keep them artificially miniaturized. To stunt their growth, the trees are provided with very little soil and water; pruning both the branches and the roots also helps. Some plants have been tended for generations and passed down to family members or other bonsai fanciers. There are many bonsai styles, and the art can be practiced even in small, confined spaces like a typical Japanese backyard or balcony.

A Ataru's father is seen caring for his bonsai in *Urusei Yatsura* (TV tp. 8, ep. 29, st. 52). • Scenes with bonsai are in *Student Days* and *Project A-Ko*.

M An old man is seen tending his bonsai in *Ranma 1/2* (vol. 8, p. 68).

BONSHŌ (BELL)

A Buddhist temple bell. Unlike Western bells, these bells have no interior clapper but are rung by striking them on the outside with a large pole or log on a special spot called the *tsukiza*, which traditionally has a lotus petal design. Bonshō have a very deep sound and are rung slowly so that the next ring comes as the preceding one has almost faded away. The ritual ringing of the bell 108 times at New Year's is called **Joya no kane**.

A Since it is rather dark inside such a bell Ataru occasionally traps Mendou there in *Urusei Yatsura* (TV tp. 13, ep. 48, st. 71). • One sees a bell in the background in *You're Under Arrest* (OVA 1) during the scene on the temple grounds. • The bells are sometimes heard but not seen, as when the **senpai** visit in *Oh My Goddess!* (OVA 3) or in *Metal Fighters Miku* (tp. 5, ep. 10), *Kimagure Orange Road* (OVA 3, ep. 1), and *Vampire Princess Miyu* (tp. 1, ep. 2).

BOSATSU (BODHISATTVA)

In Buddhism (**Bukkyō**) this is a being of great spiritual attainment who delays his ascension to Buddhahood and instead takes a vow to help all other beings reach enlightenment. Bodhisattva are considered to have unlimited compassion and appear in numerous works in the form of **Jizō** statues.

A **En no Gyōja** is a bodhisattva in *Zenki*.

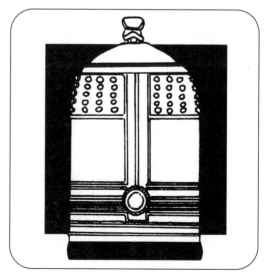

The tsukiza *is where you strike the bell and is just below the middle of this* **bonshō**.

HOMAGE TO *BLADE RUNNER*

The movie *Blade Runner*, with its dark motifs and urban setting, is well known in Japan. We also find references to it in some anime in the form of homage to the movie and its characters. There is no anime with more of these references than *Bubblegum Crisis*. Both shows have a character named Leon; interestingly enough, he is a cop in *Bubblegum Crisis* and a replicant in *Blade Runner*. Among other references in *Bubblegum Crisis* are:

the huge pyramid shaped Genome tower and Tyrell Building
the character Priss and her band The Replicants
the boomers and their dissatisfaction with being mere tools for people and a dream of freedom
a special police unit for dealing with boomers

In the BLADE RUNNER*–inspired anime* BUBBLEGUM CRISIS, *the Knight Sabers, in their street clothes, adopt a pose in front of a billboard.*

BŌSŌZOKU (GANG)

This term is sometimes translated as bikers, motorcycle gangs, speed tribes, or hot rodders. Basically these are **yankī** gangs with motorcycles and souped-up cars. Bōsōzoku are notorious for their noise, violence, and group loyalty, but in reality a great deal of bōsōzoku activity is more a public flaunting of noise and costume, with a great deal of playfulness thrown in. This does not mean that bōsōzoku cannot be dangerous but that they are more interested in fun than a lifestyle. Once a youth reaches the legal age of adulthood, 20, it is assumed that he will cease to be a bōsōzoku (if he does not, he will be looked down upon as "immature"!). Bōsōzoku gangs occasionally disband with great fanfare, going for one last group run and then ceremonially turning in their flags and emblems to the police. Claims of right wing and **yakuza** links seem unfounded, as these groups are held in disdain by many bōsōzoku.

🅐 Most of the characters in *Shonan Bakusozoku* are members of bōsōzoku groups.

BOSS COFFEE

A brand name for canned coffee beverages. The label on the tall red can reads: "BOSS MILD ROAST is made from milk, sugar and a blend of three kinds of beans."
🅐 At the game parlor in *801 TTS Airbats* (pt. 3) we see Mitaka drinking from a tall red can with a white oval and the letters "OSS" visible.

BUDŌKAN

Built in Kitanomaru Park in Tokyo for the 1964 Tokyo Olympics **jūdō** competition, this building with its soaring templelike roofs is used for a variety of public events, among

©1987 ARTMIC / YOUMEX

them rock concerts and, still, martial arts contests and exhibitions.

 In *Metal Fighters Miku* (tp. 1, ep. 1) we see the Neo-Budōkan of the future. • In *Maris the Chojo* the wrestling hall looks like the Budōkan.

BUKKYŌ (BUDDHISM)

According to *Nihon Shoki*, the earliest written history of Japan, Buddhism was introduced into Japan in 522 along with gifts from the Korean kingdom of Paekche that included a statue of the Buddha and several sutras. In the early days Buddhism was mostly a religion of the nobility, but in time it began to spread to the masses especially in the form of Pure Land Buddhism. For much of Japanese history the dominant sects were Shingon and Tendai, two esoteric Buddhist schools that still exist. For most Japanese, contact with Buddhism is occasioned by funeral rites, as these are performed far more by Buddhist than **Shintō** priests.

Often Buddhism is represented by priests, monks, or temples. Examples are found in *Urusei Yatsura*, when the priest Cherry pops up, often literally, and in *Oh My Goddess!*, in the temple where Belldandy and Keiichi live.

*Its characteristic roof design makes Tokyo's **Budōkan** a landmark easy to identify.*

An esoteric Buddhist order called the Hadja causes trouble for the heroes in *Phantom Quest Corp.* (tp. 2, ep. 4). • In *You're Under Arrest*, a neighborhood temple shows up several times. • In *Hakkenden* there are many scenes with priests and pilgrims as well as a strong Buddhist philosophical subtext to the story.

BUNRAKU

A type of puppet play originating in the merger of an earlier form of narrative storytelling called *jōruri* and puppetry, *ayatsuri*. The name comes from a famous theater in Osaka, the Bunraku-za. The performances are accompanied by music, usually a **shamisen** or occasionally a **biwa**, with the story recited by a chanter (*tayū*). The puppets are large and require three puppeteers to manipulate them. The principal operator manipulates the right arm and face, the first assistant operates the puppet's left arm, and the second assistant the legs (or in the case of the puppets of women the kimono). The puppeteers are dressed in black, much like **kurogo** in kabuki, with the assistants always having their faces veiled. It is common for bunraku plays to be adapted to kabuki and vice versa.

A large puppet of a woman is manipulated by two puppeteers and turns into an **oni** (demon) in *Urusei Yatsura* (TV tp. 13, ep. 50, st. 73).

BURŪMĀ (GYM SHORTS WORN BY GIRLS)

Burūmā allow a great deal of freedom in physical activity as they leave the legs completely uncovered. The word comes from "bloomers," a 19th-century article of clothing worn by American and European girls and women, often while active in sports.

In *Urusei Yatsura* (TV tp. 9, ep. 33, st. 56) and *Return of Lum: Sweet Revenge* (p. 20) Hanawa-**sensei** gives burūmā to Lum when he finds out she can fly so that her panties will not be visible.

Burūmā are worn by Sasami in the opening sequence of *Pretty Sammy 2* and by Akane and other

A very genki Sammy, wearing her **burūma**, jumps in her PE class in PRETTY SAMMY.

girls in *Ranma 1/2* (TV sub tp. 2, dub tp. 3, ep. 5). • Jinnai spreads burūmā about the lab room in an attempt to frame Makoto as a pervert in *Wanderers: El-Hazard* (tp. 1, ep. 1).

Ⓜ Happosai, who is a real pervert, steals gym shorts in *Ranma 1/2* (vol. 6, p. 29).

BUTSUDAN (BUDDHIST ALTAR)

 Usually, in anime, family altars in the home. They are often a niche or cabinet with doors that open outward and, inside, an image of the Buddha and memorial tablets (*ihai*) or photos of recently deceased family members. Offerings of food, flowers, and incense are regularly made at family altars.

Ⓐ We see a clear example of a family altar in *Ranma 1/2* (TV sub tp. 5, dub tp. 7, ep. 14) and again with a butsudan to Akane's mother in *Ranma 1/2* (OVA "Akane vs. Ranma!"). • We also see a butsudan with a woman's photo in *Patlabor 2* and one with a man's photo at Yamazaki's in Okinawa in *Patlabor: Original Series* (tp. 2, ep. 5).

Ⓜ There are butsudan in several of the stories in *Rumic Theater* (pp. 42, 73, 121); in *Sanctuary* (vol. 4, p. 201); and in *Domu: A Child's Dream*. • A series of events, including offering incense and ringing a bell), center on the butsudan and the photos on it in *Maison Ikkoku* (vol. 7, p. 148).

CALPIS

 A brand of soft drink made with cultured milk. Calpis water and soda are sold in cans, but you can also buy the syrup in bottles and mix your own at home. Calpis is actually quite good. Given its unappetizing name, it is sold in the U.S. as CalPico and is easy to find in Japanese and other Asian markets.

Ⓐ In *Blue Seed* (tp. 1, ep. 1) Momiji has a cold can of Calpis applied to her forehead by a classmate. We see a Calpis can poking out of a bag when Shigeo bikes in food to the SV2 in *Patlabor: New Files* (OVA 11).

CHA (TEA)

More often, *ocha*. The most widely drunk beverage in Japan. The most common form of cha is green tea; many people have several cups a day. In many offices one of the duties of the "office ladies" is to provide tea for the

The ihai *is visible behind the photo of Dr. Tofu's father on the* **butsudan** *in the* RANMA 1/2 *TV show.*

sararīman to refresh them as they work. When you visit an office you will be given cha as a matter of normal etiquette; even carpenters and gardeners are offered tea when they are working for someone. Other kinds of Japanese tea include *sencha*, which is made from more tender leaves; *bancha*, from coarser leaves; *hōjicha*, from roasted *bancha*; and *genmaicha*, a mixture of *genmai* (roasted brown rice) and *bancha*. And of course there is the tea ceremony (**cha-no-yu**) with all of its cultural significance and simple elegance; it uses *matcha*, powdered green tea. The importance of tea is also seen in the many names for things that are associated with tea. The Japanese living room is called the *cha-no-ma* or "tea room," as that is where tea is most often drunk in a home. The word *chaya*, or "tea house," may mean a dealer in tea, a roadside rest house, or a business in the pleasure quarters where **geisha** and women of less refined occupation ply their trade.

 In *Urusei Yatsura* the Moroboshi family often drinks cha at home; occasionally the monk Cherry invites himself to have some cha with them. • Green tea is clearly seen in *Zenki* (tp. 5, ep. 10).

CHABUDAI

 A traditional low (sometimes round) table used to serve tea and food. Chabudai appear in almost all anime and manga set in Japan. These tables originated in the **Meiji period** and are not to be confused with **kotatsu**, which resemble them.

 In *Ranma 1/2* much of the Tendo household action takes place around the chabudai.

 Hasukawa and Mitsuru move a chabudai in *Here Is Greenwood* (tp. 3, ep. 6), Miyu's family eats at one in *Vampire Princess Miyu* (tp. 2, ep. 4), and a chabudai is commonly used at Tenchi's grandfather's place in *Tenchi Universe* (tp. 1, ep. 2) and *Tenchi Muyo in Love*. • Chabudai are also seen in *Zenki* (tp. 4, ep. 8) and *Wanderers: El-Hazard* (tp. 1, ep. 1).

For meals, socializing, or Tendo family meetings on the RANMA 1/2 *TV show, the* **chabudai** *is an important part of the home.*

CHALK MARKS AND ILLEGALLY PARKED CARS

The population density of Japanese cities makes illegal parking a real problem. Female traffic wardens patrol the city; when they find an illegally parked car they mark the locations of the wheels with chalk on a long holder. If the car stays there too long it is towed.

 In *Phantom Quest Corp.* (tp. 2, ep. 4) we see chalk marks where Karino's car was illegally parked.

CHA-NO-YU (TEA CEREMONY)

A specialized and very formal, disciplined way of preparing and appreciating tea. The ceremony is considered a spiritual as well as aesthetic experience. Its origins lie in ancient Chinese methods of preparing powdered tea, but it has been greatly influenced by Korean sensibilities and Zen Buddhism. Its most important practitioner was Sen no Rikyu in the 16th century, and several present-day tea schools trace their lineage back to him. The tea ceremony is often performed in a special tea house or tea room that is sparsely furnished. The implements and tea cups used in the ceremony are similarly rustic and plain.

 Kuno does the tea ceremony in *Ranma 1/2: Cat-*

AGE DIFFERENCES IN MALE-FEMALE RELATIONS

There are times when age differences between characters may seem too great for intimate relationships. But again we have to remember that different cultures do not share our version of reality. No one bats an eye when Akane claims to have been seeing the much older Dr. Tofu in *Ranma 1/2* or when Yaegashi shows an interest in the much younger Momiji in *Blue Seed*. What about Yagami's interest in Godai in *Maison Ikkoku* or Prince Genji's adoption of Princess Murasaki and, years later, making love to her before going into exile? Such age differences are apparently not considered to be that great in Japan, whereas in many countries they would be considered great barriers, since one of the persons involved is a minor. And of course Godai and Kyoko's relationship in *Maison Ikkoku* is one example of a man having an interest in an older woman, not that usual in America.

Fu Fighting (ep. 1). • The tea ceremony is done by Shibano in *Metal Fighters Miku* (tp. 5, ep. 10); note the way Shibano wipes the bowl before passing it to his guest.

 In *Ranma 1/2* (vol. 5, p. 115ff) we see Takahashi Rumiko's martial arts portrayal of the tea ceremony.

CHANPON

 Mixing things, especially Japanese and Western drinks. The Japanese know what belongs where, so they have a special name for the practice of serving both traditional Japanese and Western drinks at the same event. This term is not to be confused with the traditional food dish from Nagasaki.

 The members of Unit Two on leave drink a great deal of Japanese and Western alcoholic beverages one evening in *Patlabor: New Files* (tp. 3, ep. 9).

CHAWAN (SMALL BOWL)

 A small bowl, usually ceramic, used for eating rice or for drinking tea (**cha**) in the tea ceremony (**cha-no-yu**). The term has largely replaced the other term for rice bowl, *meshi-jawan*. During the **Muromachi period** the bowls were only used for tea, but during the **Edo period** their use broadened. Each family member will have his or her own chawan and tea cup that no one else will use. To eat from a chawan you pick up the bowl in one hand and scoop from it with chopsticks (**hashi**). In anime and manga, chawan are seen in almost every household scene where a meal is served. In *Ranma 1/2* chawan show up quite often during breakfast (**chōshoku**) conversations.

CHAZUKE

A simple food dish made by pouring hot green tea, or water, over rice. Usually the rice has a topping that may include **umeboshi**, dried seaweed (*nori-chazuke*), salted cod roe (*tarako-chazuke*), salted salmon (*sake-chazuke*), or sea bream (*tai-chazuke*). Water was poured over rice in the **Heian period**, but in the **Edo period** the popularity of **cha** led to tea being used instead. We see chazuke in *Urusei Yatsura* (TV tp. 9, ep. 34, st. 57) and in *Patlabor: New Files* (tp. 1, ep. 2).

CHIBA KEN

Chiba Prefecture. The north of the prefecture comprises part of the Kantō Plain, while the south makes up the Bōsō Peninsula, with the Pacific Ocean to the east and Tokyo Bay to the west. This prefecture was created in 1875 by merging the three provinces of Shimōsa, Kazusa, and Awa. Tokyo's Narita Airport (**Shin Tōkyō Kokusai Kūkō**) is located here, as is Tokyo Disneyland. Chiba City is the capital. That Labor Police teams will be established in **Aichi Ken**, **Miyagi Ken**, and Chiba Ken is mentioned by Nagumo Shinobu in her lecture in *Patlabor 2*. • Chiba is also mentioned in *Grave of the Wild Chrysanthemum*.

CHINDONYA (MUSIC MAKER)

 The name comes from *chin*, the sound of a bell, and *don* the sound of a drum. The chindonya is a man dressed in bright, feminine colors who plays several instruments with his hands and occasionally his feet. His job is to draw the attention of people to the opening of a business, storewide sales, plays, or new products. There is usually a clarinet player as well as someone who hands out fliers. The chindonya and his band will play in front of the business that has hired them and then walk around the neighborhood handing out leaflets.

◪ We see an example of a chindonya and leaflets passed out in *Urusei Yatsura: Beautiful Dreamer.*

CHŌCHIN (HANGING PAPER LANTERN)

 Chōchin come in a variety of shapes and colors. Usually they are made of a collapsible bamboo frame of hoops with a cover of tough paper. Bars often hang red chōchin (**aka-chōchin**) out front to attract customers. A home or business may have its name or **mon** painted on its lanterns.

*Sure to draw attention, the **chindonya** is the perfect advertising medium of a pre-TV age.*

◪ An *adawara-jōchin*, or collapsible chōchin, burns on the ground during the ambush in *Sanshiro the Judoist* (pt. 1). • Chōchin are also seen above the booths at the **ennichi** in *Kimagure Orange Road* (OVA 1, ep. 1) and the **matsuri** in *Kimagure Orange Road: I Want to Return to That Day.* • We see mon on the chōchin hanging outside the Hadja temple in *Phantom Quest Corp.* (tp. 2, ep. 4).
Ⓜ Opened and collapsed chōchin are seen in *Adolf: An Exile in Japan* (p. 18).

CHOKO (SAKE CUP)

 One explanation as to why sake cups are shallow is that the early Japanese probably drank from small and shallow sea shells. When pottery came into use they simply copied what they already used. Usually sake is poured from ceramic flasks called **tokkuri**. Sometimes you see sake cups for special occasions called **sakazuki** or square wooden **masu**. There is an old custom of drinking from another's cup as a sign of friendship or to honor those of lower status. Among **yakuza** such an exchange of cups signifies a stronger bond than friendship.

◪ A tokkuri and two cups float in a wooden tray in an **onsen** in *Zenki* (tp. 4, ep. 9). • Sake cups and flasks appear in *Tenchi Muyo! Mihoshi Special*, in *Suikoden Demon Century*, and in the cat's flashback in *Urusei Yatsura* (TV tp. 14, ep. 51, st. 74).
Ⓜ Sake cups and flasks are seen in *Bringing Home the Sushi* (p. 82).

CHŌNAIKAI (NEIGHBORHOOD ASSOCIATION)

 Also called *chōkai*. Neighborhoods in Japan tend to be organized in voluntary associations that deal with issues of concern to their members. These are funded by small fees. After moving into a neighborhood one expects a visit from the local association. The work of the association is done by volunteers with some small chores rotating through the neighborhood, such as sweeping up the local garbage collection site after pickups. More complex events such as festivals and emergency drills require the cooperation of many neighbors. During WWII chōnaikai were legally required and dealt with civil defense, rationing, and suppressing dissent.

🅼 In *Ranma 1/2* (vol. 6, p. 72; *Tough Cookies*, ep. 2) what is translated as "neighborhood watch" is *chōnai* in the original Japanese. • Chōnaikai is translated as "town committee" in *Urusei Yatsura* (TV tp. 1, ep. 1, st. 2) but as just "neighbors" in *Lum Urusei Yatsura: Perfect Collection* (p. 64).

🅰 In *Kimagure Orange Road: I Want to Return to That Day*, when Madoka is asked by her sister if she has paid the fee for the **matsuri**, the word she uses is *chōkai*, which is translated as "town council."

🅼 Gen's father and family have trouble with the local chōnaikai chairman in *Barefoot Gen* (p. 10).

CHŌSHOKU (BREAKFAST)

 A traditional Japanese breakfast consists of **misoshiru** (miso soup), cooked rice (**gohan**), fish, seaweed, pickled vegetables (**tsukemono**), and, to drink, **cha** (green tea). Today other items have been added, such as eggs, toast, coffee, milk, or juice.

🅰 In *Phantom Quest Corp.* (OVA "Lover Come Back to Me") rice and **umeboshi** are all that is served for breakfast due to a lack of funds. • Kunikida-san glories in the pleasure of a traditional breakfast in an Omake Theater segment of *Blue Seed: Sea Devils*. • We get an excellent view of the food at breakfast in *Here Is Greenwood* (tp. 1, ep. 1) and in *Tenchi Universe* (tp. 1, ep. 1).

🅼 The ingredients of a traditional breakfast are seen in *Ranma 1/2* (vol. 8, p. 75); note that Akane and Ukyo are holding their rice bowls in one hand.

COMMUTER TRAINS

Trains are a major method of transportation in Japan. Primary school students, ages 6 to 12, get a half-price discount on train fares. Rush-hour commuter trains can be very crowded. One interesting detail is that **Jē Āru**

(Japan Railways) has the number of seats and seating capacity painted on the outside of its coaches. The famous "Bullet Train" (**Shinkansen**) of Japan is used more for long-distance and intercity trips than for daily commuting. It is common for trains and train-crossing signals to be heard in anime and not seen.

🅼 We see Ataru take a train to an appointment with Princess Kurama in *Lum Urusei Yatsura: Perfect Collection* (p. 311).

CRANE WIFE

There is an old story of a young man who rescues a wounded crane. A few nights later a young woman comes to his home and stays with him, becoming his wife. The couple was very poor. The wife wove some beautiful cloth and her husband sold it. He asked her to make more; she was reluctant, but agreed to try. She made her husband promise not to look into the room where she was weaving. But his curiosity got the better of him, and when he looked in on her he saw a crane plucking out its feathers and feeding them into the loom to make cloth. The crane then became angry and scolded her husband for looking into the room; it flew off, never to return.

🅰 A variant of this story is mentioned by Ataru and parodied in *Urusei Yatsura* (TV tp. 14, ep. 52, st. 75).

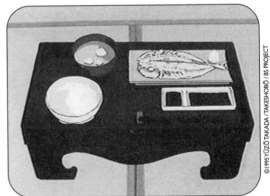

*Ah, **chōshoku**! Here we clearly see the rice, fish, and miso soup of a traditional breakfast in BLUE SEED.*

DAIKOKUTEN

 Also known as Daikoku. One of the Seven Lucky Gods (**Shichifuku-jin**). He is recognizable by his wide face, smile, and flat black hat. Often he is portrayed holding a golden mallet and seated on rice bales with mice, which symbolize a plentiful supply of food. Images of Daikoku are thus often placed in the kitchen. As the god of fortune, Daikoku is venerated by those who wish to become wealthy.

🅰 The Daikoku School of Seven Lucky Gods Martial Arts causes trouble for the Tendo and Saotome families in *Ranma 1/2: It's Fast or It's Free* (ep. 2).
• In *Growing Up* we see both the Daikoku temple and Daikokuya geisha house.
Ⓜ The Shichifuku-jin show up in the Takahashi Rumiko story "Golden Gods of Poverty" (*Rumic World Trilogy*, vol. 2, p. 14).

DAIKON (RADISH)

Daikon is the most common type of radish in Japan. The standard daikon variety is long and thick, resembling a fat white carrot. There are also round as well as long and narrow varieties. Daikon is a common ingredient in Japanese cooking. It is consumed raw, cooked, or pickled (**tsukemono**).

🅰 We see a daikon jammed in Ataru's mouth in *Urusei Yatsura* (TV tp. 6, ep. 21, st. 41).

DANNOURA NO TATAKAI

 A major sea battle at Dannoura, in the Shimonoseki Strait off the southern tip of **Honshu**. On April 25, 1185, the fleet of the

CANNED AND BOTTLED BEVERAGES

Drinks in a can are a mainstay of refreshment enjoyed by characters in countless anime. So many good conversations involve people just going to a park, sitting down, and popping open a can, playing with it as they idly converse. Go to a store in the U.S. and check out the canned and bottled beverages; you will usually just find juice, sodas, water, and beer. Go to a store in Japan and you will find beer, soda, water, juice, canned tea (green, oolong, milk tea, etc.), yogurt drinks, canned coffee (black, with sugar, with sugar and cream, etc.), and a large variety of vitamin drinks. You can even get hot tea and coffee in cans from vending machines on the street. This is beginning to change. When Japanese companies started to sell canned beverages in the U.S., American companies quickly followed and started to issue their own brands of canned coffee and tea. But the sheer variety found in Japan is not to be found here, yet.

Genji clan (**Minamoto** family) led by **Minamoto no Yoshitsune** defeated the fleet of the Heike clan (**Taira** family) in a half-day engagement.

🅰 The battle of Dannoura is shown in the beginning of the anime version of *Ghost Story*.

DARUMA

 Bodhidharma, also known as Bodai Daruma, the founder of Zen Buddhism who is famous for his devotion to sitting in meditation for long periods of time. His dedication to this one task has made him a common symbol of working toward one goal. Daruma dolls representing him are often seen in anime and manga. When starting a project, or making a wish, you buy a Daruma doll, paint in one eye, and place it in the household's or organization's shrine. Upon achieving your goal, you paint in the other eye. The present design of the doll dates from the **Edo period**, when it was used as a protection against smallpox. Daruma dolls are sold at special fairs called *daruma ichi*.

A We see a Daruma doll with both eyes painted in in one of Keiichi's fantasies at the beginning of *Oh My Goddess!* (OVA 1).

DENKI-GAMA (ELECTRIC RICE COOKER)

 The rice cooker is a common appliance in modern Japanese homes. You simply place water and rice in it and turn it on; the appliance turns itself off when the rice is ready. A housemate of mine once said after burning rice, "Why can't you just put everything in a pot and have it turn itself off when it's done?" I told her about rice cookers and she quickly bought one. You can make more than rice in a rice cooker, especially in the more expensive models with fuzzy logic chips.

A Skuld uses a "debugger" she made out of a rice cooker in *Oh My Goddess!* (OVA 4). • In *Urusei Yatsura* (TV tp. 6, ep. 22, sts. 43–44), Ataru is hit by a rice cooker.

*Waiting for the **Daruma**'s eye to be painted in. . . Will the wish be fulfilled?*

M Rice cookers are seen in *Rumic Theater* (pp. 6, 183), in "Laughing Target" (*Rumic World*, p. 91; *Rumic World Trilogy*, vol. 1, p. 165), and *Maison Ikkoku* (vol. 2, p. 172).

DENWA (TELEPHONE)

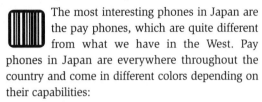 The most interesting phones in Japan are the pay phones, which are quite different from what we have in the West. Pay phones in Japan are everywhere throughout the country and come in different colors depending on their capabilities:

1. Red phones accept ¥10 coins.

2. Green phones are becoming increasingly common as they accept both ¥10 coins and telephone cards.

3. Green phones with gold bands can be used for overseas calls.

4. Gray phones have jacks for modem and fax connections.

5. Yellow phones use ¥10 and ¥100 coins for toll and long distance calls.

6. Pink phones are privately owned and are found in businesses; the owner of the business pays the phone bill with the revenue.

A In an early scene in *Oh My Goddess!* (OVA 1) Keiichi uses a pink pay phone in his dorm to receive calls and order takeout. • Kubo uses a yellow pay phone in *Otaku no Video* (pt. 1, 3rd anim. seq.). • Ataru is using a red phone to call Shinobu in *Urusei Yatsura* (TV tp. 2, ep. 6, st. 11). • In *Phantom Quest Corp.* (tp. 1, ep. 2) Ayaka uses a gray phone to download information to her Casio personal digital assistant. • Keiichi uses a green pay phone to call Belldandy in *Oh My Goddess!* (OVA 5). • Green pay phones also appear in *Blue Seed* (tp. 2, ep. 4) and *Zenki* (tp. 3, ep. 6).

M Kyoko installs a pink pay phone for the tenants' use in *Maison Ikkoku* (vol. 1, p. 243). • We see what I assume is a pink pay phone, as it's not in a regular booth, being used by Ataru in *Lum Urusei Yatsura: Perfect Collection* (p. 97).

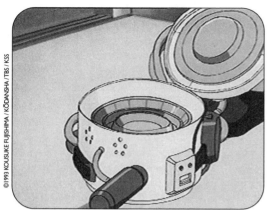

Skuld in OH MY GODDESS! has modified this **denki gama** for a very different use than it was designed for, which is cooking rice.

DEPĀTO (DEPARTMENT STORE)

While they may resemble department stores in the West, the Japanese depāto differs in several ways. Most noticeable is in the level of service, from the greeting one receives when entering, to the assistance in shopping, to free delivery in the city. Often depāto will have rooftop gardens and a floor with several restaurants. Some even have free nursery services for shoppers' children. It is not unusual for an entertainment floor to be devoted to special exhibits and events.

🅐 At the end of a *Phantom Quest Corp.* story (tp. 1, ep. 2) Ayaka comes home with her purchases carried by employees of the department store; of course she spent so much that they took both her and her purchases home.

🅜 We see the interiors of two department stores in *Maison Ikkoku* (vol. 4, pp. 37, 42).

DŌGEN

1200–1253. A major figure in Japanese Zen Buddhism and founder, in 1227, of the Sōtō sect. Originally he was trained and ordained in the esoteric tradition of Tendai Buddhism, but in 1214 he began training in the Rinzai school of Zen. In 1223 he left for China in the hope

of furthering his training in several monasteries. In 1227 he was presented with a certificate declaring him to be the Sōtō Zen successor of Zhangweng Rujing (Chang-weng Ju-ching). After returning to Japan he began to teach others in the Sōtō tradition and founded some significant Zen communities. Many of Dōgen's writings are available in English translation.

🅐 In *Zenki* (tp. 2, ep. 4) we hear a story of a jar that was made for Dōgen.

DOGS AND PREGNANT WOMEN

Due to the belief that dogs have little trouble giving birth, women go to shrines (**jinja**) on "dog days" to pray for an easy delivery.

🅐 In *Hakkenden* (tp. 1, ep. 2) Tatsuka is praying for a child. After having a vision of Princess Fuse riding on the dog Yatsufusa, she finds a puppy at the shrine.

DŌJINSHI (FANZINE)

The Japanese scene churns out a huge variety of fan-produced magazines and comics unlike those produced anywhere else in the world. There are several major conventions devoted to the sale and display of dōjinshi, the biggest being **Komiketto**.

🅐 In *Otaku no Video* (pt. 1, 1st interview) we hear mention of dōjinshi (subtitled as "fanzines").

DŌJŌ (TRAINING HALL)

The word is often translated as "place for studying the Way." Often in anime and manga the "Way" refers to the practice of martial arts, but a dōjō can also be a place to study **shōgi** or **go**. A common feature of martial arts dōjō is the **kamidana** placed high on a wall.

🅜 In *Ranma 1/2* Akane invites Ranma to the dōjō when they first meet.

🅐 In *Sanshiro the Judoist* a dōjō is seen in the very beginning of the series.

HISTORICAL PERIODS

The history of Japan is divided into periods, **jidai**, and eras, **nengō**. Periods are generally long-term cultural or political divisions. Nengō are names given to shorter spans of time within eras, usually but not always coinciding with specific imperial reigns or cultural movements. Opinions differ as to what events constitute the point where one jidai ends and a new one begins. Following is a list of the major jidai throughout Japanese history.

JŌMON, CA. 10,000 B.C.–CA. 300 B.C.
Prehistoric Japan; what little is known is based on archaeological evidence.

YAYOI (CA. 300 B.C.–CA. A.D. 300)
By this period Japan has some contact with China, and Queen Himiko rules an area known as Yamatai

YAMATO, CA. 300–710
Buddhism and writing enter Japan, laws are written down; a subperiod is Kofun, or Tumulus (250–552), named for the many large tombs; some add the Asuka period (552-645)

NARA, 710–94
The capital is moved to Nara; Buddhist and Chinese cultural studies flourish

HEIAN, 794–1185
The capital is moved to Kyōto; the arts flourish at the imperial court (this is the period of *Tale of Genji*); some add the Fujiwara period (897–1185)

KAMAKURA, 1185–1333
A military shogunate is established at Kamakura, just south of what is now Tokyo

MUROMACHI (ALSO CALLED ASHIKAGA), 1333–1568 (1573)
The Kamakura shogunate falls; culture flourishes but social instability persists; some add the Northern and Southern Courts period (1336–92) of divided rule and the Sengoku ("Warring States") period (1467–1568)

AZUCHI-MOMOYAMA, 1568–1603
The period that saw the consolidation of Japan under warlords and the eventual triumph of Toyotomi Hideyoshi and Tokugawa Ieyasu

EDO (TOKUGAWA), 1603–1867)
Japan is unified and closed to outsiders; a robust populist urban culture develops in Edo; most samurai stories date from this period

MEIJI, 1868–1912
The Tokugawa shoguns lose power to forces in favor of restoring power to the emperor after reopening Japan to the world; Westernization and industrialization begin

TAISHŌ, 1912–26
Increasing industrialization and democratization are followed by increasing political repression

SHŌWA, 1926–89
Increased right-wing political power leads to a military buildup, imperialist actions in Asia, and the defeat of Japan in WWII; this is followed by the great economic growth and globalization of the postwar period

HEISEI, 1989–
Japan's bubble economy collapses and the country experiences a period of reduced expectations; the spread of anime abroad dramatically increases

DONBURI (FOOD BOWL)

Donburi are deep ceramic bowls, often with a lid. Foods of rice topped with other ingredients are served in donburi and referred to as donburimono; colloquially they have names that end in -*don*, as in **gyūdon** (beef bowl) or *tendon* (made with tempura).

🅐 Chinese-style pork and tofu are given to Dr. Tofu

in a donburi in *Ranma 1/2* (TV sub tp. 5, dub tp. 7, ep. 14). • **Rāmen** is eaten from donburi in *Ranma 1/2: Darling Charlotte* (ep. 1), *One Pound Gospel*, and *Tenchi Universe* (tp. 4, ep. 12, st. 1). • The cook asks for his donburi back from Godai's grandmother in *Maison Ikkoku: Spring Wasabi* (ep. 1).

Ⓜ We see donburi fall from the top of a cabinet in the story "Wedded Bliss" in *Rumic World Trilogy* (vol. 3, p. 9).

DOTONBORI

A neighborhood in **Osaka** famous for its theaters, shops, restaurants, and their colorful signs. Imagine a restaurant with a 30-foot crab-shaped sign out front and you have Kanidoraku, a famous Dotonbori landmark that specializes in crab dishes.

Ⓐ The buildings and signs of the pleasure district in *Wings of Honneamise* are said to have been inspired by Dotonbori.

Ⓜ Akogiville in *Caravan Kid* is modeled on Osaka, and the parody of Dotonbori features a crab restaurant and a crab-shaped sign (vol. 1, p. 225).

DRINKS, POURING FOR ANOTHER

Filling the glass of another is a sign of courtesy, friendship, and respect. This form of social interaction is common in Japan.

Ⓐ Old man Sakaki pours Shige's beer in *Patlabor: New Files* (tp. 3, ep. 8). • Takeo pours sake for Goto, while Clancy makes a big deal over pouring sake for herself in *Patlabor: New Files* (tp. 3, ep. 9).

Ⓜ Mr. Otonashi pours beer for Godai in *Maison Ikkoku* (vol. 7, p. 152). In *Sanctuary* (vol. 3, p. 84) we see Don Mutsuo Imai overfilling Hojo's glass as a gesture of disrespect.

EBISU

One of the Seven Lucky Gods (**Shichi-fuku-jin**). He is the god of fishing, farming, and commerce. His name means "foreigner" or "barbarian." Ebisu is usually depicted carrying a fishing pole and sea bream (*tai*), and wearing a **kimono**, **hakama**, and a tall cap called a *kazaori eboshi*. There is even a Japanese beer (**bīru**) named after him using the archaic transliteration Yebisu.

Ⓐ The name Ebisu is on the roof of a Genom facility in *Bubblegum Crisis* (OVA 8). • Misato in *Neon Genesis Evangelion* consumes a rather large amount of Yebisu beer; in fact it seems to be her main beverage.

Ⓜ We meet the Shichifuku-jin in Takahashi Rumiko's story "Golden God of Poverty" (*Rumic World Trilogy*, vol. 2). • In *Lum Urusei Yatsura: Perfect Collection* (p. 159) the Shichifuku-jin are parodied.

EDO PERIOD

1603–1867; also called the **Tokugawa** period. This period dates from either 1603, when Tokugawa Ieyasu became **shōgun**, or from 1600, when he defeated his major enemies in the Battle of Sekigahara. During the Edo period Japan was under the military rule of an extensive **samurai** bureaucracy, but because of the nation's almost total isolation from the rest of the world it was a time of uninterrupted peace. Society was highly stratified, and most occupations were hereditary. The Edo period was also a time when arts and literacy flourished. Edo was the name of the administrative capital established by Tokugawa Ieyasu on the Kantō Plain in central Honshu, north of the ancient imperial capital of **Kyoto**. With the end of the

Edo period and the restoration of Emperor Meiji, the imperial capital was moved from Kyoto to Edo, which was renamed Tokyo.

🅐 *Ninja Scroll* takes place during the Edo period.

EIYŌ DRINKS (NUTRITIONAL SUPPLEMENT DRINKS)

 Commonly consumed in Japan to build up stamina while performing hard tasks at work or school, these contain vitamins, herbs, and caffeine. Some brands considered good for sexual stamina are made with snakes or snake parts.

🅐 In *Dragon Half* (pt. 2) Mink is given what is claimed to be an eiyō drink before the martial arts tournament. • Bottles of Black Viper stamina drinks are in the refrigerator at the love hotel (**rabu hoteru**) in *Patlabor: New Files* (tp. 4, ep. 12).

🅜 In *Return of Lum Urusei Yatsura* (p. 46) Mendou is sucking on several bottles of eiyō drink in an attempt to stay awake in class. • The **yakuza** Tokuda has a stamina drink in *Sanctuary* (vol. 4, pp. 7–8) as a preparation to having sex.

EKIBEN ("STATION") LUNCHES

 Boxed meals (**bentō**) sold at train stations and on trains. The word comes from *eki*, "station," and *ben*, an abbreviation of "bentō." Beginning in 1885, these were sold at Utsunomiya Station (north of Tokyo) and were simple meals of rice balls (**nigirimeshi**) with **umeboshi** fillings wrapped in a bamboo leaf (**takenokawa**). Today a variety of ekiben can be purchased at stands in the station, on the platform, on the train, or, while the train is stopped, even through an open window without leaving your seat. Ekiben come with disposable chopsticks (**hashi**), and hot tea can also be purchased to go with the meal. Many train stations have become famous for their tasty ekiben using local food specialties. Ekiben containers are often very attractive and are made of wood, plastic, or ceramic.

Kome does a rather serious job of devouring several **ekiben** *while on a train ride in* BLUE SEED.

🅐 Godai's grandmother in *Maison Ikkoku: Spring Wasabi* (ep. 1) eats from a square wooden ekiben; rice and mushrooms are clearly seen. Note that she has, according to traditional etiquette, neatly tied up the empty bentō next to her. • In *Blue Seed: Rebirth* (ep. 14) Kome and Momiji eat from ekiben on their way to Nara on the **Shinkansen** train. Notice the tea placed in the window. Later we see Kome carrying in a load of other ekiben, apparently for herself, as we again see her eating with a stack of boxes next to her. • Goemon and Murasaki eat from ekiben on a train in *Rupan III: The Fuma Conspiracy*.

EMA (VOTIVE TABLET)

 Offerings in the form of paintings on wood plaques. Often ema are pictures of horses; in fact the name consists of two **kanji**: *e*, or "picture," and *ma*, or "horse." Generally ema are small, called *koema*, with the supplicant's handwritten message thanking a Buddhist deity or **kami** or asking for a favor. These messages often deal with marriage, school exams, health, and other important occasions. Large ema, called *ōema*, are true works of art.

🅐 We see ema hung on trees in *Zenki* (tp. 6, ep. 13).

ENGAWA (VERANDA)

 The engawa is a broad veranda that extends along the perimeter of a traditional Japanese house, often facing the garden. It can be enclosed by **amado** during bad weather. There is generally no railing, and there is usually a low step up from ground level. The engawa is a place to entertain visitors, to play, to do chores, or to drink a cup of tea while enjoying the view.

🅜 Much of the action in *Ranma 1/2* takes place on or near the engawa at the Tendo home; in the winter this engawa is enclosed with glazed amado.

🅐 Keiichi and Belldandy sit on the engawa during the party at the end of the first *Oh My Goddess!* OVA.

ENKA (POPULAR SONG)

 Sad, nostalgic songs often dealing with lost love and a longing for one's hometown. Enka are thus often called the "country music" of Japan. They are the modern version of the *ryūkōka* songs that were so popular in urban areas between the **Meiji period** and the end of WWII.

🅐 Enka are mentioned in *Metal Fighters Miku* (tp. 4, ep. 9) and sung on TV in *Urusei Yatsura: Beauti-*

With the **engawa** between them and the garden, the Tendo family in the RANMA 1/2 TV show sits at their **chabudai** on a spring day.

ful Dreamer. • Enka songs are sung in *Pretty Sammy* and one opens the *Phantom Quest Corp.* series.

ENKAI (PARTY)

This five-sided **ema** from ZENKI has a picture on one side; the other side is used to write a request.

Originally these parties—which generally consist of a meal with drink and, sometimes, entertainment—were ceremonial gatherings at the court, but in time they became common, informal affairs enjoyed by everyone. Enkai are held on a variety of special occasions. There are farewell parties (*sōbetsukai*), welcome parties (*kangeikai*), parties welcoming new employees while saying goodbye to others (*kan-sōgeikai*), New Year's parties (*shinnenkai*), and year-end parties (*bōnenkai*). Sometimes enkai are held at **ryokan** when groups traveling together gather for their meals.

🅐 A party at a ryokan is the scene of the *Patlabor: New Files* story "Versus" (tp. 3, ep. 9). • A *sōbetsukai* is held for Koga-**sensei** in *Botchan* (pt. 2).

🅜 The students gather for a group meal at a ryokan while on a field trip in *Return of Lum: Sweet Revenge* (p. 99). • Yoshio attends a rowdy party of military officers with his father in *Adolf: Days of Infamy* (p. 97). • The heads of the Sagara alliance gather for a *shinnenkai* in *Sanctuary* (vol. 7, p. 104).

ANIME AND STAR TREK

The more anime you watch the more *Star Trek* references you find. *Star Trek* has been popular in Japan since the first series, and many Japanese animators have placed little tributes to the series in their work. But what about anime references in *Star Trek*? The Next Generation has an interesting number of these.

A few are:

When Riker and his father battle in "The Icarus Factor" you see banners in the background that say in **hiragana**, "Ataru," "Lum," and "Urusei Yatsura." Also visible are "Kei," "Yuri," "Akira," and "Tonari no Totoro." I wonder what the reaction was in Japan when this episode aired?

In "Ménage à Troi," a Ferengi security code begins with "Kei Yuri."

Later in "Loud As a Whisper" Geordi has a faux stone table beamed down, and the patterns in the grain of the table are distorted markings for "Kei" and "Yuri."

Other references include starships named the *Kei*, the *Yuri*, and the *Yamato* (which may or may not be an anime reference, given the existence of the real *Yamato*).

Guess what series are popular with the staff who design sets for *Star Trek*?

ENNICHI (FEAST DAY)

 Characterized by food stalls and festive activities on the grounds of shrines or temples. Originally ennichi were special days in the Buddhist or **Shintō** religious calendars. Worshipers would gather, as would merchants to cater to their needs. Some ennichi merchant stalls went on to become permanent stores, and some ennichi fairs have themselves become associated with the sale of certain products. In warm weather many people don traditional cotton **yukata** to attend their neighborhood ennichi fair. For another kind of festive worship, see **matsuri to nenchū gyōji**.

🅼 Akane and Ranma go to an ennichi fair in *Ranma 1/2: Chestnuts Roasting on an Open Fire* (ep. 1) and in the manga translation in vol. 4, p. 170.

🅰 A festival with its booths is seen in *Oh My Goddess!* (OVA 5) and *Kimagure Orange Road* (OVA 1, ep. 1).

EN NO GYŌJA

 An 8th-century ascetic and sorcerer considered a founder of **Shugendō** Buddhist practice. He is also venerated as the **bosatsu** Jinben Dai Bosatsu.

🅰 En no Gyōja is the ancestor of Chiaki, one of the main characters of *Zenki*. See also **Zenki**.

ENOMOTO KEN'ICHI

 1904–70. A popular singing comedian commonly known by his stage name Enoken. Enoken was a major innovator and performer of his time. His stage shows and radio and film roles were a major influence on Tokyo theater before WWII and on the revival of comedy in the postwar period.

🅰 Early in *Mermaid Forest* Yuta is accosted by a barker trying to get him to see a performance by Enoken.

ENOSHIMA

An island in Sagami Bay and a popular spot for tourists, about an hour southwest of Tokyo by train. Enoshima is actually connected to the mainland by a series of long sandbars and bridges. It is the location of Enoshima Shrine, which has been popular since the **Kamakura period**.

🅰 In *Ranma 1/2* (TV sub tp. 3, dub tp. 4, ep. 7) Ryoga went by the roundabout way of Enoshima to meet Ranma for a fight in the lot near their houses.

FOUR THINGS TO FEAR IN LIFE

 There is a saying in Japan that the four things to fear in life are earthquakes (**jishin**), lightning, fires, and father.

◭ Ginko says she is scared of the four biggies in *Metal Fighters Miku* (tp. 6, ep. 13).

FUDŌ-MYŌŌ

 One of the Go Dai Myōō, or Great Wisdom Kings. Originally Hindu deities, the Myōō became part of esoteric Buddhism (**Bukkyō**). Fudō-myōō is usually depicted sitting on a stone, holding a sword in his right hand, a rope in his left, surrounded by flames and looking very fierce. He uses the sword to cut through delusion and the rope to bind passions. But his role is a merciful one to aid all beings by showing them the teachings of the Buddha and leading them into self-control. This is partially indicated by the way his hair is shown gathered into seven knots and draping on his left side, a hair style for servants in Buddhist iconography. He is also seen as a protector and aider in obtaining goals in popular devotion. Temples where he is venerated regularly have a fire ritual (*goma*) devoted to him. In Shingon Buddhism he is placed among the 13 Buddhas, **bosatsu**, and deities. The Sanskrit name for Fudō is Acala Vidyārāja, which means "Immovable Radiant King."

◭ The **Edo-period** temples of the five-color Fudō-Myōō play an important role in *Tenchi Muyo in Love*.

FEBRUARY 26, 1936

 On this date a military rebellion took place in Tokyo. Many major political figures were killed. There were reports that Prime Minister **Okada Keisuke** was dead, but it turned out that it was his brother-in-law who had been shot. The rebellion failed, and many of its leaders were executed. The military was given greater power by fearful civilian politicians, and this contributed to the rise of a military dictatorship.

◭ The beginning of *Mermaid Forest* takes place during the coup attempt.

Ⓜ In *Adolf: A Tale of the Twentieth Century* (p. 116) the role of these events in the expansion of military power is mentioned in light of later developments.

FIRECRACKERS IN THE SKY

 The Japanese set off two sets of three firecrackers in the sky to let the neighborhood know something fun is happening—an upcoming festival or school field day. Often in anime all we see is the last set of explosions.

◭ Actual explosions are mistaken by Lum for a field day announcement in *Urusei Yatsura* (TV tp. 4, ep. 14, st. 27). • Fireworks heralding events are shown in *Theater of Life*, before the marathon in *You're Under Arrest* (OVA 4), before the match in *Metal Fighters Miku* (tp. 5, ep. 11), in the memories Makoto gives Ifurita in *El-Hazard* ("Seventh Night"), before the duel in *Ranma 1/2: Chestnuts Roasting on an Open Fire* (ep. 2), and before the race sequence in *Oh My Goddess!* (OVA 3).

FUGU (PUFFER FISH)

 Tasty but dangerous. The fugu contains tetrotoxin, especially in the liver and ovaries. This toxin can be fatal, but if properly prepared fugu can be quite safe. The meat is certainly attractive, white and almost transparent; often it is arranged on dishes with designs in the glaze so the patterns can be seen through the meat.

In *Urusei Yatsura* (TV tp. 6, ep. 21, st. 42) fugu is mentioned, and later some of the characters complain of a problem with numbness after eating it (TV tp. 15, ep. 55, st. 78).

FUJI-SAN (MT. FUJI)

 Mt. Fuji is one of the most impressive mountains in the world. Not only an impressive geological formation, and Japan's highest mountain, Fuji is one of the most sacred places in Japan. Climbing Mt. Fuji has been a religious pilgrimage (**junrei**) for centuries; it is not an easy climb given the altitude of the mountain, even with bus transportation up most of the way.

 In *Wanderers: El-Hazard* (tp. 1, ep. 2) Makoto speaks of having climbed halfway up Mt. Fuji and says that he hopes to go all the way some day. • We see Mt. Fuji in *GunBuster* (OVA 1), in the opening sequence in *Moldiver* (OVA 1), pictured on a phone card in *Wanderers: El-Hazard* (tp. 1, ep. 2), behind the chopper in *Patlabor 1*, after Nuku Nuku goes to school in *All Purpose Cultural Cat Girl Nuku Nuku* ("Phase 0I"), and painted on assorted **sentō** walls in several anime.

Ⓜ In *Sanctuary* (vol. 4, p. 163) a child asks Hojo if he thinks he could climb Mt. Fuji.

FUKUROKUJU

 One of the Seven Lucky Gods (**Shichi-fuku-jin**). The name denotes happiness (*fuku*), wealth (*roku*), and long life (*ju*). He is sometimes called Jurōjin. Fukurokuju represents longevity and is said to be the incarnation of the southern polestar. He is portrayed as bald with long whiskers. Often he is shown with a crane, a symbol of long life. It is said that the sacred book tied to his staff contains the life span of every person on earth. Fukurokuju can be accompanied by a black deer (an ancient legend says a deer turns black if it is over 2,000 years old).

Ⓜ The Shichifuku-jin show up in the Takahashi Rumiko story "Golden Gods of Poverty" (*Rumic World Trilogy*, vol. 2, p. 14).

FUNDOSHI (LOINCLOTH)

 Traditionally made from a long strip of white cloth, usually cotton, wrapped around the waist and between the legs. These are rarely worn these days, as Western underwear is used instead. Fundoshi are also called *shitaobi*; the special fundoshi worn by sumō wrestlers are called *mawashi*.

 In *Friendship* the men wear fundoshi when they are at the beach, as does Seita in his memories of the beach in *Grave of the Fireflies*. • Fundoshi are also worn by a boatman in *Botchan* and in *Hakkenden* (tp. 3, ep. 5).

FŪRIN (WIND BELL)

 Small bells made of metal, glass, pottery, or bamboo, from which is hung a feather or piece of paper with a poem on it (*tanzaku*) to catch the wind. Fūrin are placed under eaves or in rooms and make a pleasant sound in a summer breeze. The ones traditionally made of glass from the Tokyo area are known as Edo fūrin.

 We see Edo-style fūrin in *Oh My Goddess!* (OVA 2); *Ranma 1/2: Big Trouble in Nekonron, China*; *Blue Seed: Rebirth* (ep. 14); and *Maison Ikkoku: Love-love Story* (ep. 1). • An entire cart of them is shown going through the streets in *Urusei Yatsura: Beautiful Dreamer* (movie 2).

*A classic **bonshū**-style brass **fūrin** in OH MY GODDESS! signals that there is a breeze.*

We see several fūrin at the **Bon** Festival in *Maison Ikkoku* (vol. 3, p. 122).

FŪ-RIN-KA-ZAN

 The army banners of the famous **Sengoku period** samurai leader Takeda Shingen displayed the characters *fū* ("wind"), *rin* ("forest"), *ka* ("fire"), *zan* ("mountain"), symbolizing "as swift as the wind" (*fū*), "as silent as the forest" (*rin*), "as deadly as fire" (*ka*), and "as unshakable as the mountains" (*zan*).

In the first *Dominion Tank Police* anime series (Act 2) the tank of the Squad Leader has Shingen's banner attached to it in the scene after the police are attacked. • We also see a partially obscured banner with these characters on it after the first race in *Oh My Goddess!* (OVA 3).

FURO (BATH)

The typical bath in Japan is deep enough to be immersed in up to your neck. Japanese bathrooms usually have a separate changing room where you undress before entering the bathroom proper. Bathrooms are separate from the room with the toilet (**benjo**), unlike in the West, where the place for becoming clean is the same as that for other bodily functions. The bathroom floor is tiled and has a drain, since you wash with a shower head or a bucket of water before soaking in the tub. As you wash you sit on a small stool. Cleaning yourself before entering the tub is important, because the bath water is shared by several people during a day. Tubs are covered to keep the water hot for the next user. After washing you relax in the hot water, enjoying a moment of rest as the tensions of the day drift away. It is important to not spend too much time in the bath and get overheated. Older, traditional baths are heated by wood fires. It is still common for Japanese parents and children to bathe together. The changing room may also contain a washing machine, and some housewives will use the bath water for laundry.

Some of the members of the Nekomi Tech Auto Club from OH MY GODDESS! *Behind them is a **nobori** with the **kanji** for **fū-rin-ka-zan** on it.*

A rolled-up green bath cover is seen in *Ranma 1/2* (TV sub tp. 1, dub tp. 2, ep. 3). • In *Ranma 1/2* (TV tp. 1, ep. 1) Akane undresses before entering the bathroom. • Getting overheated in the bath is shown in *Tenchi Muyo!* (OVA 8) and *Here Is Greenwood* (tp. 2, ep. 4). • In *My Neighbor Totoro* there are two scenes with the house's old-style bath: first the girls find where the bath is, and later they take a bath with their father. • Several views of a traditional bath are in *Blue Seed: Sea Devils* (Omake Theater).

There is a bath scene in *Mai the Psychic Girl: Perfect Collection* (vol. 1, p. 34). • We can see the changing room and the stool on the wet floor of the bathroom in *Lum Urusei Yatsura: Perfect Collection* (p. 255).

FUROSHIKI (CARRYING CLOTH)

 Cloths used to wrap items for carrying. Originally furoshiki were used to carry items to and from the bathhouse (**sentō**) and opened up on the bathhouse floor while undressing (the word is made up of two parts: *furo*, "bath," and *shiki*, "spread"). Commonly children and adults will carry their **bentō** in them or will use them to wrap gifts; furoshiki used to wrap gifts are

*Mitsuru in the **furo** is a bit surprised by his unwanted "guest" in HERE IS GREENWOOD.*

returned to the giver. Furoshiki often have attractive patterns and colors dyed into the fabric.

A In *Ranma 1/2* (TV sub tp. 2, dub tp. 3, ep. 6), the furoshiki wrapping on the gift from Kasumi is mistaken for a mask by Dr. Tofu. • A furoshiki-wrapped bentō is carried by a running Ayaka to Tenchi as he leaves in *Tenchi Universe* (opening seq.).

M Ataru, with his usual patience and self-control, unwraps and eats his lunch early in *Lum Urusei Yatsura: Perfect Collection* (p. 232). • A wrapped package is next to Eiko in *Barefoot Gen* (p. 59).

FUSUMA

 Sliding doors between rooms or on closets. This traditional door is made of a wooden frame with a heavy paper on each side. A handle, called a *hikite*, is in the form of a lined recess and is located below the center of the door, since fusuma are traditionally opened and closed from a kneeling position. The fusuma will commonly have a stripe of a different color at the level of the hikite. Often pictures will be painted on the door panels to add to their beauty. Unlike **shōji**, fusuma use thick paper and let in little light. When light is needed in an interior room a fusuma may have a shōji panel built into it.

Ranma (transoms) above the fusuma may be added for ventilation.

A Fusuma are in the background as Kasumi shows Ranma-chan which room to sleep in in *Ranma 1/2* (TV tp. 1, ep. 1). • Both fusuma and shōji are seen in the coaches' quarters in *GunBuster* (OVA 4).

FUTON

 The main traditional bedding in Japan. A futon set consists of a thick cotton mattress and heavy quilted bedcover. They are laid out on the floor (futon frames are uncommon in Japan). When not in use futon are folded up and stored in a cupboard (*oshi-ire*). It is important to keep futon dry to prevent mildew, so on sunny days futon are aired out on a balcony rail or clothes pole.

M Ranma and his father sleep on futons in the *Ranma 1/2* manga and TV series. • When we first see Towa near the beginning of *Mermaid Forest* she is lying on a futon (in the manga this is on p. 196).

M Futon are seen in *Maison Ikkoku* (vol. 1, p. 68). • In *Mermaid Forest* (p. 3) we see Mana sitting up on a futon. • In *Rumic World* (p. 90) we see a young Azusa on a futon. • In *Rumic Theater* we see futon on the floor (p. 7) and then (p. 105) being hung out on a balcony rail.

*Behind Ranma and Kasumi in the RANMA 1/2 TV show we see **fusuma** with their colored stripes.*

room, or Ranma-kun does at the rich folks' house in *Ranma 1/2* (TV sub tp. 4, dub tp. 5, ep. 10). • Some loanwords heard in anime include "lucky" used by Momiji in *Blue Seed* (tp. 2, ep. 4), "bird watching" used by Ken and "partner" used by Miyuki in *You're Under Arrest* (OVA 1), "hi" and "non" used by Urd in *Oh My Goddess!* (tp. 2), and of course "Fighto, fighto, fighto" by girls running in several anime.

GAIJIN (FOREIGNER)

 This Japanese term literally means "outside person." Foreigners have a hard time fitting into Japanese society, no matter how hard they try or how well they are treated by the Japanese. Many Japanese consider their culture beyond the comprehension of outsiders, and even their language makes great distinctions between "in group" and "out group." The percentage of the population composed of foreign nationals is very small: 1,075,317 in 1990, 60% of them permanent residents, and the majority from the Koreas, China, and Taiwan. There were only 38,364 gaijin from the U.S.A. in Japan in 1990. Most foreigners, 55% in 1990, live in the industrialized, populous prefectures of Tokyo, **Osaka**, Hyōgo, and **Aichi**.

🅰 Asuka is called a "gaijin" in *Neon Genesis Evangelion* (Genesis 0:5, ep. 9), and of course she acts very much like one in many ways. Other gaijin in anime include Kanuka in *Patlabor* and Belldandy and her sisters in *Oh My Goddess!*

GAIRAIGO (LOANWORD)

 In the modern world all languages borrow words from other cultures. English would not sound like English without its words derived from French, Spanish, German, and Asian languages. Many foreign words and phrases are also used in Japanese. The words I most often notice are English or French, but I have had friends say they often hear Spanish or Portuguese words, such as *pan* for bread.

🅰 To English speakers it may seem strange to hear an anime character say "thank you" as Ranma-chan does when she is handed P-chan in the boys' locker

GEISHA

Geisha are highly skilled entertainers who from childhood learn to play music, sing old songs, and perform classical Japanese dances. Apprentices are called **maiko**, and in the past it was common for young girls to begin their training at a very early age. In the 1920s there were approximately 80,000 geisha; by 1980 the number had dropped to 10,000. The usual way to meet a geisha is by obtaining a very proper introduction from someone, usually a long-established customer. The geisha's fees are astronomical, so to be entertained by one at someone else's expense is quite an honor. Geisha are organized into groups and have their own registry office to handle their work schedules with the local entertainment establishments. Originally geisha were not women but men, also called *hōkan* or *taikomochi*, whose various skills added to the merriment of gatherings. There are few men in this profession today.

🅰 We find out that the character Orin in *Theater of Life* is to become a geisha. • A geisha is being seen by a troublesome character in *Botchan* (pt. 2). • McLaren makes a crude remark about geisha in *Bubblegum Crisis* (ep. 7), showing a foreigner's common misconception.

🅜 In *Sanctuary* (vol. 5, p. 250) we see a meeting with geisha in the **Gion** district of **Kyoto**. • In "Section Chief Kōsaku Shima" that appeared in *Bringing Home the Sushi* (p. 129) Kōsaku is introduced to a geisha and **maiko**. • The murder of a geisha with the professional name of Kinuko is an important crime in *Adolf: A Tale of the Twentieth Century* (p. 27).

GENJI

The major character of *Genji Monogatari* (Tale of Genji), known as "shining Genji." This early 11th century novel by the court lady **Murasaki Shikibu** is considered a major literary masterpiece. It devotes a great deal of space to the loves of Prince Genji. Episodes and characters from *Tale of Genji* are frequently referred to in Japanese art and literature.

🅐 We see a parody of Genji's amorous character in the form of Ataru Genji in *Urusei Yatsura* (TV tp. 3, ep. 11, sts. 21–22). • This classic tale has been adapted in the *Tale of Genji* anime.

GENKAN (ENTRYWAY)

This is an area just below ground-floor level immediately inside the entryway of a home or apartment. It is here where you remove your shoes before entering the main part of the house. You must not step in this area in your stockinged feet to prevent bringing dirt into the house. (I have even seen video footage on TV of a drug raid in Japan where the police quickly stepped out of their shoes in the genkan as they barged into the house.) As you enter the home, it is considered proper to face your shoes toward the door so that you can easily slip into them when you are ready to leave. Once inside, you will often change into slippers or shoes reserved for indoor wear. Genkan are

Genma and Ranma in the RANMA 1/2 TV show sit with their feet in the **genkan** after a morning workout.

occasionally found in other buildings, especially old-fashioned businesses. In anime, Genkan equipped with shoe lockers can often be seen at schools.

🅐 We see a genkan in the tea shop in *Phantom Quest Corp.* (tp. 1, ep. 1). • Tsurumaki is passed out after an all nighter in front of the genkan in *Otaku no Video* (pt. 1, 3rd anim. seq.). • School genkan lockers are used to pass notes in *El-Hazard* ("First Night"), *Neon Genesis Evangelion* (Genesis 0:5, ep. 9), and *Ranma 1/2: Cat-Fu Fighting* (ep. 1). • We also see genkan in *Zenki* (tp. 1, ep. 1), *Pretty Sammy*, and *Urusei Yatsura* (TV tp. 1, ep. 1, st. 1).

🅜 In *Lum Urusei Yatsura: Perfect Collection* we see a genkan (p. 31) and shoes facing out toward the door (p. 149, lower left panel). A school genkan with shoe lockers can be seen in *Return of Lum Urusei Yatsura* (p. 99). • In *Maison Ikkoku* (vol. 1, p. 10) we often see the genkan of the boarding house with a cabinet near it for storing shoes. • We see an indoor genkan at the entrance to the Bridal Chamber in "Merchant of Romance" (*Rumic Theater*, chapt. 2, p. 37).

GETA (WOODEN SANDALS)

These are wooden shoes, often with two lateral slats on the bottom, that are attached to the foot with a thong. When you see characters in **kimono** or **yukata** on the street, check their feet; odds are they will be wearing geta.

🅐 Geta are worn by the coach in *Metal Fighters Miku* and by Hyokichi in the *Theater of Life* anime. • Geta are worn in a flashback scene in *Urusei Yatsura* (TV tp. 10, ep. 37, st. 60). • We see geta from above on Nabiki's feet for a few seconds in the first music video after the ending credits in *Ranma 1/2: One Grew over the Kuno's Nest.* • Kyoko wears wooden footwear outdoors in *Maison Ikkoku: Soichiro's Shadow* (ep. 2).

🅜 Ataru gets hit in the head by a tossed geta in *Lum Urusei Yatsura: Perfect Collection* (p. 75). • In *Maison Ikkoku* (vol. 3, pp. 120–21) we see Kozue in a kimono and geta.

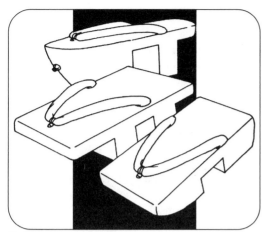

*Various forms of simple **geta** protect the feet of workers or young ladies.*

GINKGO

 This fast-growing tree is found in much of Japan. Its fan-shaped leaves turn an attractive yellow in the fall. In Jingū Gaien park in Tokyo there is a 2,500-foot-long street called Ginkgo Tree Lane, one of the landmarks of this area.
Ⓐ The challenge of climbing a ginkgo tree plays a major part in *Theater of Life*. • Ginkgo leaves are seen on the wind in *Zenki* (tp. 1, ep. 2), in *Blue Seed* (tp. 4, ep. 8), in *Kimagure Orange Road* (OVA 4, ep. 2), and, as Achika walks among the trees, in the home movie in *Tenchi Muyo in Love*.
Ⓜ Lum is depicted riding a ginkgo leaf on the cover of *Lum Urusei Yatsura: Perfect Collection*.

GINZA

 The Ginza in eastern central Tokyo is that city's most famous shopping and entertainment center. Its name comes from *gin* ("silver") and *za* ("mint"), as there was a silver coin mint built in this location in 1612. The mint is long gone but the name remains. The modern Ginza began in 1873 when two-story brick buildings and a shopping promenade were built on the street from the Shinbashi bridge to the Kyōbashi bridge in the southwestern part of Chūō Ward. The European-style brick buildings are gone, but some older build-ings are still to be seen there, the most famous being the Wakō Building with its clock tower. Today the Ginza is a shopping and office area that becomes an entertainment district at night. Chūō Street, one of the main roads in the Ginza, is blocked off to all but pedestrian traffic on holidays and Sundays.
Ⓐ The Wakō Building clock tower, a major Ginza landmark, is seen in *Patlabor: New Files* (tp. 1, ep. 1).
Ⓜ In the "'One Cup' Fisherman" story in *Bringing Home the Sushi*, we see two office ladies agree to go to the Ginza (p. 46), and we see Hamasaki and his boss take a guest to a Ginza club where they enjoy the company of **hosutesu** (p. 54).

GION

 The Gion district of **Kyoto** developed in the middle ages in front of Yasaka Shrine. Eventually this part of Kyoto became a major red light district licensed by the government. Today it is still an entertainment area and is famous for its preservation of traditional styles of architecture and entertainment. Part of the district has been declared a national historical preservation district.
Ⓜ In *Sanctuary* (vol. 5, p. 250) we see a **yakuza**

*You cannot mistake the fan-shaped **ginkgo** leaf for that of any other tree.*

meeting in the form of an **enkai** with **geisha** in the Gion district of **Kyoto**.

GISSHA (OX CART)

 In the **Heian period** it was common for the nobility, especially women, to be transported by two-wheeled, enclosed, ox-drawn carriages. In the **Kamakura period** the slow gissha was replaced by the **koshi** or palanquin.

 Mendou's mother arrives at the school in a gissha in *Urusei Yatsura* (TV tp. 4, ep. 16, st. 32). • Gissha are also seen in *Tale of Genji*.

GO

 Also called *igo*. A game that entered Japan from China, go is played on a board of 19 X 19 lines with black and white pieces that are placed on the intersections. The rules of go are very simple, but the play is quite subtle and can take years to master. Go players don't seem to mind putting in that kind of effort.

 The fathers are playing go in *Ranma 1/2* (OVA "Akane vs. Ranma!"). • The coach in *GunBuster* (OVA 4) is seen playing a game in his quarters on the ship when Amano visits him.

Go stones make a complex pattern of play in the first RANMA *movie. Black risks losing some stones, or is it white? Whose turn is it anyway?*

©1991 RUMIKO TAKAHASHI / SHŌGAKUKAN / KITTY FILM / FUJI TV

GOHAN (COOKED RICE)

 The staple of Japanese cooking, eaten with every traditional meal, and many non-traditional ones. Most scenes where breakfast (**chōshoku**) is served include gohan served in small bowls (**chawan**). Since gohan is such an essential part of Japanese cuisine, the word itself has also come to mean "a meal."

 Whether serving cooked rice or not, Kasumi uses the phrase *Gohan desu yo!* to call the family to a meal in *Ranma 1/2: Chestnuts Roasting on an Open Fire* (ep. 2). • Ataru's mother in *Urusei Yatsura* can often be heard using this phrase.

GOHEI

 Zigzag paper streamers often attached to **shimenawa** or other objects used in **Shintō** rituals. The same word is also applied to a wand decorated with paper or cloth streamers. *Harae-gushi* are sacred paper streamers—usually white—that are attached to a stick waved to the right, left, and right in a purification ritual.

 The shaking of the gohei can be seen in the wedding ritual at the beginning of the Lupin anime *Rupan III: The Fuma Conspiracy.* • In *Zenki* (ep. 1) gohei are shaken by Chiaki.

 Gohei are shaken by Sakura in an exorcism ritual in *Lum Urusei Yatsura: Perfect Collection* (p. 82).

GORYŌ (VENGEFUL GHOST)

 In Japanese tradition ghosts often haunt someone or a locality as an act of revenge against a wrong done to them while alive. "I will haunt you" thus became a threatening statement used in anger against someone. At times Buddhist ascetics and priests would be hired to perform services for those whose unusual deaths could result in a vengeful ghost. In some cases such ghosts would be deified to placate their spirits. Another name for ghost in general is **yūrei**.

 "I'm gonna go bad and haunt you" is said by a

Simple cut and folded pieces of paper attached to a stick—
gohei—*take on a ritual significance during a festival in* HAKKENDEN.

cat in *Urusei Yatsura* (TV tp. 14, ep. 51, st. 74), and he does. • A girl's ghost longs for vengeance in *Kimagure Orange Road* (OVA 2, ep. 1).

Ⓜ Kyoko dresses as **Okiku**, a famous goryō, in *Maison Ikkoku* (vol. 6, p. 3).

GYŌZA (POTSTICKERS)

 One of the many Chinese foods popular in Japan. Gyōza are made from pastry cases filled with vegetables and ground meat then fried in oil. Pork and garlic are common ingredients.

Ⓐ Potstickers with garlic are mentioned in *Urusei Yatsura* (TV tp. 8, ep. 27, st. 50).

GYŪDON ("BEEF BOWL")

 This food dish consists of rice with beef (*gyū*) on top served in a **donburi**. "Beef bowl" is how it is usually translated in anime and manga.

Ⓐ Gyūdon seems to be a favorite food of many of the characters in *Urusei Yatsura* (tp. 1, ep. 3).

Ⓜ While the translation in *Lum Urusei Yatsura: Perfect Collection* (p. 135) identifies the place Rei is eating at as a "Sukiyaki Hut," in the original text he is actually eating gyūdon.

HACHIKŌ

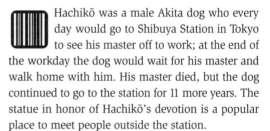 Hachikō was a male Akita dog who every day would go to Shibuya Station in Tokyo to see his master off to work; at the end of the workday the dog would wait for his master and walk home with him. His master died, but the dog continued to go to the station for 11 more years. The statue in honor of Hachikō's devotion is a popular place to meet people outside the station.

Ⓐ In *Moldiver* (OVA 3) the Hachikō statue is a meeting point. • Hachikō is mentioned in *Zenki* (tp. 5, ep. 10). • The statue is clearly visible as Ayeka walks past it in *Tenchi Muyo in Love.*

HACHIMAKI (HEADBAND)

 Usually of white or red cloth, and worn as a symbol of great exertion. One theory links early hachimaki to religious activi-

Misaki in MOLDIVER *waits for Mirai at the* **Hachikō** *statue. Where is she?*

"ASIAN WOMEN DON'T HAVE TITS THAT BIG!"

This was the sentence that began it all. It was voiced by a friend while watching the early *Ranma 1/2* TV episodes. Thank *kami-sama* I wasn't showing him the movies with Nakajima's silicone-implanted redesign of the characters. What possessed her to do that to Akane-chan I'll never understand!

Anyway, back to the subject. At the time this statement was voiced I was going out with a woman from mainland China who contradicted the statement, but not in words.

So for the next few years I did extensive hands-off research by observing and comparing East Asian women and Caucasian women. The conclusion I came to is that Asian women are not that small and Caucasian women are not all that large. If anyone doubts my unscientific conclusions let them spend some time making their own observations.

Of course the hyper-inflated breasts of *Burn-Up W* are an exception; such anatmoical excesses look like they came out of U.S. comic books rather than the majority of anime and manga.

ties. Another says that hachimaki originated in the bands worn by warriors to keep their caps on. Today, women giving birth, students studying for difficult exams (or at riots), office workers promoting a sales campaign, sushi chefs expertly carving fish, carpenters building temples, young men bearing **mikoshi**—all wear hachimaki to demonstrate their hard work and resolve. Hachimaki are often decorated with slogans—"Try hard!"

🅐 Godai wears a headband while studying in *Maison Ikkoku: Ronin Blues* (ep. 1). • In *Student Days* we see a hachimaki worn while studying for entrance exams. • Fukuhara wears a hachimaki as she draws illustrations for an anime in *Otaku no Video* (pt. 2, 5th anim. seq.).

HAGOITA (PADDLE)

Used to play **hanetsuki**, these wooden paddles are often decorated with auspicious symbols or even silk collages, making them more ornamental than functional. The use of complex silk decorations on hagoita dates from the 17th century, and while the game itself is rarely played, the craft of making decorated hagoita remains. These paddles are often sold at traditional *hagoita ichi*, a type of fair held in December. In Tokyo hagoita are sold at shrines including the Fukagawa Fudō Shrine and **Asakusa Jinja**.

Ⓜ In "One Hundred Years of Love" (*Rumic Theater*, p. 132) we see Mrs. Hoshino as a child holding a hagoita.

HAKAMA (TROUSERS)

Trousers tied over a **kimono** or **haori** and worn more often by men than women. Hakama are so loose that they can be mistaken for a skirt.

🅐 Kuno's clothes when you first see him, and often later, include hakama in *Ranma 1/2* (TV tp. 1, ep. 2). • Goemon in *Rupan III: The Fuma Conspiracy* and other Lupin anime wears hakama.

Ⓜ Kaieda in *Mai the Psychic Girl: Perfect Collection* (vol. 1, pp. 46–47) often wears hakama. • In *Sanctuary* (vol. 5, p. 26) Isaoka wears hakama at an official event.

HAKAMAIRI (GRAVESITE VISIT)

A ritual visit to a gravesite to pray. Visitors pour water over the memorial stone and burn incense. Often this is done during *higan*, the period of time around the spring and autumn equinox.

Ⓜ We see a visit to a grave in *Maison Ikkoku* (vol. 1, pp. 59–63).

HAKONE

A town west of Tokyo on the shores of the lake Ashinoko, known for its good view of Mt. Fuji (**Fuji-san**) and today a popular resort. Hakone developed as a post-station town in the **Edo period**.

🅼 In *Sanctuary* (vol. 3, p. 84) a meeting takes place in Hakone.

HAMAYA

Symbolic arrow talismans sold at shrines (**jinja**) during New Year's and kept at home during the year. Hamaya are believed to prevent bad luck and bring good tidings.

🅰 Arrows stick out of a bag held by Tsutomu in *Zenki* (tp. 6, ep. 13).

🅼 Mara gets a surprise when she steps on a hamaya in *Oh My Goddess!: Sympathy for the Devil*.

HANABI (FIREWORKS)

Fireworks-manufacturing techniques were introduced into Japan in the 16th century by the Portuguese and not by the Chinese, despite the proximity of Japan and China (this illustrates how isolated Japan was at that time). Japanese fireworks are especially noted for their variety of floral star burst rockets. Fireworks displays are common during summer festivals. The most fa-

*Loose but not so as to encumber the legs, **hakama** made excellent wear for samurai.*

mous of these is the Sumidagawa Hanabi Taikai held in Tokyo on the last Saturday in July on the banks of the Sumida River. A simple hand-held firework seen in some anime and manga is the **senkō-hanabi**.

🅰 Fireworks play a role in *You're Under Arrest* (ep. 1). • Keiichi and Belldandy watch fireworks together in *Oh My Goddess!* (tp. 5) and are seen as part of a celebration in *Theater of Life*.

🅼 We see fireworks at the **Bon** Festival in *Maison Ikkoku* (vol. 3, p. 13).

HANAFUDA

A gambling game played with 48 cards (*hanakaruta*) in 12 suits. Each card has a flower, plant, animal, or poem on it representing a month of the year. Hanafuda is a combination of a traditional court game where plants and animals associated with the seasons were matched and the Western playing cards that were introduced by the Dutch. The goal of the game is to collect as many cards from matching suits as you can.

🅰 Ataru and Lum stay up all night playing hanafuda in *Urusei Yatsura* (TV tp. 6, ep. 21, st. 42).

HANA-KANZASHI (HAIRPIN)

An ornamental hairpin shaped like dangling flowers.

🅰 We see a hana-kanzashi in Midori's hair in *Growing Up*.

HANAMI (FLOWER VIEWING)

Usually used to refer to viewing cherry blossoms (**sakura**). This pastime often takes the form of excursions and picnics in the spring. These can be quite boisterous with much consumption of food and drink and merrymaking. Some locations specially planted with flowering cherries—such as public parks (like **Ueno Kōen**) or riverbanks—are very popular for hanami parties.

🅰 In *Urusei Yatsura* a flower viewing party takes place in a classroom (tp. 5, ep. 20, st. 39).

BABES WITH BIG BAZOOKAS

I am not talking about breasts here; women with destructive armaments is the topic. One of the stupider Western stereotypes about Japan is that of submissive, meek women. Sure many Japanese women are softspoken and polite, but that does not mean they are weak. Many women in Japanese history have been strong figures, and even if Japan is still highly gender-role oriented, women often play a very strong role in their communities and in politics.

Anime and manga can also turn the expected gender roles upside down, or at least sideways, with humorous results. Who would confuse the Dirty Pair or Mew and Mica with stereotypical kimono-clad submissive women? Part of what stories can do is alter the perspective of the normal and expected by changing, exaggerating, or inverting social roles. In anime this is done for a number of reasons, but for us it means greater variety, and pleasure, in entertainment, and that's what it's really about isn't it?

Excuse me Yuri, can you pass that rocket launcher?

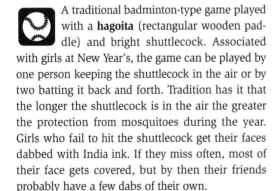

HANETSUKI

A traditional badminton-type game played with a **hagoita** (rectangular wooden paddle) and bright shuttlecock. Associated with girls at New Year's, the game can be played by one person keeping the shuttlecock in the air or by two batting it back and forth. Tradition has it that the longer the shuttlecock is in the air the greater the protection from mosquitoes during the year. Girls who fail to hit the shuttlecock get their faces dabbed with India ink. If they miss often, most of their face gets covered, but by then their friends probably have a few dabs of their own.

🅰 In the third lecture of *GunBuster* (OVA 3) Noriko gets ink dabbed on her face for not being able to answer questions.

🅜 In "One Hundred Years of Love" (*Rumic Theater*, chapt. 5, top of p. 132) we see Mrs. Hoshino as a child holding a hagoita.

HANKACHI (HANDKERCHIEF)

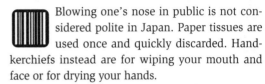

Blowing one's nose in public is not considered polite in Japan. Paper tissues are used once and quickly discarded. Handkerchiefs instead are for wiping your mouth and face or for drying your hands.

🅰 A handkerchief is used to wipe a face in *Urusei Yatsura* (TV tp. 8, ep. 30, st. 53). In *Maison Ikkoku: Call Me Confused* (ep. 1) Godai holds his handkerchief in his mouth as he washes his hands so it will be easier to get to when he dries them.

HANKO (SEAL)

Commonly called a "chop" in English. In Japan seals are used instead of signatures on legal documents. The seal can be made from any durable material; some artisans are highly skilled at carving seals and produce true works of art. The practice originated in China and at first was limited to the nobility; early records indicate that in 704 Emperor Monmu ordered each province to make and use official seals. In the **Meiji period** seals became commonly used when the government ordered the bureaucracy to accept only written documents from the public. Seals can be divided into two types, *jitsuin*, which are officially registered with the local officials, and *mitome-in*, which are unofficial seals. These seals are used in any situation that would require a signature in most other countries, from authorizing legal documents to "signing" a receipt for a package or a painting. Forgetting or misplacing a seal is thus a great inconvenience! It is a serious crime to steal or forge a hanko. (In some cases a right thumbprint may be used instead of a seal.)

🅰 Bundles of yen notes are sealed with a hanko on the seam of the paper band in *Patlabor: New Files* (tp. 2, ep. 6). • Lum uses a seal while Ten uses his handprint in *Urusei Yatsura* (TV tp. 12, ep. 44, st. 67).

◩ We see an official hanko in the story "War Council" by Takahashi Rumiko in *Rumic World Trilogy* (vol. 3, p. 63).

HAORI (JACKET)

 A jacket worn over a **kimono** or **yukata**. These are between hip or knee length. To close the front you tie two cords together. For men a formal haori will have crests (**mon**); for women haori with crests are not considered formal.
🅐 We see yukata and haori worn by SV2 members on the walkway of a **ryokan** in *Patlabor: New Files* (tp. 3, ep. 9).
◩ The characters wear haori over yukata at a **ryokan** in *Maison Ikkoku* (vol. 7, p. 109).

HAPPI (COAT)

A straight-sleeved coat made of indigo or brown cotton and imprinted with a crest (**mon**). Originally the mon represented the crest of a family and the coats were worn by its servants. Later it became common for happi to display the mon of shops and organizations. Happi are often worn by participants in festivals (**matsuri**).
🅐 Kira wears a happi in *Theater of Life*, and a red happi coat is on a **kappa** in *Urusei Yatsura* (TV tp. 7, ep. 23, sts. 45–46).
◩ We see happi coats in *Mermaid's Scar* (p. 57) worn by searchers for a missing young woman.

HARA (STOMACH, BELLY)

According to traditional Japanese medicine the belly is the center of the body and vital to health. Keeping the belly warm is thought to be especially important, so some Japanese use a band of cloth (*haramaki*) wrapped around the middle of their body or when sleeping to make sure the stomach is covered.
🅐 Tamiya in *Oh My Goddess!* (tp. 3) often wears a belly band, as do Akira in *Shonan Bakusozoku* and the old man at the souvenir stand in *Patlabor: Original Series* (tp. 2, ep. 4). • In *Urusei Yatsura* we see a belly band on an old cat (TV tp. 12, ep. 43, st. 66)

and on Ryuunosuke's father (TV tp. 17, ep. 63, st. 86). • Goto sleeps with a towel across his belly while sleeping on a couch in *Patlabor: New Files* (tp. 4, ep. 12).

HARAJUKU

A district in Shibuya Ward in western Tokyo. This is a popular area for young people and has many shops, drinking places, and restaurants. Some streets are reserved for pedestrians only on Sundays and holidays. Local landmarks include the headquarters of NHK (**Nippon Hōsō Kyōkai**), the Yoyogi National Stadium, and Yoyogi Park.
🅐 Haneda asks Yohko which is better for dinner, Harajuku or **Aoyama**, in *801 TTS Airbats* (pt. 2).

HARI (ACUPUNCTURE)

Acupuncture involves inserting needles into the body to aid the proper balance of **ki**, which insures good health. It was introduced into Japan from China in the 6th century. The needles used are classed into 10 grades depending on their thickness and length. Often hari is

*Fashionable in the past, **haori** are still worn on some formal occasions.*

*A **happi** coat is worn by Kira in THEATER OF LIFE with the **mon** clearly visible on the back.*

administered by masseurs who are certified by the government; it is not unusual for these practitioners to be blind.

 Acupuncture and moxa treatment are advertised on a sign at Tofu-**sensei**'s gate in *Ranma 1/2: Chestnuts Roasting on an Open Fire* (ep. 2).

HASHI (CHOPSTICKS)

Chopsticks are common outside of Asia, even if many of us cannot properly use them. There are several kinds of hashi; these include ordinary ones for eating (often made of lacquered wood), disposable ones (called *waribashi*) made of a single piece of wood and joined at one end so they can be broken apart, and special long wood or metal hashi, called *saibashi*, used for cooking. Disposable chopsticks are sometimes broken after use due to an old belief that spirits can attach themselves to discarded or lost hashi and make the user ill. At home, people often have their own hashi that no one else uses. Some place their hashi in a special box and take them to school or work with their lunch.

 Near the end of *You're Under Arrest* (OVA 1), Natsumi accidentally breaks her disposable hashi.
• We see red hashi used by Akane in *Ranma 1/2* (TV sub tp. 6, dub tp. 8, ep. 16).

HATA (CEREMONIAL BANNER)

 A kind of flag where the cloth hangs downward and is attached to a short pole attached crosswise at the top of another pole. These are still seen at ceremonies and shrine processions. For another kind of banner, see **nobori**.

 Hata are seen hanging in the background in *Return of Lum: Feudal Furor* (p. 81).

HATAKI

 A hataki is made up of cloth strips on a stick and is used for knocking dust off surfaces to the floor, where it can be swept or vacuumed up. While the hataki superficially resembles a **gohei** it has a more secular purpose.

 In *Urusei Yatsura* (TV tp. 3, ep. 9, st. 18) Ten uses such a duster.

 In *Maison Ikkoku* (vol. 1, top of p. 15) we see Kyoko using a hataki.

HATSUMŌDE

 Literally, "first visit." Starting after 12 A.M. on New Year's Day and for a few days afterward Japanese will visit a **Shintō** shrine or Buddhist temple to pray for what they desire in the coming year. Originally hatsumōde would be to the nearest shrine or temple in the direction considered most auspicious. Nowadays people choose to visit famous shrines or temples. Major shrines can often have over a million visitors in the first three days of the year. Part of the hatsumōde tradition is taking old amulets and talismans like **ofuda**, **omamori**, **ema**, and **hamaya** to be ceremonially burned. New ones are then bought for the coming year.

 In *Maison Ikkoku* (vol. 2, p. 81) Godai and Kyoko go to the temple for the New Year.

HAYAMA

A coastal town on the Miura Peninsula in southern Kanagawa Prefecture in central **Honshu**. Its mild climate has made Hayama a resort area with a marina.

Part of the story in *Season of the Sun* takes place in Hayama.

HAYASHI FUMIKO

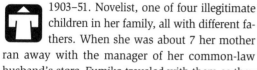 1903–51. Novelist, one of four illegitimate children in her family, all with different fathers. When she was about 7 her mother ran away with the manager of her common-law husband's store. Fumiko traveled with them as they sold goods throughout **Kyushu**. Rootless women and failed relationships are found in many of her works.

 Hayashi Fumiko is the author of *Hōrōki*, part of which is available in an anime version as *Wandering Days*.

HAZE (GOBY)

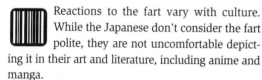 A type of fish used in tempura and sliced thin for sashimi. There are many species. The Tokyo Bay species is the *ma-haze*, which grows to a length of 8 inches.

 The mechanics in *Patlabor: New Files* (tp. 3, ep. 8) catch and dry haze.

HE (FART)

Reactions to the fart vary with culture. While the Japanese don't consider the fart polite, they are not uncomfortable depicting it in their art and literature, including anime and manga.

 We see a tough guy fart in a **sentō** (public bath) in *Patlabor: New Files* (tp. 2, ep. 7). • A guy is accused of farting in a pool in *Urusei Yatsura* (TV tp. 11, ep. 39, st. 62).

 Gen's father breaks up a spear-fighting practice session with his farts in *Barefoot Gen* (p. 9). • The first fart in *Caravan Kid* (p. 149) is in a bathtub; the ones that come later are not and are more impressive, if impressive is the right word.

ANIME IS NOT A GENRE

Another peeve of mine is people who class anime as a genre. OK, in a very broad sense of the word it can be called one, that is, if you can call cinema a genre or printed books a genre. But it is better to speak of anime as a particular medium, animation, in a particular cultural context, Japan. Then speak of Sci-Fi anime, Fantasy anime, Police anime, Historical anime, etc. I would be hard pressed to find a cinematic or literary genre that was not represented in anime. In fact the many genres recognized by critics in the West are still not enough to encompass the large variety of anime that exist, so we may have to come up with some new ones. I propose the following as a beginning:

Babes with Big Bazookas—*Dirty Pair* (I'm talking armaments here)

Romantic Martial Arts Comedy Drama—*Ranma 1/2*

Transplanted Scandinavian Goddess Romantic Comedy—*Oh My Goddess!*

Traffic Police Action Comedy—*You're Under Arrest*

Dungeons and Dragons–Based Stories—*Record of Lodoss War*

Poking Fun at Dungeons and Dragons–Based Stories—*Dragon Half*

Well, you get the idea.

HEADLIGHTS OFF

As a courtesy, drivers in Japan will often turn off their headlights at stoplights to prevent the glare from getting into the eyes of other drivers.

 We see Goto turn off the lights after stopping in a traffic jam in *Patlabor: New Files* (tp. 4, ep. 12).

HEARN, LAFCADIO

1850–1904. Writer born on the Greek island of Lefkas of an Anglo-Irish father and Greek mother. Hearn was raised in Dublin and later moved to the U.S., where he worked as a reporter. In 1889 he went to Japan, where he married the daughter of a samurai, became a Japanese citizen (taking the name of Koizumi Yakumo), and taught English literature at Tokyo University (**Tōkyō Daigaku**) until 1903. His works, although criticized today for their "exoticism," were instrumental in introducing Japanese society to the West.

A Hearn was the author of *Kwaidan*, which has been animated under the title *Ghost Story*.

HEIAN PERIOD

794–1185. The period dating from the capital's resettlement at Heiankyō (present-day **Kyoto**) until the establishment of the Kamakura shogunate (see **Kamakura period**) by the **Minamoto** family. This is the period depicted in *Tale of Genji* (see **Genji**).

A The Heian court is parodied in *Urusei Yatsura* (TV tp. 3, ep. 11, sts. 21–22).

HEIKEGANI

A species of crab (*Dorippe japonica*) whose shell has a pattern resembling a human face. It is believed that these are incarnations of the spirits of the Heike (**Taira** family) warriors who were defeated at the Battle of Dannoura (**Dannoura no Tatakai**) in the Inland Sea.

A We see crabs with the "Heike" pattern in *Ghost Story*.

HEIKE MONOGATARI

Tale of the Heike. A major literary work recounting the victories of the **Taira** (Heike clan) over the **Minamoto** (Genji clan) and their decline and destruction. *Heike Monogatari*, composed in the **biwa hōshi** style, is filled with Buddhist symbolism and references.

A In *Ranma 1/2* (TV tp. 1, ep. 2) Kuno quotes the famous opening paragraph of *Heike Monogatari*: "The sound of the bell at **Gion** echoes the impermanence of all things. The hue of the flowers of the teak-tree declares that they who flourish must be brought low." • Hōichi performs part of *Heike Monogatari* in *Ghost Story*.

HEISEI PERIOD

The name given to the reign of the present emperor, Akihito, beginning on January 7, 1989. *Hei* means "peace," and *sei* means "achievement."

A In the opening sequence of *Phantom Quest Corp.* there is mention of the Heisei period.

HIBACHI (CHARCOAL HEATER)

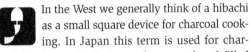

In the West we generally think of a hibachi as a small square device for charcoal cooking. In Japan this term is used for charcoal-heating units that are often round and filled with ash. Tongs (*hibashi*) are used to handle the coals. Hibachi are sometimes used to heat snacks or tea water, but their main purpose is to heat a room.

A Ataru is hit by a hibachi in *Urusei Yatsura* (TV tp. 3, ep. 11, sts. 21–22). • A hibachi is in the center of the room where Rupan and Jigen are hiding in *Rupan III: The Fuma Conspiracy*.

M Princess Kurama huddles over a hibachi in *Lum Urusei Yatsura: Perfect Collection* (p. 379). • Hibachi

We know it's cold in TALE OF SHUNKIN *when we see this ceramic* **hibachi** *with the hibashi sticking out of it.*

are seen in the *Rumic World* story "Laughing Target" and in *Barefoot Gen* (p. 54).

HIDA SANMYAKU (HIDA MOUNTAINS)

 A mountain range running through Niigata, Toyama, Nagano, and Gifu prefectures. Popular for mountain climbing, many of its famous peaks are in the Chūbu Sangaku National Park.

 Something truly evil escapes captivity in the Hida Mountains in *Ranma 1/2* (vol. 6, p. 8).

HIGUCHI ICHIYŌ

 1872–96. One of the most famous women writers of the **Meiji period**. Higuchi Ichiyō was the pen name of Higuchi Natsu, the daughter of a minor official. She was at the top of her class when her parents took her out of school after the fourth grade, believing that too much education was not good for girls. Higuchi was later able to attend a poetry school, the Haginoya, for a short time. After the deaths of her father and older brother her family fell into poverty and her childhood sweetheart's family canceled their engagement. In 1892 she published her first short story, "Yamizakura." After a year of low earnings from the sale of her stories she decided to abandon writing. At this time she, her mother, and her sister moved to the outskirts of the Yoshiwara quarter of Tokyo, an old red-light district. Here she gathered material for her story "Takekurabe," translated into English as "Growing Up." After this she began to teach at the Haginoya and wrote some of her best works. She died of tuberculosis in her mid-20s.

 There is an anime adaptation of *Growing Up*.

HINA MATSURI (DOLL FESTIVAL)

 On March 3 households with daughters display a tiered stand of dolls wearing traditional costumes representing the emperor, empress, and members of the Japanese royal court. There are two styles of arranging the dolls for the emperor and empress. The **Kyoto** style has the empress to the left of the emperor (as you face the dolls); the Edo (Tokyo) style has the emperor on the left. The doll on the right side is considered superior, and it was when a daughter of Edo became empress that the Edo style began.

 We see an example of the empress on the right in *Urusei Yatsura* (TV tp. 5, ep. 18, st. 35).

HIROSHIMA

 The capital of Hiroshima Prefecture in western **Honshu**. A port city, Hiroshima is on the Inland Sea coast. It was a castle town in the **Edo period**. It suffered extensive damage in the nuclear bombing of August 1945. Today Hiroshima is a major city known for machinery, automobiles, and food processing.

 Barefoot Gen takes place in Hiroshima around the time of the dropping of the bomb.

 Hiroshima is mentioned in *Blue Seed* (tp. 2, ep. 4).

HISAGO (GOURD)

 Large, dried-out hollow gourds are used for carrying sake, smaller ones for spices or pills. The gourd is narrower in the center than at the ends, allowing a carrying cord to be tied around it. It can also be cut lengthwise and used as a ladle.

©1995 KIKUHIDETANI /YOSHIHIRO KUROIWA / SHŪEISHA / KFACTORY /TV-TOKYO

*The **hisago** in* ZENKI *is a very versatile container. I wonder what this one contains?*

An example of drinking from a hisago is seen near the end of the *Zenki* story "Jar of Desires" (tp. 2, ep. 4). • Taisou in *Giant Robo* carries a hisago, and we know for sure it's not holding water. • In *Urusei Yatsura* (TV tp. 3, ep. 9, st. 17) we see a **tengu** drinking from a small hisago, and Ataru thinks it wants to take medicine.

HITODAMA (SPIRIT LIGHTS)

Spirits in the form of balls of fire that hover not too far off the ground, usually no higher than rooftops. Belief in hitodama goes way back; they are mentioned in such early works as *Man'yōshū*, a collection of poems from the 8th century. Seeing hitodama is also considered a sign that one will die soon, though there are ways to prevent this from happening.

 In *Hakkenden* (tp. 6, ep. 11) we see these lights burning blue over the bodies on a battlefield. • In *Ghost Story* they are seen in a haunted graveyard.

Ⓜ In *Return of Lum: Lum in the Sun* (p. 39) Ataru and Lum go on an amusement park "Horror Coaster" ride that includes hitodama among its special effects.

HIUCHI-ISHI (FLINT AND STEEL)

Flint and steel were commonly used at one time to start fires. Another use in Japan is for performing ritual purification by striking sparks on the person or object to be purified. It is this ritual use that is more likely to be seen in anime, since fires are now set by more modern methods.

 Shinobu strikes sparks at Ataru for luck in *Urusei Yatsura* (TV tp. 14, ep. 54, st. 77).

HIYAMUGI, SŌMEN (NOODLES)

Thin noodles served in a bowl of ice water. Often the bowl is of clear glass and large enough to be shared by several people. Hiyamugi and sōmen are both wheat noodles, but they are of different thicknesses, and it is very hard to tell them apart when they are shown in anime

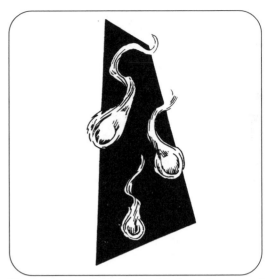

*If you see strange lights like this **hitodama**, turn around and run!*

and manga. You eat them by picking some up in your **hashi** and then dipping them in broth. Cold hiyamugi or sōmen is a summer food; after all who would eat cold noodles in the winter?

 Seita has memories of eating cold noodles on a trip to the beach in *Grave of the Fireflies*. • Hiyamugi or sōmen is shown dipped in stock and eaten from a large common bowl by the mechanics in *Patlabor: New Files* (tp. 4, ep. 13). • We see a character eating cold noodles out of season and catching hell from Ohta in *Patlabor: New Files* (tp. 3, ep. 10).

HOKKAIDO

The northernmost and second largest of Japan's four main islands. Hokkaido is known for its cold weather and large-scale dairy farming. The capital is **Sapporo**. In the **Edo period** only the southwest portion of the island had Japanese inhabitants; the rest of the island was populated by the **Ainu**. In the **Meiji period** settlers were encouraged to colonize the island.

 In *Ranma 1/2* (TV sub tp. 3, dub tp. 4, ep. 7) Ryoga is seen in Hokkaido asking directions from a dairy farmer. • Ryoko Takeuchi in *Blue Seed* (tp. 2, ep. 4) is originally from Hokkaido.

 In *Sanctuary* (vol. 2, p. 91) Hojo goes to Hokkaido to meet Mr. Ichijima.

HOMURŪMU (HOMEROOM)

 In Japanese high schools students spend the entire school day in the same classroom with the same students (except for physical education and art classes). It is the teachers who go from classroom to classroom during the day. This makes supervision easier, and allows students to keep the same desks throughout the day. Lunch is even eaten in the homeroom in most schools. For the students this means that every day they interact with the same group, and this provides a sense of security that American students often lack. Numbers outside each classroom indicate the grade level and class; for example 2-E would be second year class E, and 2-9 would be second year class 9.

Class numbers are seen outside rooms in *Project A-Ko 3*. • Nanami calls Makoto to "homeroom" in *El-Hazard* ("Fifth Night"). • In *Ranma 1/2* (TV tp. 1, ep. 2), when Kuno introduces himself he says, "I'm a junior in class 9."

Homeroom numbers are seen in *Return of Lum: Sweet Revenge* (p. 7) and mentioned in *Barefoot Gen* (p. 14).

HONSHU

The largest of Japan's four main islands. Most of the population of Japan is found on Honshu. The mountains in the center of the island make the climates of the western and eastern sides very different. The west coast has especially cold winters with lots of snow. The major urban areas of Kyoto, Osaka, and Tokyo are all on Honshu, and most anime and manga stories also take place here.

A weather report says a typhoon (**taifū**) is expected to cross Honshu in *Patlabor: New Files* (tp. 4, ep. 12).

HŌRYŪJI

 A monastery temple in the town of Ikaruga in Nara Prefecture. The temple is said to date back to the 7th century. It expanded over time and became a major religious center for the Hossō sect of Buddhism. The Hōryūji buildings house many famous works of art and are themselves major architectural treasures.

Hōryūji is seen in *Urusei Yatsura* (TV tp. 6, Spring Special 2).

HOSHI-SUNA ("STAR" SAND)

 Sand whose individual grains are shaped like stars. This rare "sand" (actually made up of tiny carcasses) is found on the beaches of the Taketomijima coast in Okinawa, where it is gathered and sold as souvenirs in small bottles.

We see a bottle of hoshi-suna in an opening sequence of *Urusei Yatsura* (TV tp. 17, ep. 65).

HOSUTESU ("HOSTESS")

 Unlike the traditional tea house modern Japanese clubs do not have **geisha**; but they do have a role for women of lesser skills. The hosutesu's job is to entertain men and make them feel important. A club may have enough of these women that every table will have a hosutesu chatting and joking with businessmen or other clients out for a drink.

Ryoko plays the role of a hostess in *Tenchi Universe* (tp. 5, ep. 16) and consumes most of the alcohol on the poor customer's tab.

Many of the scenes in *Sanctuary* (vol. 1, p. 264) take place in clubs with bar girls.

HOTARU (FIREFLY)

 Firefly viewing is a traditional pastime in Japan. Pollution has greatly reduced the numbers of fireflies and the mollusks their larvae feed on. Poems about fireflies are found in the 8th-century collection **Man'yōshū**. There is also a folk belief that the souls of the dead take the form of fireflies.

This folk belief puts *Grave of the Fireflies* in a very different light. • We see fireflies in *Hakkenden* (tp. 2, ep. 4).

HOTEI

 The Japanese pronunciation of "Pu-tai," which is the Chinese name of a 10th-century Buddhist monk. The name Hotei translates literally as "hempen sack." Hotei is well known in the West as the "laughing Buddha," and he is often portrayed with a large beggar's sack. The historical Hotei was a Ch'an (i.e., Zen) monk named Ch'i-tz'u in the province of Chekiang who was highly regarded by the people. After his death he was venerated as an incarnation of the Buddha Maitreya. In Japan he is considered one of the **Shichifuku-jin**.

M We meet the Shichifuku-jin in Takahashi Rumiko's story "Golden God of Poverty" in *Rumic World Trilogy* (vol. 2). • In *Lum Urusei Yatsura: Perfect Collection* (p. 159) the Shichifuku-jin are parodied.

IBARAKI KEN

 Ibaraki Prefecture is located on the east coast of central **Honshu**. The Kantō Plain extends into the southern part of the prefecture, and the northern part is mountainous. In the premodern administrative system Ibaraki Prefecture was known as Hitachi Province. The capital is Mito.

M Toge in *Adolf: The Half-Aryan* (vol. 3, p. 57) was born in Ibaraki.

ICHIMONJI (SPATULA)

 A scraper or spatula with a handle that is flat in relation to the blade. It is used in cooking, especially in making **okonomiyaki** and **yakisoba**.

A A bored Kubo fiddles with an ichimonji at the school festival in *Otaku no Video* (pt. 1, 2nd anim. seq.). • Ichimonji are used to prepare yakisoba in *Tenchi Universe* (tp. 2, ep. 7) and for okonomiyaki in *Ranma 1/2* (OVA "Tendo Family Christmas Scramble"). • In *Ranma 1/2: Ukyo Can Cook* Ukyo uses ichimonji of various sizes in combat and for cooking.

IKA (SQUID AND CUTTLEFISH)

 Consumed raw, cooked, or dried. The dried form, called *surume*, has been eaten since ancient times; it is an old **Shintō** offering that is traditionally used as a gift on auspicious occasions.

A Momiji makes a face as she picks up and smells an old dried squid package as she is cleaning up the office in *Blue Seed* (tp. 2, ep. 4). • An angry Kyoko struggles to bite off a piece of a whole dried squid in *Maison Ikkoku: Call Me Confused* (ep. 2).

INARI

 Inari was originally the **kami** of grains, and later the kami of commerce and success as well. The original Inari shrine is located in Fushimi in Kyoto, but over 30,000 other registered Inari shrines exist throughout Japan. Many more shrines are not registered, as they are private household shrines or on company grounds. Traditionally Inari shrines and their **torii** are painted bright red. It is not unusual to see a long tunnel made of hundreds of donated torii along the path to an Inari shrine. A statue of a fox (**kitsune**)—the messenger of Inari—is usually placed in front of an Inari shrine. Fried tofu, called *inari-dōfu*, is com-

NATIONAL HOLIDAYS

Frequently appearing in manga and anime are 15 holidays established by Japanese law:

Ganjitsu	New Year's Day	January 1
Seijin no Hi	Adult's Day	January 15
Kenkoku Kinen no Hi	National Foundation Day	February 11
Shunbun no Hi	Vernal Equinox Day	March 21
Midori no Hi	Greenery Day	April 29
Kenpō Kinenbi	Constitution Memorial Day	May 3
Kokumin no Kyūjitsu	People's Holiday	May 4
Kodomo no Hi	Children's Day	May 5
Umi no Hi	Maritime Day (Ocean Day)	July 20
Keirō no Hi	Respect-for-the-Aged Day	September 15
Shūbun no Hi	Autumnal Equinox Day	September 23
Taiiku no Hi	Health-Sports Day	October 10
Bunka no Hi	Culture Day	November 3
Kinrō Kansha no Hi	Labor-Thanksgiving Day	November 23
Tennō Tanjōbi	Emperor's Birthday	December 23

monly offered at Inari shrines since foxes are believed to like its flavor.

 A small red Inari shrine in Otsuka in the province of Musashi with primitive torii is seen in *Hakkenden* (tp. 1, ep. 2).

INORI (PRAYER)

Most personal prayer seen in anime and manga is performed silently, with the palms pressed together as the person faces a shrine, temple, or holy site, such as a **butsudan** or a grave. Some prayers in Japan take the form of chants recited out loud or silently. Each chant may be associated with particular benefits desired by the chanter. A common prayer chanted out loud is Namu Amida Butsu, the **nenbutsu** prayer of Pure Land Buddhism. When someone rubs their hands together in prayer they are imitating the motion that is often done with prayer beads (**juzu**). Prayers can also be written on an object such as an **ema** (votive tablet) and then offered at a shrine or temple. Prayers for a specific benefit, but not necessarily for the personal benefit of the person praying, are often accompanied by a promise to abstain from certain foods or alcohol (see **tachimono**).

 Ataru rubs his hands in prayer in *Urusei Yatsura* (OVA 4, pt. 1). • An old woman in a crowd prays in *Blue Seed* (tp. 1, ep. 1). • In *Irresponsible Captain Tylor* (tp. 6, ep. 19) the helmsman turns down an offer of his favorite tea, as he is abstaining until something very specific happens.

INRŌ

Containers with small compartments that are hung from a **kimono** sash and used for carrying small objects, such as seals (**han-**

49

The inrō was the wallet of earlier times.

ko), and medicine. Inrō are often works of art with complex lacquer designs on their surfaces.

Ⓜ In *Return of Lum Urusei Yatsura* (p. 6) Mendou is holding an inrō with his family crest on it, a traditional humorous design of an octopus.

INZŌ

Known in the West as mudra, these are symbolic hand positions often seen in Buddhist art. These gestures are done with and without objects held in the hands. Inzō are used in Buddhist rituals and in magical practices.

Ⓐ Inzō gestures are used by characters in *Zenki* and *Phantom Quest Corp.*

IREZUMI (TATTOO)

Criminals were once tattooed for identification, but the most famous tattoos in Japan are the beautiful multicolored art works large enough to cover most of a person's back and upper arms. These tattoos are usually positioned so they cannot be seen when the person is wearing a short-sleeved shirt. Tattoos have a certain association with **yakuza,** so the sight of them can be intimidating to the average Japanese.

Ⓐ In *Patlabor: New Files* (tp. 2, ep. 7) a tattooed yakuza is one of the customers in the **sentō.**

Ⓜ We see an example of a yakuza tattoo in *Sanctuary* (vol. 1, p. 206).

IRORI (SUNKEN HEARTH)

A traditional sunken hearth that heated the home as well as the cooking area. Irori were square pits in the floor often with a hook (**jizaikagi**) suspended over the fire to hold a cooking pot or water kettle.

Ⓐ Irori are seen in *Urusei Yatsura* (TV tp. 2, ep. 8, st. 15), *Zenki* (tp. 3, ep. 6), and *Hakkenden* (tp. 1, ep. 2).

Ⓜ Yuta and an old man sit at an irori in *Mermaid's Scar* (p. 7). • Mai sleeps next to an irori without a jizaikagi in *Mai the Psychic Girl: Perfect Collection* (vol. 1, p. 97). • We see an irori on Neptune in *Lum Urusei Yatsura: Perfect Collection* (p. 211).

IRUMA

A city in southern Saitama Prefecture, central **Honshu.** Iruma was a market and post-station town in the **Edo period.** Fa-

*Irezumi, or tattoos, evoke a tough-guy image in most cultures, and in Japan they're associated with **yakuza.***

mous for its tea, Iruma also has textile and brewing industries. It is the location of a Self Defense Forces (**Jieitai**) air base, which was once a U.S. military base.

🅰 The Self Defense Forces base at Iruma is mentioned in *Patlabor 2* and seen in *Blue Seed* (tp. 1, ep. 2).

ISE

 A city in Mie Prefecture, central **Honshu**. This is the location of Ise Shrine (**Ise Jingū**), one of the oldest and most important **Shintō** shrines in Japan. In the **Edo period** Ise was popular as a pilgrimage (**junrei**) site and for its licensed quarters. This city is still quite popular among visitors for its traditional beauty and natural surroundings. Ise is part of the Ise-Shima National Park.

🅰 A part of *Blue Seed: When Gods Walk the Earth* (ep. 17) takes place in Ise, and Miyasudakoro goes to Ise in *Tale of Genji*.

ISE JINGŪ (ISE SHRINE)

 One of most important shrines in all **Shintō**, Ise Shrine actually consists of two shrines. The inner shrine is dedicated to **Amaterasu Ōmikami**; legend has it that in the 3rd century Princess Yamatohime traveled throughout Japan for a place to enshrine the sacred mirror, part of the Imperial Regalia. At Ise she heard a voice telling her that this was the place. Every 20 years a new shrine is built as part of a special rite called the Shikinen Sengū, when the **kami** of the shrine moves to the new building. A few months after the rite the old shrine is dismantled. The outer shrine, built around the 5th century, is dedicated to Toyouke no Ōkami and is also rebuilt every 20 years. The ancient poetry anthology **Man'yōshū** contains references to Ise Jingū.

🅰 Ise Jingū is seen in *Blue Seed: When Gods Walk the Earth* (ep. 17).

ISHI-DŌRŌ (STONE LANTERN)

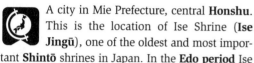 Stone lanterns come in a variety of shapes, but all have a hollowed-out upper section with an enclosed top to hold an oil lamp or candle. Lanterns are used as decorations in private, temple, or shrine gardens. Originally these were found only in Buddhist temple gardens and not in private gardens, but in the Azuchi-Momoyama period (1568–1603) tea masters (see **cha-no-yu**) started to decorate tea gardens with them.

🅰 A stone lantern is seen in the garden of a home in *Blue Seed* (tp. 1, ep. 1). • A stone lantern is seen at temples in *You're Under Arrest* (tp. 4) and *Wandering Days*. • Stone lanterns are also seen in *Hakkenden* (tp. 3, ep. 5), *Mermaid Forest*, *Zenki* (tp. 2, ep. 5), and *Kwaidan*.

Ⓜ Temples appear in *Mai the Psychic Girl: Perfect Collection* (vol. 1, pp. 66–67).

ISHIHARA SHINTARŌ

 1932–. A novelist and politician who was born in Kobe and graduated from Hitotsubashi University. He started publishing in 1954. His 1955 work *Taiyō no Kisetsu* won both the Bungakukai's Newcomer's Award and the Akutagawa Prize (**Akutagawa Shō**). In 1989 he collaborated with Morita Akio in writing the controversial *"No" to Ieru Nihon* (The Japan That Can Say No).

🅰 *Taiyō no Kisetsu* is available in an anime version as *Season of the Sun*.

ISHIKAWA GOEMON

 1558?–94? A famous thief who, legend has it, was put to death after failing to assassinate **Toyotomi Hideyoshi**. He composed a poem before his death in which he stated that thievery would never die. He was sentenced to be boiled alive along with his young son. Legend says he held his son out of the water as long as he could. Several kabuki plays have been written about Goemon.

🅰 Ishikawa Goemon also happens to be the name of Rupan's samurai sidekick whose wedding is disturbed in *Rupan III: The Fuma Conspiracy*.

IZUMI KYŌKA

 1873–1939. Novelist. He was born in Kanazawa (Ishikawa Prefecture) into an artisan family. His writings often have supernatural or fantastic themes; for example, *Kōya-hijiri* deals with the unusual experiences of a wandering monk.

🅐 Part of Izumi's *Kōyahijiri* is available as *Priest of Mt. Kouya*.

IZUMO

 One of the old provinces of Japan, Izumo now forms the northeastern half of Shimane Prefecture (**Shimane Ken**). Izumo, which is featured in many of Japan's oldest myths, is believed to have been one of the earliest cultural centers of the Japanese people. Izumo is where **Susanoo-no-Mikoto** is said to have slain an eight-headed serpent.

🅐 Momiji is from the Izumo portion of Shimane Ken, and the story of Susanoo-no-Mikoto's slaying of the Orochi-no-Orochi and rescuing of Kushinada Hime is told in *Blue Seed* (tp. 1, ep. 1).

IZUMO TAISHA

 One of the most ancient and important of the **Shintō** shrines (**jinja**) in Japan. Izumo Shrine is located in the town of Taisha in

In the first episode of BLUE SEED *we get this excellent view of* **Izumo Taisha**.

Shimane Prefecture. The architectural style of this shrine is considered to be the oldest in Japan. There are two major festivals (**matsuri**): May 14, the main festival of the shrine, and October 11–17, when the **kami** are said to all gather there for the Kamiari Matsuri.

🅐 In *Blue Seed* (tp. 1, ep. 1) we see a large **torii** with "Izumo Taisha" written on it in **kanji** and, later in the same episode, the huge **shimenawa** in front of the Worship Hall of the shrine; from this we know that Momiji is from the town of Taisha.

JAN-KEN

 Known in the west as Scissors, Paper, Stone. This is a very simple game where two or more players shout "Jan ken pon!" and shape their hand into one of three shapes. Scissors wins over paper, paper wins over stone, and stone wins over scissors. The game is often used like a coin toss in the West. I remember using jan-ken as a child in rural California more often than tossing coins.

🅜 In *Sanctuary* we see jan-ken used to make some significant decisions.

🅐 C-ko plays jan-ken with Mari in *Project A-Ko*. • Cookie and Taishi play in *Kishin Corps* (tp. 1, ep. 1). • Jan-ken is banished from SV2 in *Patlabor: New Files* (tp. 3, ep. 8). • Setsuko plays a perpetually even game with her reflection in *Grave of the Fireflies*.

The diminutive C-Ko in Project A-Ko *defeats the larger Mari in* **jan-ken,** *not the type of combat Mari planned.*

JĒ ĀRU (JR)

Japan Railways, a nationwide network of railways and related companies, formed in 1987 by the privatization of Japanese National Railways. JR is made up of the Japan Freight Railway Company (nationwide), the Central Japan Railway Company (central **Honshu**), the East Japan Railway Company (northern Honshu and the Kantō region), the Hokkaido Railway Company (**Hokkaido**), the Kyushu Railway Company (Kyushu), the Shikoku Railway Company (Shikoku), and the Japan Railway Company (Kansai area).

A Japan Rail is disrupted in *Tenchi Muyo!* (OVA 2).

JIDŌ-HANBAIKI (VENDING MACHINE)

Often located outdoors, vending machines in Japan offer a wide variety of products, including hot beverages and magazines. One even finds beer and sake vending machines; these are turned off at night when the shop that owns them closes.

A In *Robotech Perfect Collection: Macross* (TV ep. 1) there is a mobile soda vending machine of the future. • In *Urusei Yatsura* (TV tp. 3, ep. 10, sts. 19–20) we see a beer can vending machine on the street. In the first *Oh My Goddess!* OVA a vending machine dispenses hot drinks in cans.

JIEITAI (SELF DEFENSE FORCES; SDF)

The duty of the Self Defense Forces is to defend Japan from attack. The 9th article of the 1947 Constitution of Japan forbids Japan from having an army. In 1950 General Douglas MacArthur, commander of the Occupation forces in Japan, ordered the creation of the National Police Reserve to replace Allied troops sent to the war in Korea. In 1952 this force was renamed the National Safety Forces. In 1954 the forces were reorganized as the Self Defense Forces (Jieitai). The Self Defense Forces are divided into the Ground Self Defense Force (Rikujō Jieitai), the Maritime Self Defense Force (Kaijō Jieitai), and the Air Self Defense Force (Kōkū Jieitai). The SDF is a controversial institution in Japan, since many believe its very existence is unconstitutional.

A We see the SDF in *Urusei Yatsura* (TV tp. 1, ep. 1, st. 1). • In *Patlabor 2* the SDF play a major role in the story. • We see some SDF facilities in *Blue Seed* (tp. 1, ep. 1).

M The implications of the 9th article of the constitution in relation to the SDF is discussed in *Sanctuary* (vol. 5, p. 73).

JIIN (BUDDHIST TEMPLE)

The oldest Buddhist temple in Japan is said to have been founded in 552 by the conversion of a nobleman's home. In time temples were built throughout Japan as Buddhism (**Bukkyō**) spread among the populace. Until the **Meiji period** it was common for temples and shrines (**jinja**) to occupy the same plot of land or even the same buildings. The government forced the separation of the two religions and restricted the construction of new temples. After WWII these restrictions were lifted, but by then many temples had fallen into disrepair or been destroyed by bombings.

A In *You're Under Arrest* a neighborhood temple shows up several times, and in *Oh My Goddess!* Belldandy and Keiichi live in an old temple.

CINEMATIC EFFECTS IN ANIME AND MANGA

In 1977, when I first saw part of a science fiction anime in the window at the Mikado toy store in San Francisco's Japantown, I was blown away by the cinematic effects used. Angle shots, pan shots, action taking place at a distance—all in a few minutes. I had just seen *Star Wars* a few days before and was still excited by that experience when I glanced over at the TV in the window. The animation quality was poor by today's standard but for the late '70s it was comparable to what was being made in the U.S.

Today cinematic effects are even more heavily used in anime. However, in America Disney gets criticized by some reviewers for using just a few such effects.

Go figure.

JINJA (SHINTŌ SHRINE)

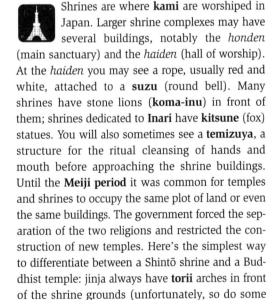 Shrines are where **kami** are worshiped in Japan. Larger shrine complexes may have several buildings, notably the *honden* (main sanctuary) and the *haiden* (hall of worship). At the *haiden* you may see a rope, usually red and white, attached to a **suzu** (round bell). Many shrines have stone lions (**koma-inu**) in front of them; shrines dedicated to **Inari** have **kitsune** (fox) statues. You will also sometimes see a **temizuya**, a structure for the ritual cleansing of hands and mouth before approaching the shrine buildings. Until the **Meiji period** it was common for temples and shrines to occupy the same plot of land or even the same buildings. The government forced the separation of the two religions and restricted the construction of new temples. Here's the simplest way to differentiate between a Shintō shrine and a Buddhist temple: jinja always have **torii** arches in front of the shrine grounds (unfortunately, so do some Buddhist temples). Often in manga and anime you will see jinja when there is a **matsuri** (festival) or **ennichi** (fair) as part of the story.

 A small red Inari shrine in Otsuka with a primitive torii is seen in *Hakkenden* (tp. 1, ep. 2). • In *Blue Seed* (tp. 1, ep. 1) we see the worship hall of Izumo shrine (**Izumo Taisha**) with its very large shimenawa; in *Blue Seed* (tp. 2, ep. 4) Momiji and Kome go to **Asakusa Jinja**.

JINRIKISHA (RICKSHAW)

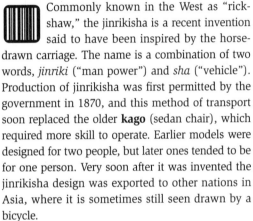 Commonly known in the West as "rickshaw," the jinrikisha is a recent invention said to have been inspired by the horse-drawn carriage. The name is a combination of two words, *jinriki* ("man power") and *sha* ("vehicle"). Production of jinrikisha was first permitted by the government in 1870, and this method of transport soon replaced the older **kago** (sedan chair), which required more skill to operate. Earlier models were designed for two people, but later ones tended to be for one person. Very soon after it was invented the jinrikisha design was exported to other nations in Asia, where it is sometimes still seen drawn by a bicycle.

A We see jinrikisha in several anime, including; *Theater of Life*, *Pretty Sammy*, *Wandering Days*, *Grave of the Wild Chrysanthemum*, *Botchan*, *Tale of Shunkin*, and *Sanshiro the Judoist* (pt. 1).

JISHIN (EARTHQUAKE)

Earthquakes are a common occurrence in Japan. The most destructive earthquake of modern times was the 1923 Great Tokyo Earthquake that resulted in over 100,000 deaths, 60,000 in Tokyo, and widespread destruction. It is estimated that this quake was 7.9 on the Japanese scale. (The Japanese scale for measuring earthquakes measures horizontal movement, unlike the Richter scale that measures vertical movement.)

M We learn that a certain significant item broke in an earthquake in *Maison Ikkoku* (vol. 7, p. 164).

JITTE (TRUNCHEON)

 Used by the **Edo period** police, a jitte consists of a short blade with a hook on one side. The hook was used to catch and break attacking swords; the blade was used to deflect thrusts. This weapon is a variant on the two-hooked *sai*.

 Jitte are seen in *Urusei Yatsura* (TV 14, ep. 54, st. 77) and *Ranma 1/2* (sub tp. 4, dub tp. 5, ep. 10).

JIYŪ MINSHUTŌ (LIBERAL DEMOCRATIC PARTY)

Since its formation in 1955 by the merger of two conservative parties, the LDP until fairly recently held a majority position in Japan's lawmaking body, the Diet.

The LDP plays a major role in *Sanctuary*.

JIZAIKAGI (POT HOOK)

 A device for suspending cooking pots over a traditional Japanese hearth (**irori**), the jizaikagi consisted of a hollow bamboo tube and an inserted iron rod. A horizontal piece attached to the rod can be adjusted to raise or lower the cooking pot or water kettle. This horizontal piece is often in the shape of a fish.

Jizaikagi appear in *Ranma 1/2* (TV sub tp. 3, dub tp. 4, ep. 7), *Hakkenden* (tp. 5, ep. 8), and *Kimagure Orange Road* (OVA 2, ep. 1).

We get a good view of a jizaikagi in *Mermaid's Scar* (p. 7).

JIZŌ

A very popular **bosatsu** who is seen as a savior of children and those suffering in hell. Small statues of Jizō are often seen by the side of the road, sometimes in groups and often with a cloth or bib around the image's neck.

Jizō show up several times in *Hakkenden*. • In *Ranma 1/2* (TV sub tp. 6, dub tp. 9, ep. 17) a statue of Jizō is used to hit Ranma. • A boy prays for rain at a Jizō statue in *Urusei Yatsura* (TV tp. 8, ep. 30, st. 53).

*An elderly rural couple in the RANMA 1/2 TV show spend some time around the **irori** and **jizaikagi** in their home.*

JOYA NO KANE

 The New Year's ringing of temple bells (**bonshō**). Buddhist temples ring their bells 108 times starting at midnight on New Year's Day. Each of the rings symbolizes one of the 108 sufferings or desires (*bonnō*) that, according to Buddhist teachings, afflict people in this world.

A temple bell is shown in the NTV broadcast of the New Year's countdown in *Patlabor: New Files* (tp. 1, ep. 3) and being rung on TV in *Maison Ikkoku: Home for the Holiday* (ep. 1).

In *Maison Ikkoku* (vol. 2, p. 81) Godai and Kyoko go to the temple for the ringing in of the New Year.

*In HAKKENDEN a statue of **Jizō** stands with a cloth bib offering wrapped around it.*

JŪBAKO (STACKING BOXES)

 Stacking lacquered wooden boxes that are used for food; they are usually in groups of two, three, or five. The most common design is black on the outside with red on the inside; they may also have painted gold designs. Jūbako are commonly used at picnics, for serving precooked food to wedding guests, or for New Year's meals (**osechi-ryōri**).

 Takeuchi brings Kunikida a meal in jūbako in *Blue Seed: When Gods Walk the Earth* (ep. 17).

Lum and Ataru's family are getting ready for the New Year's meal in *Return of Lum: Trouble Times Ten* (p. 40). Notice the soup bowls, sake cups and flasks, and the jūbako.

JŪDŌ

 "The Way of Softness." Jūdō is a technique of unarmed combat that relies on throwing (*nagewaza*), grappling (*katamewaza*), and attacking vital points (*atemiwaza*). Jūdō was developed in the late 19th century from **jūjutsu**, an older weaponless martial art, by Kanō Jigorō, who also created the system of colored belts and ranks still used today. Many schools adopted jūdō as a sport, but this was prohibited by the Occupation for a period of time after WWII. At the 1964 Tokyo games jūdō became an official Olympic sport. Skill in jūdō or **kendō** is required of all police officers in Japan, and lower-level officers cannot be promoted without showing skill in one of these.

*Open the lid of the **jūbako** and inside there is a feast.*

 We see a jūdō toss in *You're Under Arrest* (OVA 1). • Mention of a jūdō club is made at the high school in *El-Hazard* ("First Night"). • Of course *Sanshiro the Judoist* deals with the origins of this art.

JŪJUTSU

 The martial art of jūjutsu developed out of wrestling at court banquets in the Nara and **Heian** periods. While it was used by warriors during the **Kamakura period** it did not become widespread until the **Edo period**, when it was used for self-defense and by the police to make arrests. It developed a bad reputation, since bandits would use it to subdue victims. The number of jūjutsu schools grew dramatically until the **Meiji period**, when the **samurai** were abolished as a class and **jūdō** became more significant and widespread. Today most military training in the world includes close-combat techniques partly derived from jūjutsu.

 The conflict between jūjutsu and jūdō is dramatized in *Sanshiro the Judoist*.

JUKYŌ (CONFUCIANISM)

 This major Chinese philosophical tradition came to Japan through the Korean kingdom of Paekche in the early 5th century. Confucian philosophy continued to develop in Japan with the importation and publication of many Chinese texts, even during the isolation of the **Edo period**. There are various forms of Confucian thought that have played a role in Japanese society. Zen monks saw Confucianism as a secular teaching much like their own religious tradition. With its teachings of moral principle, loyalty, and self-discipline, Confucianism became widely accepted by the **samurai**.

 Several Confucian virtues are symbolized by the **kanji** for *jin* ("sympathy"), *chu* ("loyalty"), *gi* ("duty" or "righteousness"), *shin* ("faith"), *rei* ("propriety"), *ko* ("filial devotion"), *chi* ("wisdom"), and *tei* ("brotherly affection") on the beads in *Hakkenden*.

JŪNI JINSHŌ

 Twelve gods who are the guardians of Yakushi-Nyorai, the Buddhist Physician of Souls. The twelve correspond to the twelve months of the Chinese calendar. It is common for the deity associated with your birth month to be seen as your guardian deity.

△ In *Rupan III: The Fuma Conspiracy* gold-covered statues of the Twelve Guardians of Yakushi-Nyorai are found in the caves.

JUNREI (PILGRIMAGE)

 There are two major types of pilgrimage in Japan. In the first, a group of temples (**jiin**), shrines (**jinja**), or holy sites is visited in a particular order; usually this involves a circuit of 33 or 88 sites. The second type involves a pilgrimage to a single site. One of the most popular pilgrimage sites for Buddhists in Japan is visiting the 88 temples on the island of Shikoku. While these days pilgrimages may be organized by tour bus companies and take a week or two to complete, some people still take the two or three months needed for the longer pilgrimages on foot. Pilgrims are referred to as *henro*.

△ Buddhist pilgrims in traditional straw hats and white clothing with bells and staffs are seen in *Hakkenden* (tp. 6, ep. 10).

JUZU (ROSARY)

 Worshipers use "rosary"-type beads to keep count while reciting the name of the Buddha. Usually juzu have 108 beads, symbolizing the 108 evil passions that Buddhism teaches must be overcome. There are also small juzu with fewer beads.

△ The Hadja priest in *Phantom Quest Corp.* (tp. 2, ep. 4) carries a small set of these beads, as does one of the praying members of the chemistry club in *Ranma 1/2* (TV sub tp. 3, dub tp. 4, ep. 8).

ELECTRONIC RESOURCES FOR ANIME FANS

For years the world of computer bulletin board systems and the Internet has been a major communication tool for anime fans. Today the BBS scene has declined as the Internet has become more accessible and even more important in helping fans communicate. Here are some major resources on the Internet that anyone interested in anime and manga should know about:

WEB PAGES

http://www.anipike.com/
Anime Web Turnpike. The single largest and best organized collection of anime- and manga-related links there is. This is where you want to begin searching for information.

http://www.ex.org/
EX: The Online World of Anime and Manga. An electronic magazine that provides excellent coverage of the anime and manga scene. You can even get the first year on a CD-ROM disc (worth the money in my opinion).

MAJOR NEWSGROUPS

The most important resource the Internet and other networks can give you access to is other people, and newsgroups play a major role. If you are new to a newsgroup, lurk for a while, get a feel for the discussion, and then start adding your comments.

rec.arts.anime.info
Informational postings only, moderated.

rec.arts.anime.fandom
For discussion of the fan scene.

rec.arts.anime.misc
For discussion of everything else.

rec.arts.manga
For manga, that is, printed Japanese comics, not for videos from a company named Manga.

There are plenty of other resources, and the above list is just to get you started. Now dive in and have fun.

KADOMATSU (GATE PINE)

 A decoration, usually made of pine ("long life") and bamboo ("wealth"), that is placed in front of the house from January 1 until the 7th or 15th. It is considered temporary quarters for the **kami** at New Year's. Kadomatsu designs vary by region.

🅰 In *Urusei Yatsura* (TV tp. 3, ep. 11, sts. 21–22) Ataru's parents are admiring the kadomatsu they bought; it is rather small. • A kadomatsu is outside the SV facility doors in *Patlabor: New Files* (tp. 1, ep. 1) and while it snows in *Otaku no Video* (pt. 2, 4th anim. seq.).

KAEDE TO MOMIJI (MAPLE TREES)

The Japanese use two names to indicate maples, *kaede* and *momiji*. There are over 20 indigenous maple species in Japan. Their distinctive patterns and colors are commonly used in decorations and artwork, and going to view turning maples is a favorite autumnal activity.

🅰 We see maple leaves in the garden in *Tale of Shunkin*. • Red maples are very visible in *Izu Dancer*. • Kaede and Momiji are the names of the twin sisters in *Blue Seed*, where the maple-leaf motif often shows up.

KAGO (SEDAN CHAIR)

A kago is a seat suspended from a single cross beam and carried by two men. It is usually used to transport one person at a time. The front and back of the kago are covered and the sides can be left open or enclosed with fold-up screens. The kago is not the same as the **koshi**.

🅰 We see an example of a kago in *Hakkenden* (tp. 2, ep. 3).

KAI-AWASE (SHELL-MATCHING GAME)

 In the **Heian period** this game simply involved matching shell halves. Later, players tried to match shells that were painted with pictures or poems. It is easy to see that this game influenced the development of the card game **uta karuta**.

🅰 Painted shells used in the game are seen in *Tale of Genji*.

KAIMYŌ

Buddhist name for the deceased. The custom of taking on a Buddhist name to help guide one in life developed in Japan in the 14th century. Later this custom evolved into the granting of Buddhist names to persons who have died. Funeral services in Japan are largely handled by Buddhist priests, so a tablet with the deceased's Buddhist name on it is usually on the memorial altar (**butsudan**).

🅼 There are butsudan with kaimyō on tablets in *Rumic Theater* (chapt. 2, p. 42; chapt. 4, p. 121).

*Maple (**kaede** or **momiji**) viewing is popular in the fall, and the bright red colors can be stunning.*

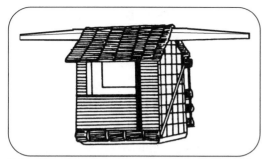

*Before there was the taxi there was the wheeled **jinrikisha**; before the jinrikisha there was the sedan chair, or **kago**.*

KAISHAKUNIN

 An assistant who ceremonially lops off the head of a person who is committing ritual suicide (**seppuku**), after he has slit his stomach but before he has died from the wound.
 In *Urusei Yatsura* (TV tp. 4, ep. 14, st. 27) and *Return of Lum Urusei Yatsura* (p. 24), after his defeat by Ataru, Mendou prepares for seppuku with one of his family servants in the role of kaishakunin.

KAKEMONO (HANGING SCROLL)

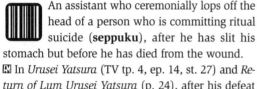 Also called a *kakejiku*. Hanging scrolls were introduced into Japan from China in the 6th century. At first they were Buddhist pictures hung in temples; over time they came to be hung in the home and to include a variety of seasonal subjects in both paintings and calligraphy. You will usually see a kakemono hung in the **tokonoma**.
 We see a kakemono in the tokonoma behind Ataru's dad in a **ryokan** in *Urusei Yatsura* (TV tp. 19, ep. 73, st. 96) and behind Soun Tendo at dinner in *Ranma 1/2: One Grew over the Kuno's Nest*.

KAKIGŌRI-KI (SHAVED ICE)

 A popular summertime treat is some shaved ice with fruit syrup flavoring poured on top. In the spirit of research I had some Japanese-style shaved ice and found that it is not at all like American snow cones, as the Japanese ice is so thinly shaved that it quickly melts in your mouth. (Next time I think I'll have it with *azuki* beans.) Often what you see in anime and manga is not the shaved ice but the characteristic banner used to advertise it. The banner has a single character, and often waves are painted at the base.
 Hotta-**sensei** treats Botchan to shaved ice in *Botchan* (pt. 1). • We see a shaved-ice banner held by Ataru in the beginning of *Urusei Yatsura: Beautiful Dreamer*. • Ranma and Akane eat it in *Ranma 1/2: Darling Charlotte* (ep. 1) as do Godai and Kintarō in *Maison Ikkoku: Playing Doubles* (ep. 2).
 We see a banner in English in the translation of *Return of Lum: Lum in the Sun* (p. 176).

KAMAKURA

 Located in southeastern Kanagawa Prefecture (**Kanagawa Ken**) not too far south of Tokyo. Kamakura has been an important city since the 12th century, when it became the seat of the Kamakura shogunate. The city is famous for its historical buildings and Buddhist temples.
 Part of *Friendship* takes place in Kamakura. • Kamakura is mentioned in Shino's father's story of the Murasame sword in *Hakkenden* (tp. 1, ep. 2).

KAMAKURA PERIOD

 1185–1333. This period in Japanese history is named after the city of **Kamakura**, near present-day Tokyo. It was the capital of the Kamakura shogunate, dominated by the Genji (**Minamoto**) and Hōjō families.
 The Kamakura period is mentioned in *Maison Ikkoku: Ronin Blues* (ep. 1) and in *Zenki* (ep. 41).

KAMI

 The word "kami" is impossible to translate directly into English, but attempts include: god, deity, spirit, "superior and mysterious force." Kami are the focus of most **Shintō** ritual. In subtitled anime you commonly hear the word "kami" spoken, often in the form *kami-sama*, which is usually translated as "God." Whenever you see characters clap twice (**kashiwade**) and pray they are praying to a kami.

KAMIDANA (SHINTŌ ALTAR)

The word literally means "**kami** shelf." Kamidana are placed high on a wall and resemble a miniature shrine. Offerings to the kami, usually of rice, salt, and water, are placed in front of it and on special occasions may include sake and other foods. Kamidana are found in homes, shops, restaurants, offices, ships, and martial arts halls (**dōjō**). Usually the kamidana enshrines the local kami and perhaps a kami connected in some way to the family.

Ⓜ Kamidana are in the dōjō in *Ranma 1/2* (TV tp. 1, ep. 1; vol. 1, p. 22), and its falling is seen as a bad omen (*Ranma 1/2: Evil Wakes*, ep. 1; vol. 6, p. 10). Ⓐ You see a kamidana in Princess Kurama's control room in *Urusei Yatsura* (TV tp. 3, ep. 12, st. 24), behind Hamaji when she visits Shino's home in *Hakkenden* (tp. 2, ep. 3), and in the dōjō in *You're Under Arrest* (OVA 1).

KAMINARIMON

The Gate of Thunder, the famous entryway to the temple **Sensōji** and the shrine **Asakusa Jinja** in Tokyo. Notable is the huge red lantern weighing more than 200 pounds and about 10 feet tall. Inside the gate is the Nakamise shopping arcade that leads to the main hall of the temple.

Ⓐ We see this gate when Momiji and Kome go to Asakusa Jinja (identified erroneously as Kaminarimon Shrine) in *Blue Seed* (tp. 2, ep. 4). • In *Tenchi Muyo in Love* the students visit this temple and shrine on their field trip. • The gate and lantern are visible in the flashback when Ryoga looks for Ranma in *Ranma 1/2*.

KANA (SYLLABARY)

Japanese writing systems in which each syllable has one character. Writing in Japan was originally based on imported Chinese characters (**kanji**). But not all Japanese words could be easily rendered with Chinese, so several kanji would be used phonetically to "spell out" the Japanese word. In time kana developed as a simpler way to write down the sounds of words. Today there are two groups of kana, each with 48 characters representing the sounds of the Japanese language. *Hiragana* is cursive and used mostly for verbal endings and native Japanese (and some Chinese) words. *Katakana* is more angular and generally used for foreign loanwords (**gairaigo**). Modern Japanese texts may be written in a combination of kanji, hiragana, katakana, and Roman letters. Some books use very small kana (*furigana*) next to kanji as an aid to those who do not know the kanji or for readings that are irregular or uncommon.

Ⓐ Both forms of kana commonly show up on signs in stories with modern settings. In *Here Is Greenwood* (tp. 1, ep. 2) the word "tobacco" on a shop sign is written in hiragana rather than the usual katakana for foreign words. This is an example of an occasional playful use of different scripts for writing words.

KANAGAWA KEN

Kanagawa Prefecture, on the southern fringe of the Kantō Plain with Tokyo Bay on the east and mountains in the west. Under the old provincial system this area was called Sagami Province. The capital is Yokohama; other major cities include **Kamakura**, Kawasaki, Fujisawa, Sagamihara, Yokosuka, and Hiratsuka.

In RANMA 1/2 *the* **kamidana** *in the Tendo* **dōjō** *is often visible.*

The huge lantern of the gate of the **Kaminarimon** Shrine, seen here in Blue Seed, is one of the most famous symbols of old Tokyo.

◭ The story in *Shonan Bakusozoku* takes place in Kanagawa Prefecture. • That Labor Police teams have been established in **Osaka** and Kanagawa is mentioned by Nagumo Shinobu in her lecture in *Patlabor 2*.

KANJI (CHINESE CHARACTERS)

 The Japanese began to use Chinese characters in about the 5th century. Before that there was no written script. A single kanji character can have more than one "reading" (pronunciation): *on* readings approximate the original Chinese pronunciations, while *kun* readings are indigenous Japanese words applied to imported Chinese characters with the same meanings. Thus the Japanese character for "dog" is pronounced *ken* (*quan* in Chinese) in the *on* reading and *inu* in the *kun* reading. The existence of *on* and *kun* readings makes for some interesting word play in Japanese texts. The list of commonly used kanji characters prescribed by the Ministry of Education was set at 1,850 in 1946 and expanded to 1,945 in 1981. Kanji are used in conjunction with the phonetic scripts known as **kana**.
◭ The bat tells Dracula which kanji he should use in his letter in *Urusei Yatsura* (TV tp. 8, ep. 27, st. 50).

KANTŌ CHIHŌ (KANTŌ REGION)

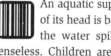 An area consisting of **Chiba**, Saitama, **Kanagawa**, Tokyo, Gunma, Tochigi, and **Ibaraki** prefectures. The major geographical feature of the area is the vast Kantō Plain (Kantō Heiya). This is the most heavily populated area in Japan, and it played a major role in politics and warfare during the period of the civil wars (**Sengoku jidai**).
◭ The Kantō region is mentioned in Shino's father's story of the Murasame sword in *Hakkenden* (tp. 1, ep. 2) and in *Blue Seed* (tp. 4, ep. 8).

KAPPA

An aquatic supernatural creature. The top of its head is bald and holds water. Should the water spill the kappa becomes defenseless. Children are warned not to play near rivers as kappa may drown them. Kappa are said to be fond of cucumbers (**kyūri**) and **sumō**.
◭ Kappa are mentioned in *Urusei Yatsura* (TV tp. 2, ep. 8, st. 15). • We see kappa with a feast of cucumber dishes in *Urusei Yatsura* (TV tp. 7, ep. 23, sts. 45–46). • Washu turns Ryoko and Ayaka into kappa in *Tenchi Universe* (tp. 1, ep. 4). • Kappa,

The **kappa**. Not something you want to be grabbed by in the middle of the night.

translated as "water imps," are mentioned in *Blue Seed* (tp. 2, ep. 3) and later seen (*Sea Devils*, ep. 15).

KAPPŌGI (COOKING APRON)

 This gownlike piece of clothing with baggy sleeves drawn right below the elbow covers the front of the wearer and extends to the knees. Originally designed to protect **kimono** while cooking it is now worn occasionally outside the kitchen and on short shopping trips for groceries.

🅐 The old woman at the **ryokan** wears a kappōgi in *Tenchi Muyo!* (OVA 9), as does the aunt in *Grave of the Fireflies* and Nozomu in *Moldiver* (OVA 1). • In *Vampire Princess Miyu* we see a kappōgi on a servant (tp. 1, ep. 2) and on Miyu's mother (tp. 2, ep. 4).

🅜 We often see a kappōgi on the mother in *Barefoot Gen*.

KARAOKE

 The word means literally "empty orchestra." Prerecorded music minus the vocal track allows anyone to be the singer. This is a very popular pastime in bars, clubs, and even homes. The quality of one's singing is not as important as the willingness to join in the fun.

🅐 A karaoke machine is in a cab at the beginning of *Phantom Quest Corp.*, "End of the World" (tp. 1, case 2). *Pretty Sammy* begins with the mother singing to a karaoke recording at home. • Kiyone

As Seita enters his aunt's home in GRAVE OF THE FIREFLIES he finds her wearing a **kappōgi**.

and Mihoshi enjoy karaoke in a private room in *Tenchi Universe* (tp. 2, ep. 6), as do several characters in *Macross Plus* (OVA 2).

KARASU (CROW)

There are several species of crow in Japan. Two live there year round; the rest are migratory. The crow is considered an evil omen and bearer of bad luck. Loud croaking or the gathering of many croaking crows is a sign of disaster; croaking crows in the evening are especially feared. The crow, however, is also considered a messenger of some **kami**, for example the kami of the Kumano Shrine, the Suwa Shrine of Shinano, and the Hiyoshi Shrine of Ōmi. The crowing of a crow at the hours of 6 A.M. and noon is a good omen. Crows are also seen as symbols of filial piety, as it is said that crows care for their aged parents.

🅐 A crow cawing in the opening scene of *Otaku no Video* (pt. 1, 1st anim. seq.) might be a bad omen, given the changes in life to come for Kubo. • We also hear a crow during Keiichi's **senpai** visit in *Oh My Goddess!* (OVA 3), at the beginning of *Tenchi Universe* (tp. 1, ep. 1), and in *Urusei Yatsura* (TV tp. 1, ep. 1, st. 1).

KARĒ RAISU (CURRY RICE)

 Powdered curry was introduced to Japan in the late **Edo period** by the British. During the **Meiji period** the dish curry rice was developed; it is today among the most popular curry dishes in Japan.

🅐 Curry rice is one of the Earth foods listed by Ataru in *Urusei Yatsura* (TV tp. 8, ep. 29, st. 52). • Curry rice is seen being served by Kasumi early on in *Ranma 1/2: Big Trouble in Nekonron, China* and is cooked by Madoka for Kyosuke in *Kimagure Orange Road* (OVA 4, ep. 2).

KASA (UMBRELLA)

There is a prehistoric wall painting in a Japanese tomb that shows an umbrella being used. Originally umbrellas were made with cloth and not used so much for protection from rain and sunlight but to indicate the status of the owner, usually a noble or Buddhist cleric. It was near the end of the 16th century that the folding rain umbrella came to Japan. A common type is the oiled paper umbrella or *karakasa* (the name literally means "Chinese umbrella," reflecting its origin). In the **Edo period** the umbrella became more refined, using painted oiled paper on a bamboo frame. Today these are valued as works of art and are not often seen in daily use.

🅐 The daughter of an umbrella maker plays a major role in *The Martyr*. • An umbrella is often seen in *Hakkenden* (tp. 5, ep. 8). • Other places umbrellas appear in anime are *Urusei Yatsura: Beautiful Dreamer*, *Grave of the Wild Chrysanthemum*, and *Student Days*.

KASHIWADE

Clapping hands at chest height in worship. Commonly this is done twice but the ritual can vary at some shrines. A **Shintō** custom, this is generally not done at Buddhist temples.
🅐 Kashiwade can be seen in *Tenchi Muyo!* (OVA 1) after the explosion at the school and in *Blue Seed* (tp. 2, ep. 4) when Momiji and Kome go pray at **Asakusa Jinja**.

*Mmm, **kashiwa mochi**. Don't eat the wrapping (although it is biodegradable).*

MACS IN ANIME

I have to start this one by stating that after years of working with DOS and Windows I stand firmly on the side of the Macintosh in the desktop computing religious wars.

But have you ever noticed when Macs pop up in anime?

Usually 'puters in anime and manga are some generic unidentifiable box. But Macs stand out either in their interface or case design. In the "lecture" segments in *GunBuster* the graphics in the background are HyperCard stacks, and in *All Purpose Cultural Cat Girl Nuku Nuku* Kyusaku uses a Mac in several scenes.

But the ultimate Mac reference is in *Pretty Sammy 2*, right down to a new operating system called Mach-8. I won't say any more about this one; you'll have to watch it yourself for the rest of the references to Macintosh and the evil American software-company-owning billionaire out to control the world.

KASHIWA MOCHI

A round, filled piece of **mochi** (rice cake) wrapped in an oak leaf and commonly eaten on Children's Day (**Kodomo no Hi**). The oak leaf symbolizes "not withering."
🅐 In *Urusei Yatsura* (OVA "I Howl at the Moon") Ataru remarks that Lum's mochi looks like kashiwa mochi. • We also see kashiwa mochi in *Tenchi Muyo!* (OVA 13).

KASŌ (CREMATION)

Cremation was introduced into Japan with Buddhism (**Bukkyō**). Used first for the disposal of the remains of priests, it was adopted by the nobility and spread to the larger populace. The bereaved do not retain all the ashes but preserve only certain bones in an urn.
🅐 In *Grave of the Fireflies* we see cremations, in-

HAIR OF A DIFFERENT COLOR

Japanese hair is naturally dark brown, black, or even rarely a very dark red.

But in anime one sees a riot of color: brown, black, blond, red, blue, green, pink . . .

Why?

Well in manga it is very hard to distinguish different characters if everyone has similar dark hair, even if you use the variety of textures that naturally and artificially exist in Japan. So characters are often drawn with light hair; remember, manga are almost always black and white. When a manga character design is transferred to anime or to a colored manga illustration, the colors selected can be quite interesting. Of course in some cases, such as Lum, the non-human origin of the character makes an unnatural hair color more believable.

Related to this is a conversation I was having with a friend a few years ago. She was commenting on the blond characters in anime as we were watching the Japanese news on TV (we get such programming in the San Francisco Bay Area). All of a sudden there was a story about schools with pictures of the students leaving for the day. My friend stopped mid-sentence, pointed at the TV, and said, "Look there's a blond, another one, a redhead!" This must have been an unusual high school given how few foreigners live in Japan.

Now if you have trouble with anime characters walking around with pink, blue, or green hair come to the S.F. Bay Area and look me up. I'll show you real characters with such hair; in fact until recently it seemed that only Asians had solid hair colors rather than just a streak or colored tips.

cluding one with a wicker casket for a child, and the containers where ashes or bones of the dead are stored.

 Bones play a role in the *Rumic Theater* story "Hidden in the Pottery" (chapt. 4, p. 127).

KASŌ (GEOMANCY)

 Better known in the West by its Chinese name *feng shui*, kasō is, among other things, a belief system for discovering the most auspicious way of selecting building layouts and locations. One important part of kasō is *kimon*, or inauspicious direction. This is generally the northeast, and builders will avoid putting doors or certain rooms on that side of the structure.

🅰 In *Blue Seed* (tp. 2, ep. 4) we see kasō used in connection with the removal of a hill and new construction.

KATA (FORM OR SEQUENCE)

 Kata are most commonly known in the West as a series of stances done in sequence during martial arts training. Kata in karate and aikidō are a series of movements used in attack and defense, but kata are found in other areas of Japanese culture and society as well, from sword making, the tea ceremony (**cha-no-yu**), and kabuki drama, to writing kanji strokes in sequence, correctly serving a bottle of beer to a customer, choosing seating arrangements in a room, or the interactions between two people of different social status. The subject gets so complicated that Boye Lafayette De Mente wrote an entire book, *Behind the Japanese Bow*, explaining Japanese culture from the standpoint of kata.

🅰 Kata are in the "pattern" used by the coach in Noriko's mecha training in *GunBuster* (OVA 4). • Several women are going through tennis kata in *Maison Ikkoku: Playing Doubles* (ep. 1).

KAWABATA YASUNARI

1899–1972. Japan's Nobel Prize winner for literature (1968). Many of his short stories and novels are available in English translation. Kawabata, who was also a master of the literary essay, is known for his emotional expressiveness and for the poignant beauty of his imagery. Much of his work is marked by a kind of bittersweet eroticism. While his death in 1972 shocked the nation

*The technique for ringing a **kei** is shown here in* Tenchi Universe; *note the cushion it sits on.*

and was ruled a suicide, many of his friends believed it was an accident.

🅐 Kawabata is the author of *Izu no Odoriko*, which is available in anime (and in film) as *Izu Dancer*.

KAYU (RICE PORRIDGE)

Frequently, *okayu*. It is primarily a breakfast (**chōshoku**) dish. Sometimes ingredients other than rice are included for flavor, such as egg, **umeboshi**, salmon, and roe.

🅐 Ataru is served okayu in *Urusei Yatsura* (TV tp. 6, ep. 21, st. 42).

KEI (BELL)

A bowl-shaped bell on a small cushion, also called *kin* or *kinsu*. Used in Buddhist services, it is often seen on a **butsudan**, where it is rung before offering prayers.

🅐 In *Tenchi Universe* (tp. 2, ep. 5) Kiyone rings a kei at an improvised butsudan to Mihoshi; the grandfather rings one at the family butsudan in *Tenchi Universe* (tp. 6, ep. 17). • Tofu-**sensei** rings a kei at his butsudan in *Ranma 1/2* (sub tp. 5, dub tp. 7, ep. 14).

🅜 In *Barefoot Gen* (p. 125) we see a Buddhist priest ring a kei in a rural temple.

KEIO PURAZA HOTERU (KEIO PLAZA HOTEL)

Located in Shinjuku Ward of western Tokyo, the Keio Plaza Hotel building is over 500 feet or 47 stories tall.

🅐 The Keio Plaza Hotel is near the headquarters of the You-Gen-Kai-Sya in *Phantom Quest Corp.* (tp. 1, insert).

KEISHICHŌ (TOKYO METROPOLITAN POLICE DEPARTMENT)

Formed in 1874 the Keishichō is the police for the entire capital district of Tokyo. It is headed by a superintendent general who is appointed by the National Public Safety Commission and approved by the prime minister and the Tokyo Metropolitan Public Safety Commission. The main building of the National Police Agency is located in the Kasumigaseki area of central Tokyo. Some 18 stories tall and completed in 1980, its distinctive circular tower housing a transmission antenna and its wedge shape are clearly visible from the air and the ground.

🅐 The headquarters building is seen in *Phantom Quest Corp.* (tp. 1, ep. 1), in *Patlabor 2*, and in *Blue Seed* (tp. 2, ep. 4). • "TMPD" is on the back of several jackets in *Blue Seed* (tp. 1, ep. 1) and *Patlabor 2*.

🅜 The headquarters is also seen in *Sanctuary* (vol. 6, p. 5).

*This end view of the **Keishichō**, the Police Headquarters in Tokyo, is the one seen again and again in anime and manga, as it is here in* Blue Seed.

KEIZAI KIKAKU CHŌ (ECONOMIC PLANNING AGENCY)

 This small cabinet-level advisory agency was established to create economic plans for the nation. The execution of these plans is left to other agencies. Most of the work of the Keizai Kikaku Chō consists of economic and statistical studies that are published as papers on specific issues of concern to the Japanese government. **A** Yoshiki was at the Keizai Kikaku Chō before being transferred to TAC (Terrestrial Administration Center) in *Blue Seed* (tp. 3, ep. 6).

KEMARI (JAPANESE "FOOTBALL")

 Sometimes called *shūkiku*, kemari came from China in the Nara period and became especially popular among court nobles in the **Heian period**. The game is played by 4, 6, or 8 people who stand in a circle and keep a 10-inch deerskin ball in motion. The game is slow and dignified. In 1881 the Kemari Preservation Society was formed, as Emperor Meiji was concerned that the game might die out. One occasionally sees kemari "performed" by people wearing ancient court costumes. **A** We see kemari played by Princess Murasaki in *Tale of Genji*. • Sasami plays the game by herself in *Tenchi Universe* (tp. 4, ep. 11); this is possibly a reference to Princess Murasaki.

KENDAMA (CUP AND BALL TOY)

 A toy consisting of a handle with two shallow cups and a spike. A wooden ball with a hole in it is held in a cup, tossed, and caught on the spike. The ball is attached to the handle by string to keep it from getting lost. **A** A kendama falls from Mousse's clothing during his duel with Ranma in *Ranma 1/2: Chestnuts Roasting on an Open Fire* (ep. 2). • Sasuke uses a kendama as a weapon in *Ranma 1/2: Goodbye Girl-Type* (ep. 1). • Godai plays with a kendama in *Maison Ikkoku: Love-love Story* (ep. 2).

KENDŌ ("WAY OF THE SWORD")

 Kendō is Japanese fencing based on samurai two-handed sword-fighting styles. In the 18th century protective equipment and a bamboo sword (**shinai**) were introduced to reduce injuries. Skill in either kendō or **jūdō** is required of all police officers in Japan; a lower-level officer cannot be promoted without showing skill in one of these practices. Unlike some other martial arts, kendō does not use a system of colored belts to signify the ranking of the practitioners. **A** We see Ishihara Kyoko successfully practicing a kendō attack in *Sanctuary*. • In his introduction in *Ranma 1/2* (TV tp. 1, ep. 2) Kuno notes that he is a practitioner of kendō. **M** We see kendō training in *Ranma 1/2* (vol. 4, p. 38).

KEN'ETSU (CENSORSHIP)

 Government censorship from the **Edo period** to the end of WWII was mostly political in nature. After the war the old censorship laws were eliminated and replaced by new regulations. Unlike the prewar period, the focus of censorship in modern Japan has been on sexual matters in print, illustration, cinema, and anime. The most common restriction has been to prevent the publication of works that show genitalia and pubic hair. More recently this restriction has been relaxed, but the rules are still much stricter than in

*An insistent Princess Murasaki plays **kemari**, not a girls' sport, in* TALE OF GENJI.

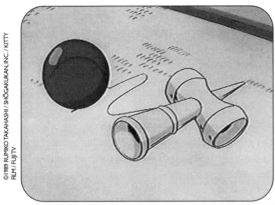

*A **kendama** of traditional design lays on a **tatami**-covered floor in MAISON IKKOKU.*

many other countries. Some anime and manga available in English have had, in the case of anime, the censoring removed or, in manga translations, the genitals added so that we are seeing items not visible in the original Japanese release.

🅰 In the **sentō** sequence in *Patlabor: New Files* (tp. 2, ep. 7) towels are worn until the fight, when black dots appear over the crotches; in the sequence viewed from the top of the wall dividing the men's and women's sections you see several articles tossed in the air, including some of those dots. • A computer-altered pixelated crotch is seen in *Blue Seed: Sea Devils* (Omake Theater).

KETSUEKI-GATA (BLOOD TYPE)

In Japan blood type plays a role much like that of astrological signs in the United States. There is thus a whole "science" of how blood types correspond to personality types and how compatible one blood type is with others. Some authors use a hybrid system of Western astrology and blood type.

🅰 The blood type is given for the TAC folks in *Blue Seed* (tp. 2, ep. 4). • In *Here Is Greenwood* (tp. 1, ep. 2) we find out that Mitsuru's type is A, Shinobu's is AB, and Hasukawa's is A; in *Pretty Sammy 2*, Sasami identifies hers as A.

KI (SPIRIT, LIFE FORCE)

A very abstract yet important term used in conjunction with other words to indicate a variety of mental states or "life energies." I'll limit this entry to some broad examples. Known in Chinese as *qi* or *chi*, ki is central to such medicinal arts as acupuncture (**hari**), where treatment of illness involves restoring a balance to the ki in the body. In martial arts the ki must be controlled before a person can be effective in action; the word aikido refers, roughly, to the principle of ki acting in harmony. One common way ki is symbolized in anime and manga is as flames, as a larger-than-life image of a person's "battle aura," or as someone sensing a person's "battle spirit." In some stories ki can actually be projected out of the body to deliver a physical blow against an opponent.

Ⓜ Happosai's rather dramatic "battle aura" is seen in *Ranma 1/2* (vol. 6, p. 36) and *Ranma 1/2: Evil Wakes* (ep. 1).

🅰 Shampoo's Great Grandmother senses Ryoga's battle spirit—ki, that is—in *Ranma 1/2: Breaking Point* (ep. 2). • We see flames behind Shinobu's eyes when he warns Nagisa in *Here Is Greenwood* (tp. 1, ep. 2), and behind the eyes of Miku and Aquamarine in *Metal Fighters Miku* (tp. 6, ep. 12). • A ki blast is used against an opponent in *Zenki* (tp. 2, ep. 4).

*Practiced by many police officers, **kendō** requires fitness, agility, and quick reflexes. Here it is seen in SANCTUARY.*

KI-AI (SHOUT)

 A focusing of **ki** by means of an abrupt shout, used in martial arts as well as in religious and magical practices.

A We see a **tanuki** use a ki-ai when attempting to turn leaves into money in *Urusei Yatsura* (TV tp. 14, ep. 52, st. 75). • In *Ranma 1/2* and *Suikoden Demon Century* we see a ki-ai used before striking. • In *Phantom Quest Corp.* (tp. 1, ep. 2) Rokkon uses a ki-ai as part of an exorcism.

M A psychic uses ki-ai during a ritual in *Domu: A Child's Dream*.

KIDŌTAI (RIOT POLICE)

 While the typical Japanese policeman at the local **kōban** is very friendly, the padded, armored members of the Kidōtai look more like people you want to avoid. Kidōtai duties are not just limited to riot containment but include rescue operations and simple crowd control.

A Riot police block off a street in *Roujin Z*. The 2nd, "Hell's Own," and 4th riot squads are mentioned and their large black buses seen in *Patlabor: Original Series* (tp. 1, ep. 2).

KIKU (CHRYSANTHEMUM)

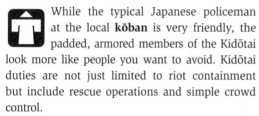 Chrysanthemums have been grown in Japan since ancient times. They were introduced for medicinal use from China in the 5th century. Ornamental varieties were introduced in the 8th century. The flower is considered a symbol of autumn, although some varieties bloom at other times of the year. The crest of the imperial family is a stylized chrysanthemum. An edible variety is *shokuyōgiku*.

M Kyoko takes chrysanthemums to Soichiro's grave in *Maison Ikkoku: Spring Wasabi* (ep. 2) and in vol. 7 (p. 178).

A Masao gives Tamiko wild chrysanthemums in *Grave of the Wild Chrysanthemum*.

KIMONO

 A traditional robelike garment worn by both men and women. The word is occasionally used for Japanese traditional clothing in general. Women's kimono tend to be more colorful than men's. A light cotton version of the kimono is a **yukata**; a heavy outer kimono for indoor wear in cold weather is a *tanzen*. The kimono is always worn with the left side overlapping the right; corpses are dressed in the reverse. One of the unfortunate results of flipping images in manga translations is that we have people walking around wearing kimono in the style used to dress the dead.

M Kimono are worn by Nabiki when Ranma first arrives in *Ranma 1/2* (TV tp. 1, ep. 1) and by Ranma and Akane when they go to the fair (vol. 4, p. 170).

A Lum wears a kimono in *Urusei Yatsura* (TV tp. 5, ep. 18, st. 35). • Several scenes in *Tale of Genji* have layered kimono in the tradition of the nobility; Ayaka wears this style in *Tenchi Universe* (tp. 4, ep. 11).

M Kyoko wears a kimono in *Maison Ikkoku* (vol. 2, p. 81). • We see layered kimono on Shinobu in *Return of Lum: Feudal Furor* (p. 88).

KINGYO (GOLDFISH)

 Goldfish are believed to have been first introduced into Japan from China in the 16th and 17th centuries. Other varieties were introduced by Dutch traders in the 18th century. In the Bunka and Bunsei eras (1804–30), goldfish became very popular and vendors carrying tubs would walk through neighborhoods chanting "Kingyo, kingyo!"

A Goldfish sellers carrying tubs on a pole are seen in *Wandering Days* and *Urusei Yatsura* (TV tp. 19, ep. 73, st. 96). • Several kinds of goldfish are in *Kimagure Orange Road* (OVA 1, ep. 1).

KINGYO-SUKUI (GOLDFISH DIPPING)

 An entertainment commonly seen at festivals (**matsuri**) and fairs (**ennichi**). Players try to catch goldfish in a tank using a "spoon" made of a handle with a loop of wire and paper over the loop. This takes a great deal of skill; otherwise you break the paper. The trick apparently is in the angle used to scoop up the fish.

 In *You're Under Arrest* (OVA 2) kingyo-sukui is listed by Natsumi as one of the activities she wanted to do that summer. • It is seen in *Ranma 1/2: Chestnuts Roasting on an Open Fire* (ep. 1), in *Kimagure Orange Road* (OVA 1, ep. 1), and in *Tenchi Universe* (tp. 2, ep. 7).

 We see Ranma playing a round of kingyo-sukui in *Ranma 1/2* (vol. 4, p. 170). • In *Maison Ikkoku* (vol. 3, p. 122) Godai and Shun both try it at the **Bon** Festival.

KINKAKUJI (TEMPLE OF THE GOLDEN PAVILION)

 Built in 1397 by the **shōgun** Ashikaga Yoshimitsu on his estate in western **Kyoto**, it is called the "Golden Pavilion" because the inside and outside of the second and third stories are decorated with gold leaf. One of Yoshimitsu's last wishes was that the pavilion be turned into a Buddhist temple. Named Rokuonji, it belongs to the Shōkokuji branch of the Rinzai Zen sect. The temple survived the massive destruction of the Ōnin war (1467–77), natural disasters, and WWII. It was destroyed by an arsonist in 1950 and replaced by a replica in 1955.

 We see an old man drinking tea while looking at the Golden Pavilion in *Urusei Yatsura* (TV tp. 6, Spring Special 2).

KINTARŌ

Kintarō—literally, "Golden Boy"—was the childhood name of Sakata no Kintoki, one of the retainers of the warrior **Minamoto no Yorimitsu**. In Japanese folklore, depending on the version of the story, he was born either the son of a mountain witch or an exiled noblewoman. As a child he is said to have carried an ax and wrestled with bears and other animals.

In *Urusei Yatsura* (TV tp. 1, ep. 4, st. 1) and *Re-*

turn of Lum: Feudal Furor (p. 153) we see Kintarō portrayed as an alien child come to Earth.

KIRISUTOKYŌ (CHRISTIANITY)

Christianity was introduced into Japan by Francis Xavier, who landed at Kagoshima in 1549. The warlord Oda Nobunaga supported the missionary efforts of the Jesuits. In 1587 **Toyotomi Hideyoshi** outlawed Christianity in Japan and had 26 martyrs executed in Nagasaki. The ban continued to be upheld through the **Edo period**, during which time the persecution and execution of Christians continued, especially after the Shimabara Uprising in 1637. Many Christians, called Kakure ("Hidden") Kirishitan, continued to live in Japan, concealing their faith from the government until 1873, when the ban was lifted. Many of these Christians lived in the vicinity of Nagasaki, which con-

WHERE DID THAT COME FROM!?

Anime is created for the Japanese market, so much that we see is unfamiliar to us. In many cases this unfamiliarity adds to the pleasure of watching anime. I attempt to explain some of these details in this book and its online supplement, but there is one class of items I do not talk about much: allusions to other shows.

Anime is often sprinkled with references to other shows as a way of showing homage. Studio Gainax is known for this, especially in *Otaku no Video* (for example, just look at the variety of outfits worn by the characters at the school festival) and *GunBuster* (the posters in Noriko's room).

The early *Project A-Ko* OVAs also have several references, such as those to *Fist of the North Star* and the Captain Harlock stories, and *Blue Seed* (tp. 11, Omake Theater) has a reference to the Ghidrah movies right down to the style of the previews you would see in the theater.

So if you don't get it, you may have to simply try to expand your knowledge of Japanese pop entertainment, especially science fiction and samurai films.

tinues to have a large Christian community to this day. The Nagasaki area also had few **Shintō** shrines and Buddhist temples until the Meiji period due to continued arson from the Hidden Christians in the area. In some cases Christian communities migrated to distant areas to avoid detection and suppression. In the remote communities of Kyushu, Christianity combined with elements of Buddhism and Shintō to create an interesting mixture of these traditions. It is estimated that less than 1% of the population of Japan is Christian today.

🅜 *One Pound Gospel* has a major character who is a novice nun.

🅐 The distrust of Christianity by the Japanese is shown in *The Martyr*.

KISERU (TOBACCO PIPE)

 Tobacco (*tabako*) smoking is believed to have been introduced into Japan in the late 16th century. The kiseru is made up of a metal bowl and mouthpiece joined by a length of hollow bamboo or metal pipe. The bowl is small, holding only enough for a few puffs. Women often smoke from longer kiseru, as the length of the stem makes the smoke cooler.

🅐 A pipe is smoked by Sato, when he is first seen in *Student Days*, by the grandfather in *Kimagure Orange Road* (OVA 2, ep. 1), and by Shampoo's great grandmother in *Ranma 1/2: Chestnuts Roasting on an Open Fire* (ep. 1).

🅜 A pipe is smoked, and used as a weapon, by Happosai in *Ranma 1/2* (vol. 6, p. 20).

KISSATEN (COFFEEHOUSE)

 The first kissaten in Japan, Kahii Sakan, was opened in the **Ueno** district of central Tokyo in 1888. Soon others opened, mostly in the **Ginza**. Kissaten are a bit like American coffee shops, serving meals and pastries as well as beverages. Many kissaten have adopted a theme in decor or music. There are even kissaten with hostesses (**hosutesu**). Coffee in kissaten is expensive, as much as $4 to $5 a cup. But customers are not expected to leave right away and can order a single cup of coffee and stay as long as they like without ordering anything else. Their water glass will be kept full so they don't get thirsty. Friends often meet in kissaten to spend hours relaxing and talking. Businessmen also use kissaten to meet clients outside the office. Many shops provide racks of magazines and newspapers for customers to read.

🅐 Godai and some friends discuss their exams in a kissaten in *Maison Ikkoku: Ronin Blues* (ep. 1). • Ohta takes a break in a kissaten in *Patlabor: New Files* (tp. 3, ep. 10); notice the man at the next table reading a book. • Ataru, displaying his total lack of knowledge of coffee, orders American coffee, extra strong, in *Urusei Yatsura* (TV tp. 16, ep. 60, st. 83). • Of course there is the coffee shop ABCB in *Kimagure Orange Road*.

KISU (KISS)

In Japan kissing is a highly intimate act, so intimate that parents will not kiss in front of their children. Kissing in Japan is not a sign of affection or closeness but suggests sexual foreplay or strong romantic love. For this reason indirect kissing, such as sharing a soda straw or touching lips to anything that another's lips have touched, has an emotional content that is difficult for many non-Japanese to comprehend.

Akane kisses P-chan, and Ranma, who knows who P-chan really is, gets upset in *Ranma 1/2* (sub tp. 4, dub tp. 5, ep. 10; vol. 2, p. 36). Later in the series Shampoo's kiss of Ranma is shocking to everyone, especially Akane and Ranma, in *Ranma 1/2* (sub tp. 5, dub tp. 8, ep. 15; vol. 3, p. 120).

In *GunBuster* (OVA 3) Noriko blushes after she absentmindedly drinks from the bottle Smith Toren left with her. • Ryoko, in her characteristic style, offers Tenchi sake in a bottle while saying—"It's like indirectly kissing"—in *Tenchi Muyo!* (OVA 11). • Hikaru and Kyosuke have their first kiss after going out for years in the movie *Kimagure Orange Road: I Want to Return to That Day.* • In *Urusei Yatsura* (TV tp. 16, ep. 62, st. 85), Lum has a cold and Ataru sells the surgical mask she has been wearing to several students, who take turns wearing it out of a desire for an indirect kiss. Of course they also catch her cold.

KITSUNE (FOX)

 Foxes have supernatural abilities, including the ability to change shape and to be messengers of **Inari**, the **kami** of cereal crops. One finds small shrines to foxes as well as fear of possession by fox spirits. Fox shrines have a statue of a sitting fox, and Inari shrines often have statues of foxes nearby. The most sacred foxes are white.

Murphy, a shape-changing fox with seven tails, is in the story "Maris the Chojo" (*Rumic World,* p. 120ff; *Rumic World Trilogy,* vol. 1, p. 113), which has also been animated.

We see fox statues in *My Neighbor Totoro* during the scene where the girls wait for their father at the trolley stop. • Fox-spirit possession is diagnosed in *Vampire Princess Miyu* (tp. 1, ep. 1).

In *Lum Urusei Yatsura: Perfect Collection* (p. 80) you can see a fox statue near the **torii;** there is also a fox statue on a **Shintō** altar along with a mirror (**seidōkyō**), paper slips on the wall (**senja-fuda**), and a statue of a **tanuki** (p. 82).

KIYOMIZUDERA

 Founded about 798 by the monk Enchin, Kiyomizudera is a temple of the Hossō sect of Buddhism. The most famous feature of this temple, its veranda on a cliff overlooking **Kyoto**, is often what is pictured in anime and manga. There is a saying about doing something "with as much determination as if leaping off the veranda of Kiyomizu Temple."

Kiyomizudera is shown and the "jump from the stage of Kiyomizu" is mentioned in *Urusei Yatsura* (TV tp. 6, Spring Special 2).

KŌBAN (POLICE BOX)

Small police substations are found throughout Japan and are staffed by one or two police officers, or ten or more in busy districts. The kōban system was created when the old *tsujiban* system of corner guards in busy areas was modernized in the **Meiji period**. Each kōban has an office area and, in urban areas, sleeping quarters. In the countryside the kōban are like small houses for the policeman and his family. Officers at the kōban not only fight crime but give directions and help find lost objects; if you find something on the street simply take it to your local kōban! Kōban officers also patrol the neighborhood on bicycle and on foot.

A kōban is seen in *Urusei Yatsura* (TV tp. 12, ep. 46, st. 69). • Kyosuke borrows a bike from a kōban in *Kimagure Orange Road* (OVA 3, ep. 2). • A kōban is seen when Ohta is standing in the rain while an old woman talks to the officer on duty in *Patlabor: New Files* (tp. 3, ep. 10). • Due to wartime regula-

ON THE CUTTING OF MANGA STORIES

Oh I hate this!

A manga you have been dying to see translated starts coming out and they skip several chapters to make the action flow faster. The result is often a loss of continuity and character development. She was pissed at Him in chapter 1 and now all of a sudden She is all loving in chapter 2. What has happened is that a stack of chapters was cut in between and you are really reading chapter 12! Or they don't even start with chapter 1 but skip several ahead. I can understand removing an occasional sex scene to be able to sell the translation in some states with restrictive laws on publishing, but cutting large sections is another matter.

Now if they would only go back and put in the cut chapters in a graphic novel format special edition for collectors or something I would not gripe as much.

tions the kōban in *Grave of the Fireflies* is kept dark at night.

 Yuta asks for directions at a kōban in *Mermaid's Scar* (p. 39).

KODOMO NO HI (CHILDREN'S DAY)

Before WWII, May 5 (the 5th day of the 5th month) was a festival for boys; now it is a national holiday in honor of all children. The day is still a bit boy-centered, especially since there is a Girls' Day Festival (see **hina matsuri**). On Children's Day parents fly **koinobori** (carp streamers) and put up small displays in the home with replicas of ancient weapons, swords, armor, bows and arrows, or samurai helmets as symbols of strength.

 Children's Day is celebrated in *Urusei Yatsura* (TV tp. 7, ep. 26, st. 49).

KOI (CARP)

 Carp is both eaten and bred as an ornamental fish in Japan. Special breeds of pond koi have a variety of colors and patterns. The word "koi" is a homonym of the word for "love," and this is the cause of puns and confusion.

 We see examples of ornamental koi in ponds in *Ranma 1/2* (TV tp. 1, ep. 1) and in *Zenki* (tp. 2, ep. 4), in the temple pond in *Ghost Story*, and in *All Purpose Cultural Cat Girl Nuku Nuku* ("Phase 0III").
• In *Here Is Greenwood* (tp. 3, ep. 5) Hasukawa uses the word "koi" while speaking to himself, and a friend thinks he is referring to the carp in the nearby pond.

KOINOBORI (CARP STREAMER)

These banners are flown outside houses on May 5, Children's Day (**Kodomo no Hi**). Carp (**koi**) are noted for their strength in swimming upstream, and it is hoped that sons will show such perseverance in their lives. Often there are several koinobori in the following order: black, symbolizing the father; red symbolizing the mother; and small ones, often blue, the children. Often an "arrow wheel" will top the post and spin in the wind.

 In *Urusei Yatsura* (TV tp. 1, ep. 4, st. 1) Lum is "airing out" the family koinobori in autumn, the wrong time of year. We later see koinobori displayed at the proper time in *Urusei Yatsura* (TV tp. 7, ep. 26, st. 49). • A public service announcement gives koinobori safety tips in *Urusei Yatsura* (TV tp. 6, after Spring Special 1).

KOKKAI (DIET)

 The Japanese legislative branch is a bicameral system divided into the Shūgiin (House of Representatives or lower house) with 512 members serving four-year terms and the Sangiin (House of Councillors or upper house) with 252 members serving six-year terms. Members of the Diet always wear a special pin that identifies their status. Deep purple pins are worn by members of the House of Councillors, and maroon pins are worn by the members of the House of Representatives. In *Sanctuary* (both the manga and anime) much of the story involves political maneuvering in the Kokkai. Construction on the distinctive Diet building in the Kasumigaseki area of central Tokyo began in 1920 and ended in 1937.

🅰 The Kokkai holds a special meeting to discuss a problem with strong economic and political repercussions in *Patlabor 1*; the Diet building is surrounded by troops in *Patlabor 2* as tensions between the government and military increase.

Ⓜ In *Sanctuary* (vol. 1, pp. 34, 164–67) many scenes take place outside of and in the Diet building. The members pin is also seen (vol. 1, p. 174).

KŌKŌ YAKYŪ (HIGH SCHOOL BASEBALL)

 Baseball is the major school sport in Japan. Every year in March and April the National Invitational Senior High School Baseball Tournament takes place. In August the All-Japan High School Baseball Championship—also known as the "Japanese High School World Series"—is held at Kōshien Stadium in Nishinomiya near Osaka. The event is so popular that in August the combination of air conditioners and televisions in use sometimes causes power outages. One tradition is for the losing team to gather dirt from the Koshien field to scatter on their home playing grounds to inspire themselves to work harder for the next season.

🅰 Lum watches the High School World Series in *Urusei Yatsura* (TV tp. 11, ep. 39, st. 62). • The Kōshien Stadium baseball quarterfinals second game between Sakiyama High and Kase High is on TV in *Maison Ikkoku: Love-love Story* (ep. 1).

Ⓜ The High School World Series is mentioned in *Return of Lum: Lum in the Sun* (p. 92).

KOMA-INU

 A pair of sculpted animals, sometimes referred to as lions or as dogs, often placed opposite each other in front of shrines and temples for protection from evil. The one on the right, known as "A," always has its mouth open; the one on the left, known as "Un," has its mouth closed.

🅰 Koma-inu are seen in *Tenchi Muyo! Mihoshi Special*; *Hakkenden* (tp. 5, ep. 8); *Blue Seed: Sea Devils* (ep. 16); *Vampire Princess Miyu* (tp. 2, ep. 4); and *Student Days*.

Ⓜ In *Sanctuary* (vol. 3, p. 313) koma-inu can be seen in front of the shrine.

KOMIKETTO

 Komiketto, or Comic Market, is the major **manga** convention in Japan. It has been held every August and December in Tokyo since December 1975. Komiketto is organized as a nonprofit and is run by fans for fans. In 1995 nearly 300,000 people attended the three-day event, with over 60,000 sellers of **dōjinshi**.

🅰 Comic Market is mentioned in the elevator scene in *Otaku no Video* (pt. 1, 1st anim. seq.).

KONGŌSHŌ (VAJRA)

Vajra has several levels of meaning in Buddhism. In esoteric Buddhism vajra symbolizes the delusion-destroying power of wisdom. Stylized thunderbolt implements, often made of cast brass, symbolize vajra and are used in rituals, along with the proper **inzō** (hand positions).

*The classical structure of the granite front of the **Kokkai** (Diet) Building as seen in BLUE SEED.*

An example of this kind of ritual implement is seen at the right and left edges of the titles scene at the beginning of *Zenki*. Also in *Zenki* Chiaki is told of the Vajra power in her heart (tp. 1, ep. 1).

KON'IN (MARRIAGE)

Marriages in feudal Japan were often arranged by families to strengthen alliances. Arranged marriages still exist, as they do elsewhere in the world. A go-between (*baishakunin* or *nakōdo*) handles communication between the families and often arranges the initial meeting (**omiai**) between the couple. You don't have to marry the person you meet at an omiai, but family pressure may be brought in the case of a very good prospect. Omiai are useful in breaking the ice in a traditional gender-defined culture, and while the custom of arranging an omiai and using a matchmaker is declining, it is not unusual for a couple to have someone act out the role of the go-between at the wedding and reception.

🅜 At times arranged marriages take place without the services of a go-between, as in the engagement between Ranma and Akane in *Ranma 1/2*. • An arranged engagement plays a role in the story

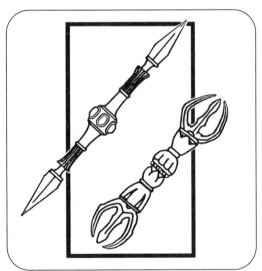

Originating in the ancient Mediterranean world, the **kongōshō** *changed little in shape as it moved eastward.*

Laughing Target in the *Rumic World* anthology and in an anime version.

KONNYAKU (DEVIL'S TONGUE ROOT)

 Konnyaku is the name of both the plant and the jelly made from its starchy bulb. The jelly is made into blocks. Konnyaku jelly slices are used in *nimono* (simmered dishes) like **oden**. It is also made into thin noodles (*shirataki*) and thick ones (*ito konnyaku*). Shirataki is an ingredient in stewlike dishes such as **sukiyaki**.

🅐 Goto and Nagumo make a side trip to get some konnyaku in Shimonita in *Patlabor: New Files* (tp. 4, ep. 12).

KŌSEISHŌ (MINISTRY OF HEALTH AND WELFARE)

 Formed in 1938 by the merger of bureaus of the Home Ministry and later reorganized under the Occupation, this ministry does general planning for the health, welfare, and pension systems. It also oversees accreditation of health professionals and institutions, and regulates medicines and drugs. Its offices are in the Kasumigaseki government district in central Tokyo.

🅐 The ministry plays a major role in *Roujin Z*.

KOSHI (PALANQUIN)

 A koshi is a covered palanquin on long horizontal poles carried by men. Originally only the imperial family rode in koshi, but eventually it was used by commoners. Later it was replaced by the **kago**. The only kind of koshi still in use today is the **mikoshi** used in **matsuri**.

🅐 In *Hakkenden* (tp. 4, ep. 7) we see someone carried in a koshi.

🅜 In *Mermaid Forest* (p. 19) Mana is about to be placed on a primitive koshi.

KOTATSU

 Low tables with a heat source beneath them. In the past the heat came from a small charcoal pit or from a **hibachi** under

the table. Nowadays kotatsu have an electric heater installed on the bottom of the table frame. The table top is removable, and in winter a quilt is draped between the frame and the top to hold the heat in. **Chabudai** look much like kotatsu but don't have a heating unit. Among poor families, the kotatsu may be a room's sole source of heat.

 We see a kotatsu on Mihoshi's ship in *Tenchi Muyo!* (OVA 4) and at Ryoko's hideout in *Tenchi Muyo! Mihoshi Special*, including a view of its bottom with the electric heating unit built in. • In *Otaku no Video* characters are often seated around a kotatsu. • In *Patlabor 2* we see a kotatsu while the alert is being broadcast on TV. • Kotatsu often show up in the dorm in *Here Is Greenwood* (tp. 1, ep. 1).

Ⓜ Kozue and Kyoko sit at a covered kotatsu in Kyoko's apartment in *Maison Ikkoku* (vol. 2, p. 27). • A kotatsu is seen in *Lum Urusei Yatsura: Perfect Collection* (p. 16).

KOTO

 A 13-stringed musical instrument associated with refined tastes. Based on the Chinese *cheng*, the koto was introduced to Japan in the 11th century. Once an instrument of the nobility, it continues to be played in modern Japan. The strings are plucked by small picks worn on the thumb and first two fingers of the right hand; the left hand is used to change the pitch of the strings. Compositions for the koto are still written today, and there are many schools of instruction.

 We see and hear koto in *Tale of Genji*. • In *Ranma 1/2: Goodbye Girl-Type* (ep. 1), Kodachi plays the koto and uses the picks as a weapon.

KŌYA-SAN (MT. KŌYA)

 A mountain in northern Wakayama Prefecture in central **Honshu**, famous for the headquarters of the Shingon sect of Buddhism and its many temples. The over 111 temples on Kōya-san are often visited by devout Buddhists on pilgrimages (**junrei**).

On a cold December night in MAISON IKKOKU, Godai and Kyoko drink some tea while staying warm at the **kotatsu**.

Ⓜ In *Mermaid's Scar* (p. 272) a story is told about the priest **Saigyō** on Kōya-san.

KUJI

 The nine magic syllables, a spell of Taoist origin that in Japan is recited while moving the hand through a sequence of **inzō** (hand positions). The kuji in Japan have evolved a different interpretation from their use in **Shugendō**, perhaps influenced by Chinese Buddhist interpretations.

 The kuji are recited and some of the accompanying inzō are done by Rokkon at the beginning of case 4 of *Phantom Quest Corp.* (tp. 2, ep. 4).

Shunkin plays the **koto** for a client in TALE OF SHUNKIN.

KUME MASAO

 1891–1952. A novelist and playwright who attended Tokyo University (**Tōkyō Daigaku**) with **Akutagawa Ryūnosuke**. His plays and novels became very popular. He also wrote haiku poetry under the name of Santei.

🅰 Kume Masao is the author of *Gakusei Jidai*, available in an anime version as *Student Days*.

KURAGE (JELLY FISH)

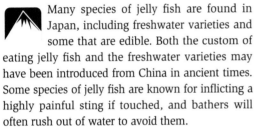 Many species of jelly fish are found in Japan, including freshwater varieties and some that are edible. Both the custom of eating jelly fish and the freshwater varieties may have been introduced from China in ancient times. Some species of jelly fish are known for inflicting a highly painful sting if touched, and bathers will often rush out of water to avoid them.

Ⓜ Kyoko runs into kurage while swimming in *Maison Ikkoku* (*Playing Doubles*, ep. 2; vol. 1, p. 173).

🅰 People rapidly empty out of a public pool once jelly fish are found in it in *Hyperdoll* (Act 1). • An *aragami* jelly fish causes trouble in *Blue Seed* (tp. 3, ep. 5).

KURAMA TENGU

 A fictional character from a novel of the same name. He was known as a mysterious samurai who rescued patriots from the Shinsen-gumi, a group who opposed the changes that led to the Meiji Restoration in 1868.

Ⓜ Kurama Tengu makes a brief appearance at the disco in *Lum Urusei Yatsura: Perfect Collection* (p. 353).

KURAMAYAMA

 A hill in northern **Kyoto** legendary in Japanese history for its occupation by robbers and evil spirits. It is here that **Minamoto no Yoshitsune** is said to have been trained by **tengu**.

🅰 In *Urusei Yatsura* (TV tp. 3, ep. 12, st. 24) Ushi-wakamaru (Minamoto no Yoshitsune) is shown on Kuramayama being trained by the tengu.

KURISUMASU (CHRISTMAS)

 With less than 1% of its population Christian it may seem strange that Christmas is celebrated in Japan. But the holiday has been adopted by the Japanese, who manage to make it fit into their culture quite well. Many homes are decorated with fir tree branches, and people eat "Christmas cake." Gift giving seems to be mainly for children and close friends and relatives. Stores of course promote gift giving, as Christmas comes just about the same time that workers receive their December bonus (**shōyo**).

🅰 Christmas presents play a role in *Urusei Yatsura* (TV 3, ep. 10, sts. 19–20). • In *Oh My Goddess!* (OVA 4) we hear a newscaster mention Christmas cake.

Ⓜ In *Maison Ikkoku* (vol. 2) Godai has trouble giving a Christmas present and we get to see a Christmas party (vol. 4, p. 35).

KUROGO (STAGEHAND)

 Kabuki stagehands, more properly known as *kōken*. They are dressed all in black (the term kurogo means "black costume"). In some plays they have to step on stage to remove parts of costumes; the audience assumes these shadowy figures, since they are not part of the story, are not really there.

🅰 In *Urusei Yatsura* kurogo drop petals on Ran in a flashback (TV tp. 9, ep. 31, st. 54) and interfere with a baseball game where no one notices them (TV tp. 18, ep. 70, st. 93).

Ⓜ A kurogo appears on the stage during a Shakespeare play in *Ranma 1/2* (vol. 7, p. 35).

KUSHAMI (SNEEZE)

 There is a common belief that you will sneeze if someone talks about you.

Ⓜ Akane sneezes when she is being talked about in the *Ranma 1/2* manga (vol. 3, p. 8) and TV series (*Ranma 1/2: Darling Charlotte*, ep. 2).

A Ayeka sneezes when talked about by Ryoko in *Tenchi Muyo!* (OVA 2). • A-ko sneezes in her sleep when B-ko talks about her in *Project A-Ko*. • Nene sneezes when Lisa is asking folks about her in *Bubblegum Crisis* (OVA 8). • Ataru sneezes when talked about in *Urusei Yatsura* (TV tp. 6, ep. 22, sts. 43–44).

KUSHI (COMB)

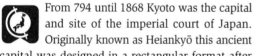 Japanese combs are not only functional but sometimes very beautiful works of art made with lacquered wood, or tortoise-shell and mother of pearl inlay. Combs were made with a large variety of materials depending on the social status of the wearer.

A In *Tale of Genji* we see several women wearing or using combs. • Okoto wears hairpins and a comb in *Tale of Shunkin*. • A red comb is in Otomi's hair in *Sanshiro the Judoist* (pt. 1).

KYOTO

From 794 until 1868 Kyoto was the capital and site of the imperial court of Japan. Originally known as Heiankyō this ancient capital was designed in a rectangular format after the Tang China capital of Chang'an. Kyoto is famous to this day for its architecture and cultural heritage.

A **Heian-period** Kyoto is parodied in *Urusei Yatsura* (TV tp. 3, ep. 11, sts. 21–22). • Kyoto is mentioned in Shino's father's story of the Murasame sword in *Hakkenden* (tp. 1, ep. 2). • *Tale of Genji* takes place in Kyoto as does part of *Vampire Princess Miyu*.

M P-chan returns from Kyoto in *Ranma 1/2* (vol. 2, p. 99). • In *Sanctuary* (vol. 5, p. 250) we see a meeting being served by **geisha** in the **Gion** district of Kyoto.

KYŪ (MOXIBUSTION)

 A medical treatment in which cones of moxa (made from the hairs that grow under the leaves of a variety of mugwort)

INTERROGATE YOUR FOOD

So you're a strict vegan and plan to enjoy visiting Japan, eh?

Better bring lots of cash or arrange for your own cooking facilities.

Most vegetables in Japan are cooked in a stock made with a fish base (*dashi*). Traditional Japanese food involves lots of seafood as well as vegetables and rice. The only place you will find completely meat-free cooking is in a few Buddhist monasteries, at a high price, or at special vegetarian restaurants, at a high price—unless you are lucky enough to find an occasional small place in a side street run by members of some unusual new religious sect (**shinkō shūkyō**) who walk around muttering mantras all the time and try to get you to join before, while, and after you eat your meal. But then it's probably worth it just for the experience of being proselytized in broken English in another country.

are placed on acupuncture (**hari**) points and ignited. This treatment is believed to help cure illness by restoring a proper balance of **ki**.

A Moxa treatment is advertised on a sign at Dr. Tofu's gate in *Ranma 1/2: Chestnuts Roasting on an Open Fire* (ep. 2).

KYŪDŌ (JAPANESE ARCHERY)

 Literally, "the way of the bow." Targets are shot at from a standing position, with an emphasis on form and etiquette. The military form, *kyūjutsu*, is often done from horseback.

M We see examples of kyūdō when Yuzuru is the team captain in the *Rumic World* story and video *Laughing Target*.

A Jinnai corners Makoto in the school archery range in *El-Hazard* (tp. 1, "First Night"). • Akane borrows a bow from another student in *Ranma 1/2: Cat-Fu Fighting* (ep. 1).

STARS

As you watch your favorite fantasy anime, *Zenki*, *Phantom Quest Corp.*, or something by Clamp, do you ever consider that those pentagrams and Stars of David are not part of Japanese culture? Search as you can and you will not find examples in Japanese art before the opening of Japan in the **Meiji period**, probably not much before the 1980s (with the one exception of an obscure **mon** done in a pentagram style, but this one is believed to have been a result of contact with European sailors before the **Edo period**).

These symbols, referred to by some as universal archetypes, are in fact of Middle Eastern origin and from there spread to Europe and North Africa. The reason you see them in anime and manga is that they are considered exotic occult symbols from the West that add an air of mystery.

KYŪRI (CUCUMBER)

 The Japanese cucumber is longer and more slender than the European varieties. It is eaten mainly in salads and pickled. The supernatural animal **kappa** is known to be very fond of kyūri.

🅰 We see Ataru offered a feast of cucumbers in *Urusei Yatsura* (TV tp. 7, ep. 23, sts. 45–46).

KYUSHU

 The third largest and most southern of the four main islands of Japan. Kyushu is subtropical and has lots of rainfall, and is an area of developing high-tech industries.

🅰 Ryoga travels to Mt. Aso (**Asosan**) in Kyushu in *Ranma 1/2* (TV sub tp. 3, dub tp. 5, ep. 9). • The story of *Wandering Days* takes place in Kyushu.

MAGATAMA (BEADS)

 Crescent-shaped beads found in many ancient archaeological sites and mentioned in legendary literature. Green magatama seem to have been important status symbols in prehistoric times.

🅰 Mamoru Kusanagi has several of these implanted in his body in *Blue Seed*.

MAIKO (APPRENTICE GEISHA)

 The word, used in the **Kyoto** and **Osaka** areas, means "dance child." Maiko have distinctive hairstyles and manners of dress, including long-sleeved (*furisode*) **kimono** with a dangling **obi**. They cover their faces in white powder as a sign that they have yet to attain the status of geisha. The training maiko undergo includes classical dance and playing traditional drums. In the past maiko started their apprenticeship between the ages of 13 and 18; today with education compulsory through middle school, a maiko can be in her early 20s.

Ⓜ In "Section Chief Kōsaku Shima" in *Bringing Home the Sushi* (p. 129) we see maiko in a **Gion** district tea house.

MĀJAN (MAH-JONGG)

 A Chinese game that has become popular in Japan since its introduction in the 1920s. Mah-jongg is played with 136 small tiles used much like cards in Western games. There are usually four players, and money often changes hands. Businessmen play mah-jongg to socialize with their clients. The Chinese characters for mah-jongg literally mean "house sparrow," after the sound the tiles make when they are mixed on the table.

🅰 Mah-jongg is in Ataru's dream in *Urusei Yatsura* (TV tp. 6, ep. 21, st. 42). • A game and magazine are in *Blue Seed* (tp. 6, Omake Theater). • The coach plays a mah-jongg computer game in *One Pound Gospel*.

Ⓜ We see an example of mah-jongg in *Return of Lum Urusei Yatsura* (p. 144). • Two cops on patrol talk about a game in *Domu: A Child's Dream*.

MAKUDONARUDO (MCDONALD'S)

 That McDonald's can be found almost anywhere in the world is often used as a symbol of American multinational business activity. The chain has been so successful in Japan that a McDonald's in Santa Clara, California, was opened under Japanese management. Often the McDonald's trademark of the golden arches is inverted on bags and signs in anime, probably to prevent visits from American lawyers.

🅰 Igarashi waits for Mitsuru at a McDonald's in *Here Is Greenwood* (tp. 3, ep. 5). • Kome has a bag

*The exact significance of simple yet enigmatic **magatama** beads has been lost in prehistory.*

with inverted golden arches in *Blue Seed* (tp. 5, ep. 10) as do Ranma and Akane in *Ranma 1/2* (sub tp. 2, dub tp. 3, ep. 6).

MAKURA (PILLOW)

In olden times Japanese pillows were made of stone. Later, wood pillows (*komakura*) or grass bundles came into use. Pillows made of cotton cloth stuffed with buckwheat chaff, down, or kapok are common today. Pillows filled with processed buckwheat chaff have a cover that is open at both ends. An old belief held that the soul left the body in sleep and entered the pillow; many Japanese still will not throw pillows or step over them.

🅰 Old-fashioned hard pillows are in *Tale of Genji*, *Hakkenden* (tp. 6, ep. 10), and *Ghost Story*. • Godai hugs his buckwheat chaff pillow so hard it breaks open at one end in *Maison Ikkoku: Welcome to Maison Ikkoku* (ep. 1). • Buckwheat chaff pillows are also in *All Purpose Cultural Cat Girl Nuku Nuku* ("Phase 0II"), *Metal Fighters Miku* (tp. 6, ep. 12), *Urusei Yatsura* (TV tp. 11, ep. 39, st. 62), *Patlabor: New Files* (vol. 3, ep. 9), *Mermaid Forest*, *Vampire Princess Miyu* (tp. 2, ep. 4), *One Pound Gospel*, and *Tenchi Universe* (tp. 3, ep. 9).

Ⓜ Buckwheat chaff pillows are in *Rumic Theater* (chapt. 1, pp. 7–8), *Maison Ikkoku* (vol. 1, p. 95), and *One Pound Gospel* (vol. 1, p. 84).

MANEKINEKO ("BECKONING CAT")

A small statue of a sitting cat with one paw raised. Made of ceramic or papier mâché, these talismans are often seen near business entryways, as they are felt to bring good fortune in the form of customers.

🅰 A manekineko is used in a fight in *Urusei Yatsura* (TV tp. 6, ep. 21, st. 42).

Ⓜ We see a beckoning cat statue near the bottom right in a restaurant in *Lum Urusei Yatsura: Perfect Collection* (p. 70). • In *Ranma 1/2* (vol. 4, p. 54) a manekineko is seen behind Ranma as he assumes a "cat fist" position.

MANGA (JAPANESE COMICS)

 The word "manga" can mean any kind of illustrated story but is usually used for Japanese comics. Manga are read in massive quantities by people of all ages, from school children to adults. They are almost always published in serialized forms in magazines and, if popular enough, collected into books as both paperbacks and hardcovers. Major genres include *shōnen* (boys'), *shōjo* (girls'), *seinen* (young men's), *redisu* (ladies'), and *seijin* (adult, mainly men's erotic manga). The best books in English on manga are Frederik L. Schodt's *Manga Manga* and *Dreamland Japan*.

A In *Otaku no Video* (3rd anim. seq.) we see shelves of manga in Tanaka's apartment when Kubo goes to visit him. This is not surprising since Tanaka is such an otaku. • In *Tenchi Muyo! Special: The Night before the Carnival*, girls' romantic manga play a major role in the story when they are assumed to be Earth's relationship manuals.

MANJŪ (BUN, DUMPLING)

 Usually steamed, made of wheat or buckwheat flour and filled with a sweet bean paste called *an*. Some varieties have other ingredients added to the dough to change its consistency. The *manjū* was introduced from China and thus is similar to some dim sum varieties.

A A manjū offering on a tray is seen in *Urusei Yatsura* (TV tp. 6, ep. 21, st. 41). • The *momiji manjū* (maple-shaped manjū), a specialty of **Hiroshima**, is seen in *Blue Seed* (tp. 2, ep. 4) and *Ranma 1/2* (sub tp. 4, dub tp. 6, ep. 12).

*The traditional **manekineko**, portrayed here in the first* RANMA *movie, is easy to recognize. Are all cats this friendly?*

©1991 RUMIKO TAKAHASHI / SHŌGAKUKAN

MAN'YŌSHŪ

 "Collection of Ten Thousand Leaves," the oldest existing collection of Japanese poetry. There are 4,516 numbered poems in the collection; the most recent poem is dated New Year's Day of A.D. 759, and the older poems claim to predate Japanese writing. The text is written with Chinese characters (**kanji**) but in Japanese, using the sound of the characters to "spell out" Japanese words. The collection also contains notes, letters, and other information in Chinese.

A A poem from Book 1—"As I gaze at the moon, the mountains look like kingdoms, and it reminds me of my love, far away"—is quoted by B-ko to her father in *Project A-Ko 4*.

M A poem by **Ōtomo no Yakamochi** from *Man'yōshū* is quoted in *Adolf: 1945 and All That Remains* (p. 201).

MASU (BOX MEASURE)

 The masu, a square wooden box formerly used for measuring rice and beans, is sometimes used for drinking cold **sake** (ask for *masuzake*). Masu are usually made of cypress. Sometimes a little salt is placed on a corner, tequila style.

A A corner of a masu is seen on a table at the reunion in *You're Under Arrest* (OVA 3). • We see masu in *Roujin Z* and near a sleeping Happosai in *Ranma 1/2* (TV tp. 14, ep. 33).

M A drinking contest using masu is seen in *Maison Ikkoku* (vol. 6, p. 77). • Happosai drinks sake from a masu in *Ranma 1/2* (vol. 6, p. 19).

*Happosai empties a **masu** in the RANMA 1/2 TV show. I don't advise using this drinking style unless your mouth is as wide as his is. Drink from the corner and be safe.*

MATOI (BANNER, STANDARD)

 This traditional banner dates back to the days when fires were fought by local brigades. Matoi often have interesting designs and cloth strips hanging down from the emblem at the top of the pole.

🅼 The standard on the roof of Kodachi's school (St. Bacchus in the translated manga, St. Hebereke in the anime) in *Ranma 1/2* (TV tp. 4, ep. 11; vol. 2, p. 114) is a matoi.

🅰 In *Project A-Ko 3*, during the mobilization near the end of the story we see one of the robots dramatically land while it is holding a matoi. • In *Patlabor: Original Series* (tp. 2, ep. 4) we see Shinshi shaking a matoi in celebration when the SV2 is told they are temporarily relieved of duty.

MATSURI TO NENCHŪ GYŌJI (FESTIVALS AND ANNUAL EVENTS)

 Holidays in Japan are often divided into two main categories. Matsuri are **Shintō** festivals that occur on set dates. Nenchū gyōji are annual and seasonal observances often of Chinese or Buddhist origin. Some events have elements of both and do not fall clearly into one or the other category. See also **ennichi** (fairs).

🅰 In *Tenchi Universe* (tp. 2, ep. 7) we see both the festivities and the ritual offering of gifts to the local **kami**.

MEIJI JINGŪ (MEIJI SHRINE)

 Located in Yoyogi in Shibuya Ward of western Tokyo, Meiji Shrine is dedicated to the memory of Emperor Meiji and Empress Shōken (see **Meiji period**). The Japanese Diet (**Kokkai**) passed a resolution for its construction in 1913. It was destroyed in an air raid in 1945, and reconstruction was completed in 1958. Meiji Shrine is the most popular shrine in Japan, with 2,412,250 visitors on New Year's Day of 1986.

🅰 In *Maison Ikkoku: Soichiro's Shadow* (ep. 1) Ikuko shows Godai a photo of herself during the **Shichi-go-san Festival**, when she got to go to Meiji Shrine.

MEIJI PERIOD

 1868–1912. The Meiji period marked the beginning of modern Japanese history. Toward the end of the **Edo period**, after more than 250 years of self-imposed isolation, Japan opened its ports and began a new era of interaction with the rest of the world. During the Meiji period, the emperor was restored to power, feudalism was abolished, a postal system was created, Western thought and technology were introduced, and the national capital was moved to Edo, which was renamed Tokyo.

🅰 Some of the anime that take place in the Meiji period are *Tale of Shunkin*, *Priest of Mt. Kouya*, *Theater of Life*, *Growing Up*, and *Dancing Girl*.

MEINICHI (DEATH ANNIVERSARY)

 The anniversary of a person's death, commemorated by their loved ones. Common practices include prayers (**inori**), visiting the gravesite, and placing a favorite object of the deceased at the household altar.

🅼 We see a visit to the graveyard in *Maison Ikkoku* (vol. 1, p. 59) with the bereaved pouring water over the memorial stone, burning incense, and praying.

Sakura in Blue Seed, *with her training in the U.S. and somewhat aggressive manners, is not your conventional* **miko**.

MEISHI (BUSINESS CARD)

 Cards bearing a person's name were first used at the beginning of the 19th century. Business persons usually exchange cards immediately upon their first meeting to determine their relative status.

🅐 In *Phantom Quest Corp.* (tp. 1, ep. 1) Ayaka hands a girl her business card. • Mr. Invader, Lum's father, gives Ataru his card in *Urusei Yatsura* (TV tp. 1, ep. 1, st. 1). • Mujaki gives Lum his business card in *Urusei Yatsura: Beautiful Dreamer.*

🅜 One of Mendou's bodyguards exchanges cards with Sakura in *Return of Lum: Lum in the Sun* (p. 218).

MIKAN

 Similar to a mandarin orange or tangerine, the mikan is very popular as a winter snack. Large quantities are consumed in Japan, even to the point that some people actually start to turn a little yellow due to their bodies absorbing too much carotene from the fruit. More crop land in Japan is devoted to mikan production than to any other fruit. The proper way to peel a mikan is to pull the skin in four sections down away from the stem, leaving the peel connected at the bottom. Any uneaten parts can then be placed inside the peel.

🅐 Ataru refers to eating mikan in *Urusei Yatsura* (TV tp. 15, ep. 58, st. 81).

🅜 In *Maison Ikkoku* (vol. 7, p. 18) we see mikan on the table in Kyoko's room as the Maison folks discuss their New Year's plans.

MIKO (SHRINE MAIDEN)

 Supplementary priestesses found at **Shintō** shrines. Miko wear a long-sleeved top called a *chihaya*, and *hibakama* over their legs. In ancient times miko were often powerful figures and in some cases rulers. Some miko still perform ancient shamanistic roles but usually independently of shrines and often in neo-Shintō popular faiths.

🅜 Sakura introduces herself as a miko and we see her later in traditional garb (*Urusei Yatsura*, TV tp. 2, ep. 5, st. 9; *Lum Urusei Yatsura: Perfect Collection*, p. 77); in the anime, "miko" is translated as "sorceress."

🅐 Miko garb is worn by Sakura Yamazaki in *Blue Seed* (tp. 4, ep. 8). • A miko in white at a wedding with a traditional wrap around her hair is visible in *Rupan III: The Fuma Conspiracy.* • A shrine and a woman dressed as a miko are seen in Key's vision in *Key the Metal Idol* (tp. 2, ep. 4).

🅜 A miko hands Kozue and Godai their fortunes in *Maison Ikkoku* (vol. 4, p. 61).

MIKOSHI (PORTABLE SHRINE)

The mikoshi is actually a palanquin (**koshi**) for carrying a **kami** on travels and visits and at festivals (**matsuri**). The name is written with the characters for "kami" and "koshi." During festivals the mikoshi is hoisted on the shoulders and carried around the neighborhood with much boisterous yelling and pushing; it looks like fun.

🅐 In *You're Under Arrest* (OVA 2) Natsumi mentions, in her list of things undone that summer, wanting to help carry a mikoshi in the Sumida Festival. • The *Blue Seed* TV series ends with a matsuri and the carrying of mikoshi.

MIKUJI (FORTUNE STICK)

 Also known as *omikuji*, a common fortune-telling method found at many shrines and temples. A stick is shaken through a small hole in the corner of a canister. The number on the stick corresponds to a slip of paper with a printed fortune on it. Mikuji originated in China, and many of the fortunes are taken from the *I Ching*. The mikuji paper is often tied to a tree on the temple or shrine grounds in the hope the fortune will not come true if bad or will come true if good.

🅐 We see Momiji and Kome use mikuji at the temple **Sensōji** (identified erroneously as the Kaminari-mon Shrine) in *Blue Seed* (tp. 2, ep. 4). After this they walk past a tree with fortunes tied to it.

🅜 In *Maison Ikkoku* (vol. 4, pp. 55, 61) Godai draws a fortune stick while he is with Kyoko and later with Kozue. • In *Return of Lum: Trouble Times Ten* (p. 27) we see mikuji tied to branches.

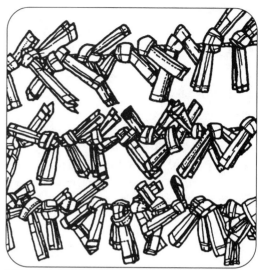

Mikuji are tied on branches at shrines. Will it be a good or bad fortune?

MIMIKAKI (EAR SCOOP)

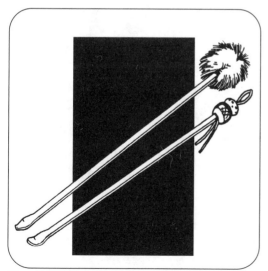 This is a simple bamboo scoop used to remove excess wax from inside the ear. To Americans, who have been warned since childhood not to put anything smaller than a foot-ball in their ears, such a tool may seem dangerous. But in reality it is an effective and pleasant device for cleaning the ears and provides moments of affection between couples or children and parents. Ear cleaning—either by a mother for a child or by a woman for a man—is an instantly recognizable symbol of intimacy and happiness.

🅐 Ataru's ears are being cleaned by Shinobu in *Urusei Yatsura* (TV tp. 14, ep. 54, st. 77), • A mimikaki is used by Shampoo's Great Grandmother in *Ranma 1/2: The Breaking Point* (ep. 1).

MINAMOTO

One of the four great families of Japanese history, also known as Genji. An offshoot of the imperial family, the Minamoto were defeated by the **Taira** family in 1160. They eventually defeated the Taira at the Battle of Dannoura (**Dannoura no Tatakai**) under the leadership of **Minamoto no Yoshitsune**.

🅐 The Battle of Dannoura is shown in the beginning of *Ghost Story*. • The Genji clan is mentioned in Shino's father's story of the Murasame sword in *Hakkenden* (tp. 1, ep. 2).

The **mimikaki** is used to clean the ears. Very simple, and very pleasant.

MINAMOTO NO YORIMITSU

 948–1021. A **Heian period** military leader who aligned himself with the Fujiwara family. His skill as a warrior and archer are mentioned in *Konjaku Monogatari*.

◢ A story of how Yorimitsu's men killed the running demon is told in *Zenki* (tp. 3, ep. 7).

MINAMOTO NO YOSHITSUNE

 1159–89. Known as Ushiwakamaru as a child, Yoshitsune was a military commander of the Genji family (**Minamoto** family) in their struggles against the Heike clan (**Taira** family) in the 12th century.

◢ His legendary training by **tengu** on **Kuramayama** and the famous battle on a bridge against **Benkei** are depicted in *Urusei Yatsura* (TV tp. 3, ep. 12, st. 24).

MINO (RAINWEAR)

Mino is rainwear woven from plant stalks or straw, sedge, or other plants. There are several different types of rain gear. The *koshimino* covers the waist and hips, the *katamino* covers the shoulders and the entire back, the *dōmino* goes from the shoulders to mid-calf, the *marumino* covers the body from the shoulders down, the *seimino* covers only the shoulders and top of the back, and the *minobōshi* covers the head and upper torso.

◢ We see such a raincoat in *Hakkenden* (tp. 5, ep. 8). • Amamori's father wears a mino raincoat when we first see him come home in *Urusei Yatsura* (TV tp. 8, ep. 30, st. 53).

MINSHATŌ (DEMOCRATIC SOCIALIST PARTY)

 This moderate party is largely supported by labor unions and small businesses. Its stated goal is to improve social welfare programs and reduce unemployment. For much of its history as an opposition party that cooperated with the Liberal Democratic Party (**Jiyū Minshutō**),

its power has been larger than the numbers of its representatives in the Diet (**Kokkai**).

Ⓜ In *Sanctuary* (vol. 5, p. 118) a representative from this party attends a small back room meeting with a major figure in the Liberal Democratic Party as part of a political plot.

MISMATCHED FOODS

 There is an old folk tradition in Japan that eating certain foods together is unhealthy. Mismatched foods are said to include eel and sour plum, and tempura and ice water. While the belief is no longer as strong as it used to be, some older Japanese still refer to it.

◢ In *Urusei Yatsura* (TV tp. 6, ep. 21, st. 41) there is a reference to mismatched foods.

MISO (SOYBEAN PASTE)

 Miso is made by taking steamed soybeans and mixing them with *kōji*, a fermenting agent, and salt. Introduced to Japan from China in the 7th century, miso is used as a flavoring agent in Japanese cooking and as a base for miso

*Reeds and grasses are easy to obtain and are cleverly put to use in making **mino**, or rainwear.*

OTAKU QUIZ
MIKO MADNESS!

Without looking at any entry in this book identify six of the following items that are in this picture of a miko.

chihaya	gohei
hibakama	jinja
kamidana	obi
pinkku bira	seidōkyō
suzu	tabi
yukata	

ANSWERS

suzu, tabi, obi, chihaya, hibakama, gohei

soup (**misoshiru**), a common part of a traditional Japanese breakfast (**chōshoku**). Miso is also used as a preservative and, mixed with other ingredients, as a dressing. There are hundreds of varieties of miso made throughout Japan.

🅐 In *Urusei Yatsura*, Miso soup is served at the first breakfast scene in the movie *Beautiful Dreamer* and in the TV show (tp. 6, ep. 21, st. 42).

Ⓜ Hanako attempts to make miso soup in spite of certain interference in *Rumic Theater* (p. 183).

MISOGI (PURIFICATION)

 In the Shinto tradition, water is used to cleanse body and mind of sin (*tsumi*) and pollution (*kegare*). There are many specific forms of misogi depending on the circumstances. Forms include *mizugori* (standing under a waterfall) and *shubatsu* (sprinkling salt water). Related customs are tossing salt into the ring at a sumo match and sprinkling water at the gate of one's home in the morning and the evening. Also related is the

Japanese practice of the daily bath. The origin of such purification rituals is said to be the kami Izanagi no Mikoto bathing himself in the sea after his visit to Yomi, the land of the dead.

🅐 In *Ranma* (TV tp. 1, ep. 2), on the way to school Ranma gets wet when she steps in front of an old woman sprinkling water at her gate.

MISOSHIRU (MISO SOUP)

 Miso is the main flavoring; other common ingredients include soup stock, tofu, dried bonito, and vegetables. Miso soup, often seen in anime at breakfast (**chōshoku**), can be served at any meal.

🅐 In *Urusei Yatsura*, Miso soup is served at the first breakfast scene in the movie *Beautiful Dreamer* and in the TV show (tp. 6, ep. 21, st. 42). We also see instant miso soup squeezed from a tube by Kiyone in *Tenchi Universe* (tp. 2, ep. 6).

Ⓜ Hanako attempts to make miso soup in spite of certain interference in *Rumic Theater* (p. 183).

MIYAGE (SOUVENIR)

 Often called *omiyage*. In the past pilgrims would return home from temples and shrines with amulets (**ofuda**) and talismans (**omamori**). Nowadays travelers return home from trips with more secular items for family, neighbors, friends, and coworkers. An omiyage should be something unique from the place you have traveled to, like food, crafts, or folk art. If you are taking an extended trip you may receive a farewell gift (*senbetsu*) and it is expected you will bring omiyage in return.

🅐 Miyuki brings back snacks as souvenirs from a school reunion and Ken gives her an **omamori** he bought on a trip in *You're Under Arrest* (OVA 3). Lum shops for omiyage in *Urusei Yatsura* (TV tp. 6, Spring Special 2). • Some characters carry souvenir bags as they leave the **ryokan** in *Patlabor: New Files* (tp. 3, ep. 9).

MIYAGI KEN

 Miyagi Prefecture, in northern **Honshu** on the Pacific coast. The economy is based on agriculture and fishing. The main crop is rice and the majority of the fishing is done for sardines, tuna, and mackerel. The capital is Sendai.

🅐 That Labor Police teams will be established in **Aichi**, Miyagi, and **Chiba** prefectures is mentioned by Nagumo Shinobu in her lecture in *Patlabor 2* • Yoshiki Yaegashi is identified as being from Miyagi Prefecture in *Blue Seed* (tp. 2, ep. 4).

MIYAMOTO MUSASHI

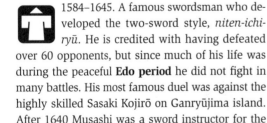 1584–1645. A famous swordsman who developed the two-sword style, *niten-ichi-ryū*. He is credited with having defeated over 60 opponents, but since much of his life was during the peaceful **Edo period** he did not fight in many battles. His most famous duel was against the highly skilled Sasaki Kojirō on Ganryūjima island. After 1640 Musashi was a sword instructor for the Hosokawa daimyō clan in Kumamoto. Miyamoto Musashi was also a skilled painter and metal worker; several of his artistic works are in museums today. Legend has it that on his deathbed he gave his disciple his book on swordsmanship, *Gorin no Sho*, translated into English in 1974 as *The Book of Five Rings*. Artistic works based on his life include a kabuki play by Tsuruya Nanboku, a best-selling novel by Yoshiwara Eiji, and the Samurai Trilogy film series directed by Inagaki Hiroshi.

🅐 The Samurai Trilogy film series is parodied in *Urusei Yatsura* (TV tp. 15, ep. 55, st. 78) with the regular cast as characters from the film and Onsen Mark as Miyamoto Musashi.

MIYAZAWA KENJI

 1896–1933. Miyazawa Kenji is best known for his many children's stories. His first collections failed to sell well but brought him to the attention of the literary world. He also wrote a sizable body of poetry, much of which was published after his death. A devout Buddhist, Miyazawa also worked as an agricultural high school teacher and researcher and struggled to improve the lives of the poor farmers in his native Iwate Prefecture.

🅐 Miyazawa's best-known children's story *Ginga Tetsudō no Yoru* is available as the anime *Night on the Galactic Railroad*. More recently an anime based on his life has been released in Japan under the title of *Iihatove Gensō: Kenji no Haru* (The Illusion of Iihatove: Kenji's Spring).

MIZUGORI (WATERFALL PURIFICATION)

Literally, "removing impurities by water." This ascetic practice is related to **misogi** and is done by standing under a waterfall or by pouring buckets of cold water over oneself. It can serve to express religious devotion or, as is often the case for martial artists, as a form of mental or physical discipline.

Ⓜ Princess Kurama has Ataru doing **mizugori** under a waterfall in *Lum Urusei Yatsura Perfect Collection*

(p. 298) and in *Urusei Yatsura* (TV tp. 3, ep. 9, st. 17). **A** In *Ranma 1/2* (OVA "Akane vs. Ranma!") Soun Tendo is pouring water on his shoulder as part of a prayer for his daughter's success in the kitchen. • In *Blue Seed* (tp. 1, ep. 1) we see Momiji pouring water on herself in the sacred cave; the water must be quite cold as it is winter in this scene. • An image of a warrior meditating under a waterfall is shown in *Metal Fighters Miku* (tp. 5, ep. 11).

MIZUHIKI (DECORATIVE CORDS)

 Twisted paper strings used for ornaments or wrapped around gifts. The style of knots used varies with the occasion, as does the color: ordinary happy occasions call for red and white (**aka to shiro**) mizuhiki, weddings for gold and silver or gold and red, and funerals for black and white.

A Notice the red and white cords on Pretty Sammy's baton in *Tenchi Muyo! Mihoshi Special* and in *Pretty Sammy*.

MOCHI (RICE CAKE)

 Mochi is made by pounding steamed rice in a mortar or by using an electric mochi machine until the grains have been completely formed into one glutenous mass. Mochi is traditionally made and eaten at New Year's and at **matsuri** or **ennichi**. There are many varieties and styles (see **kashiwa mochi**). Mochi takes some chewing to break it down, and each year there are reports of people choking to death by trying to swallow it too soon. Mochi can be easily dried and stored. Dried mochi will be soft if reheated, and mochi toasted over a flame will swell up in the middle. Flat rice crackers (**senbei**) are made with thin-sliced fried mochi.

A Noa eats soft puttylike mochi from a bowl in the *Patlabor: Original Series* (tp. 2, ep. 5).

M We see mochi swelling up as it toasts on a **hibachi** in *Barefoot Gen* (p. 151).

QUEERS IN ANIME?

Sure, homosexuality is found all over the world, in spite of what is often stated by some "representatives" of other cultures. In Japan homosexuality is neither well accepted or looked down upon; rather it seems to be something to keep private and not be too open about. But in anime a few gay and lesbian characters crop up. In *Bubblegum Crisis* we have Daley, who is in a position of authority in the AD Police and quite open about being gay. In *El-Hazard* the easily impressed Alielle often shows unwanted attention to other female characters, much to their discomfort and our amusement. Her lover, Princess Fatora, has a less pleasant personality, but both of the characters are treated as humanly as the others in the series. That the Japanese feel uncomfortable about gay life shows up in *Here Is Greenwood* when Mitsuru and Shinobu, who are not gay, tease Kazuya by pretending they are. But perhaps the most sympathetic portrayal of a strong lesbian character is Akane in *Kimagure Orange Road*, who shares an interest in the same woman as her cousin even if she does nothing about it.

MOKUGYO

 A fish-shaped wooden percussion instrument often associated with the rhythmic Buddhist chanting done to its beat.

A Early in *Rupan III: The Fuma Conspiracy*, Zenigata is beating a mokugyo while chanting sutras. • In *Sanshiro the Judoist* (pt. 1) you hear the priest hitting a mokugyo and chanting.

MOMOTARŌ (PEACH BOY)

A character from folklore who was found by an old couple inside a giant peach. When he was older he left home with a

OTAKU QUIZ
ACTOR—CHARACTER—ANIME MATCH!

Match the actor to the character and to the show.

ACTOR	CHARACTER	SHOW
Amano Yuri	Alfin	*Armitage III*
Fuchizaki Yuriko	Asako	*Bubblegum Crisis*
Hidaka Noriko	Becky Farrah	*Crusher Joe*
Hiramatsu Akiko	Jean	*Dagger of Kamui*
Hiroyuki Sanada	Jiro	*Ghost in the Shell*
Hisakawa Aya	Kubo	*GunBuster*
Masutani Yasunori	Kusanagi Motoko	*Gunsmith Cats*
Sasaki Run	Morisato Megumi	*Oh My Goddess!*
Tamagawa Sakiko	Nene Romanova	*Otaku no Video*
Tanaka Atsuko	Ross Sylibus	*Ranma 1/2*
Tsujitani Kōji	Takaya Noriko	*Secret of Blue Water*
	Tendou Akane	*Ushio and Tora*
	Tsujimoto Natsumi	*You're Under Arrest*

ANSWERS

ACTOR	CHARACTER	SHOW
Amano Yuri	Asako	*Ushio and Tora*
Fuchizaki Yuriko	Morisato Megumi	*Oh My Goddess!*
Hidaka Noriko	Jean	*Secret of Blue Water*
Hidaka Noriko	Takaya Noriko	*GunBuster*
Hidaka Noriko	Tendou Akane	*Ranma 1/2*
Hiramatsu Akiko	Nene Romanova	*Bubblegum Crisis*
Hiroyuki Sanada	Jiro	*Dagger of Kamui*
Hisakawa Aya	Becky Farrah	*Gunsmith Cats*
Masutani Yasunori	Ross Sylibus	*Armitage III*
Sasaki Run	Alfin	*Crusher Joe*
Tamagawa Sakiko	Tsujimoto Natsumi	*You're Under Arrest*
Tanaka Atsuko	Kusanagi Motoko	*Ghost in the Shell*
Tsujitani Kōji	Kubo	*Otaku no Video*

dog, a pheasant, and a monkey to fight a group of demons on an island and returned with their treasure for his foster parents.

A In *Urusei Yatsura* (TV tp. 1, ep. 2, st. 1) Ataru's family finds a giant peach with a surprise inside. Ataru yells "Momotaro!" as the peach is opened. • Momotaro's abilities are parodied in *Urusei Yatsura* (TV tp. 3, ep. 11, sts. 21–22).

MON (FAMILY OR ORGANIZATIONAL CREST)

 The family crest (*kamon*) system originated in the warring period of the 12th century. Warriors used designs on their banners and camp equipment to identify who they were; soon mon were added to clothes. The custom spread to the nobility and, especially in the **Edo period**, to commoners. The mon is designed in two colors, usually black and white. Many of the designs are of natural objects that have special significance, but abstract patterns and manmade objects are also used. Catalogs of mon, called *monchō* or *monkan*, display thousands of designs. Mon are often seen on formal **kimono** at the front just below the shoulder, between the shoulder blades, and on the sleeves. Crests can also be seen on paper lanterns (**chōchin**) to make a house identifiable in the dark and on **noren** at the entrance to businesses.

Mon are seen on the chōchin hanging outside the Hadja Temple in *Phantom Quest Corp.* (tp. 2, ep. 4). These seem to be, on the left, the "five-seven-five" paulownia blooms and, on the right, three commas. In Happosai's memory of his trip to China you see a mon on a kimono in *Ranma 1/2* (vol. 8, p. 129).

MORI ŌGAI

1862–1922. Born Mori Rintarō. While he trained to be a doctor Mori Ōgai also studied and read literature. After graduating he began his medical career in the army. In 1884 he was sent to study medicine in Germany for four years. There he also read and studied European literature. Upon returning to Japan he supported the development of medical research in Japan and published a medical journal and a literary journal, *Shigarami Sōshi*. He went on to serve in the Sino-Japanese war, the Russo-Japanese War (**Nichiro Sensō**), Manchuria, and Taiwan. He eventually rose to the rank of surgeon general and head of the medical division of the Army Ministry.

Mori Ōgai is the author of *Maihime*, published in 1890, which is available in an anime version as *Dancing Girl*.

MOTHER-IN-LAW

In ancient Japan the husband moved in with the family of the bride. In medieval times, with the increased importance of male lineage in higher-class families, the wife began to move into the home of the groom. The mother-in-law had great power and usually controlled the household, reducing the role of the wife to a minor one, or even servitude. In some areas separate housing would be built for the parents, or there would be separate cooking facilities in one home. In the modern world problems still exist since mothers are often closely bonded to their sons. Given the low birthrate in Japan a bride almost always has a mother-in-law to deal with unless there is an older brother whom the mother lives with. Common ways a mother-in-law interferes include telling the bride how to clean, cook, and raise the children and complaining to the neighbors over her poor treatment.

In *Return of Lum Urusei Yatsura* (p. 65) Ataru tries to warn Shinobu to stay away from Mendou by warning of the dangers of having a domineering upper-class mother-in-law. • A classic troublesome mother-in-law is seen in the "Hidden in the Pottery" story in *Rumic Theater*. A nicer mother-in-law, but still with problems, is in the "Extra Large Size Happiness" story.

MURASAKI SHIKIBU

The court lady of the Heian period who is best known as the author of the masterpiece of Japanese literature, *Genji Monogatari* (Tale of Genji). She was a member of the powerful Fujiwara family and after being widowed became a lady-in-waiting for the Empress Akiko. Lady Murasaki is parodied in *Urusei Yatsura* (TV tp. 3, ep. 11, sts. 21–22).

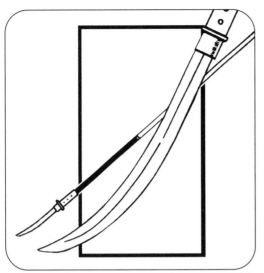

*At one time the **naginata** was a popular weapon used by warriors, monks, and women.*

MUROMACHI PERIOD

 1333–1568 (or 1573). In 1333 the Kamakura shogunate (**Kamakura period**) was destroyed by the forces of Ashikaga Takauji. This produced a period of both cultural development and wars that lasted until Oda Nobunaga captured Kyoto in 1568. The Muromachi period is also known as the Ashikaga period after the Ashikaga family that held the shogunate until 1573.

🅰 The Muromachi period figures in *Project A-Ko*, in Shino's father's story of the Murasame sword in *Hakkenden* (tp. 1, ep. 2), and in *Zenki* (tp. 5, ep. 11).

MUSHANOKŌJI SANEATSU

 1885–1976. A painter, playwright, poet, and novelist, Mushanokōji was part of the influential literary group Shirakaba. His works are characterized by a strong individualism in many of the characters.

🅰 The 1920 novel *Yūjō* is available in an anime version as *Friendship*.

MY CITY

 A prominent building located just outside **Shinjuku** station in western Tokyo.

🅰 In *Otaku no Video* (pt. 1, 1st anim. seq.) we see My City shortly after the tennis game. • Late in *Patlabor 2* My City is seen, from the street, behind the officer who is ordering the evacuation to higher areas.

NAGASAKI

 The capital of Nagasaki Prefecture on the island of **Kyushu**. Nagasaki has been a major port since 1571, when it became the major entry point for foreign trade. When Japan secluded itself during the **Edo period** Nagasaki was the only port open to foreign trade, and that trade was only Chinese and Dutch. Given this foreign connection, Nagasaki is a major center of Christianity (**Kirisutokyō**) in Japan. During the **Meiji period** the first modern shipyards in Japan were built here. After the destruction of WW II Nagasaki returned as a center of industry, shipbuilding, and fishing.

🅰 Nagasaki is mentioned in *Wandering Days*. • Nagasaki is the location of *The Martyr*, which makes sense given the religious nature of the story.

NAGINATA (HALBERD)

 A weapon consisting of a 4- to 8-foot shaft with a 1- to 2-foot blade that allows it to slice much like a sword. From the 11th century until almost the 16th century the naginata was the main weapon of foot soldiers and Buddhist warrior monks. Not only men but samurai women and children were trained in its use. During the **Edo period** several martial arts schools were devoted to the study of *naginatajutsu* or *naginata-dō*. The All Japan Naginata Federation was formed in 1955; today this martial art is primarily a woman's sport. Practice is done with armor and bamboo naginata just as **kendō** uses armor and bamboo swords.

 Genpachi uses a naginata when we first see him fight in *Hakkenden* (tp. 2, ep. 4). • We see school girls with naginata in **hakama** and white tops secured with **obi** in *Ranma 1/2: Evil Wakes* (ep. 2). • A naginata is used by Ayaka in *Tenchi Universe* (tp. 4, ep. 11). • Naginata are seen in *Urusei Yatsura* (TV tp. 3, ep. 11 sts. 21–22).

Ⓜ A girl is holding a naginata in the background in *Ranma 1/2* (vol. 7, p. 104, top frame).

NARUTO

 Boiled fish paste with a pink swirl in the center. When cut into slices the swirl becomes visible. Naruto is commonly served in soba, **rāmen**, or udon dishes.

Ⓐ Naruto is seen in cup rāmen in *Maison Ikkoku: Soichiro's Shadow* (ep. 1). • Shigeo is holding naruto in his **hashi** while talking to the mechanics at night in *Patlabor: New Files* (tp. 4, ep. 11). • A naruto is tossed by Ranma at an offensive person in *Ranma 1/2: Darling Charlotte* (ep. 1). • Naruto are seen in an udon dish in *Urusei Yatsura* (TV tp. 19, ep. 73, st. 96).

Ⓜ A naruto is stuck to Kosaku's face in *One Pound Gospel* (vol. 1, p. 94).

NASU (EGGPLANT)

 Eggplant was introduced to Japan from China around the 8th century. Several varieties exist. Nasu are commonly pickled and can be cooked in several ways. Nasu halved and grilled is called *shigiyaki*.

Ⓐ Masao goes to the fields to pick eggplants in *Grave of the Wild Chrysanthemum*.

NATSUME SŌSEKI

1867–1916. A **Meiji-period** novelist and critic. He studied to be a scholar of English literature at Tokyo University (**Tōkyō Daigaku**). After teaching for a couple of years he went to England to study further until 1903, when he returned to Japan and replaced **Lafcadio Hearn** at the First Higher School and Tōkyō Daigaku. In 1907 he quit his teaching positions and devoted himself to writing. His stories often deal with the issues raised by individualism, especially intellectuals living in a changing society. His most famous works are *I Am a Cat* (Wagahai wa Neko de Aru, 1905–6) and *Botchan* (1906).

Ⓐ A two-part anime was based on *Botchan*.

It is not proper, in the RANMA 1/2 TV show, to toss your **naruto**—*or any food—at someone . . . unless you are sending a challenge.*

NATTŌ

 A food made by taking boiled or steamed soybeans and fermenting them with an agent known as *nattō-kin*. Nattō is generally eaten on rice with soy sauce, mustard, and spring onions. Nattō is soft and brown, and also very sticky. Among non-Japanese, it is one of the least favorite of all Japanese foods.

Ⓐ Isamu chooses nattō as part of his breakfast in the cafeteria line the day after the fire in *Macross Plus* (OVA 2); nattō is also seen on his tray. • Nattō is one of the foods served at the first breakfast scene in *Urusei Yatsura: Beautiful Dreamer*. • Mihoshi and Kiyone have nattō as part of their breakfast in *Pretty Sammy*; nattō's sticky nature is well illustrated in this scene.

NEBUTA MATSURI (NEBUTA FESTIVAL)

 Held August 1–7 in Aomori, the Nebuta Festival is famous for its gigantic paper lantern floats in the shape of animals and kabuki figures. The floats sometimes need as many as 30 men to carry them. At the end of the festival they are tossed into the sea or local rivers.

Ⓐ We see the Nebuta Festival in the flashes of scenes symbolizing Japan early on in *Blue Seed* (tp. 1, ep. 1).

Honestly, Kiyone in PRETTY SAMMY *should know better than to get into an angry discussion with Mihoshi while eating* **nattō**.

©1995 AIC / PIONEER LDC INC.

NEKO (CAT)

 Cats were rare in Japan until around the 12th century. The common Japanese cat, even in old descriptions, seems to have been short haired with white fur and black and brown spots. During the **Edo period** short-tailed cats were so popular that long-tailed cats became scarce and were feared. Sailors and fishermen prize tortoiseshell tomcats as a protection from shipwreck. Black cats are believed to have the power to cure disease. Folk tradition says cats that have been killed come back for vengeance and will haunt their killer for seven lives. There are also stories about **bakeneko**, supernatural monster cats.

Ⓐ A vengeful ghost (**goryō**) of a cat shows up in *Urusei Yatsura* (TV tp. 14, ep. 51, st. 74). • A short-tailed brown and white neko is fed by Priss in *Bubblegum Crisis* (OVA 5).

NENBUTSU

 The practice of chanting Namu Amida Butsu, a prayer that expresses the hope of being reborn in the Buddhist Pure Land. Namu Amida Butsu was popularized by the Priest Hōnen in the late 12th and early 13th centuries and is often seen in anime when a character is praying or someone else is in danger or has died.

Ⓐ We see Namu Amida Butsu translated as "Praise the name of Amida Buddha" in *Ranma 1/2* (TV sub tp. 5, dub tap. 7, ep. 14). • Cherry often chants Namu Amida Butsu in *Urusei Yatsura* (TV tp. 2, ep. 6, st. 11). • Eimi prays after the shuttle leaves with her on it in *All Purpose Cultural Cat Girl Nuku Nuku* ("Phase 0VI").

Ⓜ The chant shows up in *Barefoot Gen* (p. 125) and *Barefoot Gen: The Day After* (p. 27).

NENGAJŌ (NEW YEAR'S CARD)

 The custom of sending out special cards at New Year's dates from 1874. New Year's is a major event in Japan and the sending of nengajō to a large number of people is part of the week-long celebration. You send cards to your family members and to most of your acquaintances; businesses send cards to their customers. The average family sends out about 100 cards every year. Many of the cards sent are printed by the government with a lottery number on each card. Some families will have custom cards of their own design. Special New Year's post cards also are printed by the government and cost more than usual, with the difference going to charity. Cards mailed between December 15 and 25 are held by the post office and delivered at one time on January 1.

Ⓜ Ataru is told to get the New Year's cards from the mailbox in *Return of Lum: Trouble Times Ten* (p. 41).

NICHIRO SENSŌ (RUSSO-JAPANESE WAR)

 As the Russian Empire spread its influence into East Asia, the Japanese felt that a major conflict was inevitable. With Russian influence and military actions in Manchuria increasing Japan decided to act and on February 8, 1904, attacked the Russian fleet at Port Arthur in Manchuria. Most of the war took place in Manchuria and Korea, but when the Japanese destroyed the Russian fleet in the battle of Tsushima on May 27–28, 1905, the war was nearly over. On September 5, 1905 the Treaty of Portsmouth was signed with U.S. President Theodore Roosevelt as mediator.

Ⓐ *Theater of Life* begins with celebrations of the Japanese victory.

Ⓜ Yuta remembers some events that took place just before the Russo-Japanese War in *Mermaid's Gaze* (p. 28).

NIGIRIMESHI (RICE BALL)

 This simple food consists of a rice ball— round, cylindrical, or triangular—with a filling of salted fish, fish eggs, or salted plum (**umeboshi**). Nigirimeshi can be wrapped in sheet seaweed (**nori**) or have sesame seeds sprinkled on top. The name is a combination of two words: *nigiri*, which means gripping or squeezing, and *meshi*, which means cooked rice.

THE SOUNDS OF JAPAN

The sounds of Japan are often heard in anime, and they're even seen in manga through "sound" words. These sounds help us understand the season of the year, the feelings of characters, and what is going on out of sight. But such sounds are not always easy to identify.

One sound that is common in Japan but unusual for non-Japanese is the high-pitched repetitious call of the **semi**, or cicada. When you hear the semi you know it is summer and hot. Other sounds are mostly manmade, such as that of the **fūrin**; this small hanging bell, with a piece of paper attached to the clapper to catch the breeze in hot weather, tells you it's summer.

A much larger bell is the **bonshō**, the Buddhist temple bell. It has a very deep sound and is rung slowly so that the next ring comes as the preceding one has almost faded away. Bonshō can be used to highlight dramatic moments or to indicate a hard impact, such as when Kyosuke and Hayakawa ram their heads together by accident in the *Kimagure Orange Road* OVA story "Spring Is for Idols."

Or there may be a scene next to a garden where you don't see a **shishiodoshi** (deer scare) but you can hear its regular hollow wooden sound as it slowly hits a rock. In fact you may not even see the garden at all but be observing a scene inside a wealthy house that naturally would have such a garden attached to it.

Another sound associated with summer is vendors wandering the streets chanting "Kingyo, kingyo!" ("Goldfish, goldfish!") as they walk among the neighborhoods with tubs of goldfish on a pole. The goldfish seller, now rarely seen) is also a symbol of the past here.

Then there is the sound of the **shōji** being slid open or closed, which lets you know someone has entered or left a room without your seeing them. The sound of the shōji can also serve to convey emotion, as when an angry character slams the shōji open or closed.

So the next time you watch anime or read manga pay attention to the sounds, and see what else you can hear that gives the story its distinctive Japanese cultural context.

*Rice shaped by hand then wrapped in **nori** to create a **nigirimeshi** makes for a quick meal or snack in OH MY GODDESS!*

 D eats nigirimeshi in *Project A-Ko*. • Akane unpacks nigirimeshi wrapped in **takenokawa** in *Ranma 1/2: An Akane to Remember* (pt. 2). • Nigirimeshi are seen in *Urusei Yatsura* (TV tp. 6, Spring Special 2) and in *Wandering Days*.

NIHONBASHI

 This central Tokyo bridge, originally built in 1603, is the zero marker used in measurements of the Japanese road system. The present Western-style bridge with its ornate lamps was built in 1911 and has elevated freeways over it. Nihonbashi is also the name of the upscale shopping district in the vicinity of the bridge.
 We get a clear view of this bridge under the freeway in the helicopter sequence near the end of *Patlabor 2*.

NIHON KŌGYŌ KIKAKU (JAPANESE INDUSTRIAL STANDARDS)

JIS are the officially established standards for mining and industrial products. They were established to encourage productivity through standard terminology, symbols, signs, and quality of goods. Foreign-made goods have been subject to JIS since 1980, and goods that qualify are allowed to carry a JIS label. JIS specifications are set by MITI, the Ministry of International Trade and Industry (**Tsūshō Sangyō Shō**).
We see the Japanese Industrial Standards label on the bottom of the bottle of Chinese-made shampoo that Ranma got from Shampoo in *Ranma 1/2* (TV sub tp. 6, dub tp. 9, ep. 17).

NIHONKOKU KENPŌ (CONSTITUTION OF JAPAN)

The present Constitution of Japan was largely written after WWII by non-Japanese in the Government Section of the General Headquarters of the Supreme Commander for the Allied Powers. The Japanese had their own commission working on a new constitution but progress was slow and General Douglas MacArthur felt the result would not be democratic enough. The Japanese government largely accepted the document MacArthur presented to them with few changes, the most significant being the two-house structure for the Diet (**Kokkai**). Of special interest is Article Nine of the constitution, which, among other things, states that "land, sea, and air forces, as well as other war potential, will never be maintained." This article is interpreted by some to mean that the

*The lamp post is the most recognizable part of the bridge at **Nihonbashi**.*

Japanese Self Defense Force (**Jieitai**) may not even be a legal institution.

 Amending Article Nine of the constitution is proposed in *Sanctuary* (vol. 5, p. 71).

NIHON KYŌSANTŌ (JAPAN COMMUNIST PARTY)

 Founded in 1922, Nihon Kyōsantō operated illegally until after WWII. The party survived the anti-communist purges of government and industry ordered by the Occupation forces in the early 1950s. It continues to be an active player in Japanese politics.

 In *Sanctuary* (vol. 3, p. 25) we see an election poster for a Communist Party candidate.

NIHONTŌ (JAPANESE SWORD)

 Steel swords in Japan go back to the 8th century; many of the earliest swordsmiths were not just workers skilled in creating laminated carbon steel blades but **yamabushi** who lived a religious life with their apprentices. From the 10th century the signature, location, and date of the swordsmith were chiseled into the tang of the blade. Sword manufacturing requires many foldings (like kneading) of the metal, and as a result the polished blade has a grainlike wood texture with thousands of layers of steel. The older blades are almost always straight and short, intended to stab rather than slash. The sword is more than just a weapon in Japan and demands aesthetic, even spiritual, respect. Some swords are collected as works of art. Sword hilts and cases display remarkable workmanship. During the **Edo period** swords could only be carried by **samurai**. With the ending of the old class system in the **Meiji period** the wearing and making of swords was even more restricted. After WWII the Occupation forces ordered the destruction of all swords not in museums, shrines, and private collections or that had historical, artistic, or religious value. Many swords were destroyed or sold to foreigners as souvenirs. Today all swords must be registered with the police, and swordsmiths are attempting to revive some of the ancient techniques.

 We see swords put to practical use in *Rumic World: Fire Tripper.*

 Of course *Hakkenden* has a lot of swordplay in it.

• A sword is used by Colonel Shinkai in *Kishin Corps* (tp. 1, ep. 1).

NINGYO (MERMAID)

 There is a legend of a young maiden in the 5th century named Yaohime who ate meat that her father had been given by a strange man. It was the flesh of a mermaid, and for 800 years Yaohime continued to look like a 15-year-old girl. After her death a shrine was built in her honor, and later other shrines to her were constructed around Japan.

 Long life as a result of eating the flesh of a ningyo is the theme of *Mermaid Forest* and *Mermaid's Scar.*

NINJUTSU

 Also known as *shinobi*, the military art of the ninja was used to spy on enemies, assassinate opponents, and stage commando-style raids. To do this ninja had special training and used special tools and weapons. Many of the tools were for easy entrance and exit. One tool that contributed to legends of the ninja's amazing powers was a small spring board that could be concealed near a wall so, if in danger of being caught, the ninja could use the board to leap higher and escape. The ninja costume was suitably nocturnal: tight dark clothing (that wouldn't snag on tree limbs or furniture) with only the eyes uncovered. Ninja were mostly used in the civil wars of the **Sengoku period**. During the peaceful years of the **Edo period** ninja techniques were refined into a formal martial art to prevent them from being lost. In popular culture ninja have been elevated to superhero status.

 Female ninja play a significant role in a story in *Urusei Yatsura* (TV tp. 6, Spring Special 2; *Return of Lum: Sweet Revenge*, p. 71).

 Sasuke is a ninja in *Ranma 1/2: Cat-Fu Fighting*

(ep. 1). • To cover up his abilities Kyosuke claims his ancestors were ninja in *Kimagure Orange Road* (tp. 2, ep. 2). • One of the best examples of a ninja story in anime is *Dagger of Kamui*. • *Ninja Scroll*, another well-known ninja anime, owes more of its style to the excesses of kabuki theater than to conventional ninja stories or movies.

NIPPON DENSHIN DENWA (NIPPON TELEGRAPH AND TELEPHONE CORPORATION)

 Japan's largest telecommunications company. Originally there was the Nippon Telegraph and Telephone Public Corporation, a government-run monopoly. In 1985 it was privatized and became Japan's largest joint-stock company.

Ⓜ We see "NTT" on a pay phone in *Maison Ikkoku* (vol. 5, p. 72).

NIPPON HŌSŌ KYŌKAI (JAPAN BROADCASTING CORPORATION)

 Known as NHK, the major public broadcaster in Japan. NHK also broadcasts via satellite and local transmission to the rest of the world in over 20 languages. NHK was formed from three radio stations in 1926 and was the sole broadcaster in Japan until 1951.

Ⓐ We see an NHK TV van early on at the school in *El-Hazard* ("First Night"). • An NHK sticker is on the name plate of Nagisa's apartment in *Here Is Greenwood* (tp. 1, ep. 2).

Ⓜ In *Domu: A Child's Dream* an NHK sticker is on the name plate at old man Cho's apartment, and NHK trucks are seen at the police station.

NOBORI (BANNER)

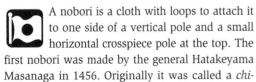 A nobori is a cloth with loops to attach it to one side of a vertical pole and a small horizontal crosspiece pole at the top. The first nobori was made by the general Hatakeyama Masanaga in 1456. Originally it was called a *chi-*

*A **nobori** of the Satomi clan stands against the sky in* HAKKENDEN.

tsuke-hata, or banner with loops. Nobori, commonly used as military banners, are now also used at businesses, sumō matches, temples, and shrine festivals (**matsuri**), where they are treated with great respect. Another kind of banner, called a **hata**, has cloth attached to a pole set crosswise at the top of another pole.

Ⓐ A nobori is seen on Ataru's back in *Urusei Yatsura* (TV tp. 19, ep. 72, st. 95), along an old-fashioned street in *Blue Seed* (tp. 3, ep. 5), and along the path leading to the shrine in *Tenchi Universe* (tp. 2, ep. 7).

NOODLE SLURPING

 Noodle slurping is a common way to cool hot noodles when eating them but is not considered proper behavior among the more cultivated classes. Most Japanese don't mind, however.

Ⓜ Ataru is not bothered by such refined niceties in *Urusei Yatsura* (TV tp. 2, ep. 5, st. 9; *Lum Urusei Yatsura: Perfect Collection*, p. 71).

NOREN (SPLIT CURTAINS)

 Split curtains used in for entryways to indicate that businesses are open or to separate the kitchen from the rest of the house or the back of a shop from the area where customers are served. Noren usually come to chest or neck height to block the view but not passage and ventilation. Some noren can drape almost all the way to the ground and in some cases are even held in place by weights or tied to stakes. *Nawa noren*, which are noren made of cords rather than curtains, usually indicate a drinking establishment.

 Noren are seen at the entrance to the kitchen in much of *Ranma 1/2* (ep. 1; vol. 1, p. 27).

 Noren are seen in front of a business in *Ranma 1/2* (TV sub tp. 1, dub tp. 2, ep. 3), in front of a shop in *Theater of Life*, and in *Zenki* (tp. 3, ep. 6). • We see noren used to separate the back room from the store in a souvenir shop in *Urusei Yatsura* (TV tp. 6, Spring Special 2). • In *Zenki* (tp. 3, ep. 7) during the first nocturnal running sequence we see a large noren attached to the ground and tied to weights.

 Noren in front of a restaurant can be seen in *Lum Urusei Yatsura: Perfect Collection* (p. 70). • Other ex-

*Red **noren** and Chinese motifs are traditionally hung outside of **rāmen** restaurants, such as this one in* MAISON IKKOKU.

amples are in *Maison Ikkoku* (vol. 1, p. 100) and *Rumic Theater* (chapt. 6, p. 182). • Nawa noren are seen in *Maison Ikkoku* (vol. 1, pp. 262–63) and *Rumic Theater* (chapt. 2, p. 39).

NORI (SEAWEED, LAVER)

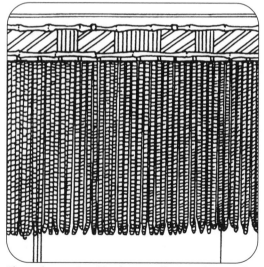

*The cord **noren** is said to be very effective at keeping flies out.*

For an island nation like Japan nori is a common food source. The term is used both for seaweed in general and for a particular type of seaweed, *asakusanori*, that is dried in thin sheets. These sheets are used to make rolled **sushi** (*makizushi*), rice balls (**nigirimeshi**), **chazuke**, and other dishes. They can also be cut up and sprinkled on soba and rice dishes. Traditionally shops that deal in tea also sell nori, presumably because both products need similar handling to protect them from moisture. Nori is popular in the gift-giving seasons of *chūgen* (midsummer) and *seibo* (year end).

 Nori strips are visible in a clear container above the rice in the breakfast scene at Mihoshi and Kiyone's in *Tenchi Universe* (tp. 2, ep. 6).

 Kyoko rolls some *makizushi* to take with her in *Maison Ikkoku* (vol. 7, p. 174).

OBI (SASH, BELT)

 The obi is tied around the waist to hold a **kimono** or a **yukata** in place. Men's obi are narrower and plain compared to women's obi, which can even be made of expensive brocade. There are many styles of tying an obi, and these vary depending on the kimono or mood of the wearer. The decorative patterns on obi often mirror the season, with maple leaves in the fall and plum blossoms in the spring, for example. In the past single women tied their obi in back and married women in front. Today most women tie their obi in back. In anime and manga you see obi whenever you see kimono or yukata.

🅐 Obi and kimono are seen in *Growing Up*. • A bow-shaped obi is seen in *Kimagure Orange Road* (tp. 2, ep. 1) and on Nabiki in *Ranma 1/2* (TV tp. 1, ep. 1).

🅜 Kyoko's elaborate obi is being tied by Mrs. Ichinose in *Maison Ikkoku* (vol. 6, p. 4); note that the kimono and obi have chrysanthemum patterns.

ODEN

 A dish made of a variety of ingredients boiled for some time in a kelp and soy sauce broth. Common ingredients include **daikon**, tōfu, hardboiled eggs, *chikuwa* (grilled fish paste tubes), and potatoes. Oden is commonly served at street stalls (**yatai**).

🅐 We see oden cooking in Ryuu's stand in *Urusei Yatsura: Beautiful Dreamer*.

🅜 Godai and Mr. Ichinose have a few at a **yatai** serving oden in *Maison Ikkoku* (vol. 6, p. 73).

OFUDA

 A kind of talisman. This can be made of a tapering piece of wood or paper that has the name of a deity written or stamped on it in red and black ink. These are then wrapped in white paper and tied with colored thread. Ofuda are distributed both by **Shintō** shrines and Buddhist temples. Those obtained from shrines are regarded as a symbol of the particular **kami** and are often placed on the **kamidana** at home or work. The purpose of the ofuda is to attract good fortune. A related type of charm is the **omamori**, which performs some of the same functions as ofuda.

ŌGI (FOLDING FAN)

 The folding fan is a Japanese invention of the early **Heian period** (794–1185). These are made in several ways. One is by having a series of wide ribs held together at one end and bound together by thread; in this design the ribs make up the fan. Another design uses silk or paper between narrow ribs fixed together in such a way that the fan can be opened. There are a variety of ōgi designs including iron-ribbed ones used by samurai.

🅐 We see ōgi with a red sun pattern in *Oh My Goddess!* (OVA 1), *Tenchi Muyo!* (OVA 6), *Tale of Shunkin,* and *Urusei Yatsura* (TV tp. 6, Spring Special 2).

🅜 Ōgi are seen in *Maison Ikkoku* (vol. 1, p. 21).

OJIGI (BOW)

Bowing is part of a respectful greeting in Japan. In the most common form, such as between two businessmen, you stand with your hands at your sides and bend forward at the waist while keeping your back straight. How deeply you bow depends on the relationship between the persons involved or the formality of the occasion. When visiting a home a more formal bow may be seen, with the host or hostess kneeling on his or her knees and bending forward with palms flat on the floor. The most formal such bow involves the head lowering far enough to touch the hands and is called *zarei*.

 Compare the bows of Godai and Yotsuya to Kyoko when she introduces herself in *Maison Ikkoku: Welcome to Maison Ikkoku* (ep. 1; vol. 1, p. 10).

 Goemon bows on his knees and asks for a favor of Rupan in *Rupan III: The Fuma Conspiracy*, Goto bows in apology to angry Nagumo Shinobu in *Patlabor 2*, and Lum bows to Mako after giving her tea in *Urusei Yatsura* (TV tp. 16, ep. 59, st. 82).

OKADA KEISUKE

 1868–1952. Prime Minister of Japan from 1934 to February 28, 1936. He narrowly escaped death on **February 26, 1936** when rebels attacked his residence. He later played a major role in the overthrow of the Tōjō Hideki cabinet near the end of WWII.

 The beginning of *Mermaid Forest* takes place during this coup attempt and has a newspaper wrongly reporting his death.

OKAME

 A mask of a homely but good-natured woman often accompanied by a mask of Hyottoko, a rather funny-faced man. Players wearing masks of these two will often put on short funny plays at shrine and temple festivals. The Okame mask shows a young woman with fat cheeks, small mouth, and small upturned nose and narrow eyes. A popular view is that the mask symbolizes Ameno-uzume-no-mikoto, who danced in front of the cave that **Amaterasu Ōmikami** hid herself in. The Hyottoko mask shows a man with a spouting mouth and sometimes one eye smaller than the other. To call someone by these terms is insulting but can be done in a joking sense.

 We see Okame masks on Ton-chan's cheerleaders in *Urusei Yatsura* (TV tp. 18, ep. 70, st. 93).

THE HONORIFIC O-

Many common Japanese words are preceded by the prefix o-. The prefix serves two purposes, as an honorific and "softener" (making requests or statements seem less abrupt). Some words are rarely heard without the prefix. Examples are *ocha* (for "tea") and *otearai* (for "toilet"). If you're looking for a word in this book and can't find it, try dropping the o- and looking under the next letter, for example under **cha** instead of *ocha*.

OKIKU

 Okiku was a maid of the samurai Aoyama Tessan. The story goes that he entrusted her with the care of 10 rare dishes that were a gift from Dutch visitors. He became enamored with her beauty, and when she rejected his advances he took and hid one of the dishes. Then he demanded she bring out the set. He said he would forgive the loss of one of the dishes if she became his mistress, but she still refused. In anger he killed her and tossed the body into an old well. Every night her ghost (**goryō**) would come out of the well, count to 9, and scream. Eventually a neighbor exorcised her ghost by waiting by the well and, when she had reached the count of 9, yelling, "10!" The ghost then screamed and never returned.

 Kyoko dresses as Okiku-san in *Maison Ikkoku* (vol. 6, p. 3).

OKINAWA KEN

The chain of approximately 60 islands, known also as the Ryūkyū islands. The island of Okinawa is the largest of the chain. The kingdom on the islands paid tribute to the Chinese since the 15th century. In 1609 the Shimazu family conquered the islands but kept them outside of the supervision of the **Tokugawa** shogunate and the islands continued to pay tribute to China. During the **Meiji period** the Japanese government established formal control of the islands. The Chinese did not recognize Japanese sovereignty until the treaty of 1895. In 1945, during WWII, Okinawa was invaded with the loss of a quarter million Japanese and 12,500 American lives during an 82-day battle. The United States administered the islands until 1972, when they were returned to Japan. Today Okinawa's warm climate has made it a popular tourist spot.

🅐 Yamazaki is from Okinawa and we see him visiting his family home there in *Patlabor: Original Series* (tp. 2, ep. 5). • In *Neon Genesis Evangelion* a school trip to Okinawa is mentioned and we see some of the students depart (Genesis 0:5, ep. 10).

🅜 Tokai invades Okinawa in his own way in *Sanctuary* (vol. 3, p. 50).

OKONOMIYAKI

 Okonomiyaki "pancakes" are made from a batter of flour, eggs, and water, with shredded cabbage and any of several meats or seafood. Customers cook their own on a griddle built into their table. Toppings usually include a sauce and perhaps ginger, bonito flakes, or seaweed.

🅐 Okonomiyaki are in *Ranma 1/2* (OVA "Tendo Family Christmas Scramble," 2nd kitchen scene) and in *Hyperdoll* (Act 2), where their use is unconventional.

🅜 In *Ranma 1/2* (vol. 8, p. 16) Ukyo is seen cooking okonomiyaki.

OKURIBI (RITUAL BONFIRE)

A fire set at the end of the **Bon** Festival to send the souls of the dead on their way. In the Daimonji Okuribi, held in **Kyoto** on August 16, huge fires are lit on five mountains overlooking the city.

🅐 In *Moldiver* (OVA 5) you can see the okuribi on Mt. Nyoigatake that forms the character *dai* ("large"). • We also see the Mt. Nyoigatake okuribi in the early part of *Blue Seed* (tp. 1, ep. 1) when the scenes representing Japan flash by.

OL ("OFFICE LADY")

 Female office workers who serve tea, make copies, and do various odd office jobs. OLs tend to have a college degree and be between the ages of 18 and 28. Married office ladies are a rarity. Since many office ladies live at home or in company dorms they have money to spend on overseas travel and entertainment.

🅐 The two most dangerous OLs in anime are found in *All Purpose Cultural Cat Girl Nuku Nuku*.

🅜 In *Bringing Home the Sushi* we see some short stories concerning office ladies (pp. 69–78); notable also are the stories about two OLs planning to go to the **Ginza** (p. 46) and Section Chief Shima finding out what happens when you annoy the OLs with a rude comment, even if unintentional (p. 118).

OMAMORI (AMULET)

 Omamori, believed to ward off disaster and bad influence, are a major source of revenue for many shrines and temples and are often bought by pilgrims as souvenirs (**miyage**) for friends and family. They are small pieces of paper with the name of the shrine or temple and a few words describing the benefit of the charm. Traditionally omamori come in a brocade bag with a drawstring, but there are now omamori telephone cards. Large omamori are kept at home, while smaller ones can be carried in a purse or pocket. Children may carry talisman bags, *omamori-bukuro*, for protection. Themed omamori exist for special purposes like traffic safety or school exams. Omamori don't expire, but some people buy new ones every year, usually during their New Year's shrine or temple visit (**hatsumōde**). See also **ofuda**.

🅐 Ken gives Miyuki an omamori for traffic safety in *You're Under Arrest* (OVA 3). • An omamori is around the neck of an old cat in *Urusei Yatsura* (TV tp. 12, ep. 43, st. 66). • An omamori for success in exams is purchased at the beginning of *Student Days*.

OMIAI

 An arranged meeting between a man and a woman who are seeking marriage partners. Such meetings can be held at a home or restaurant. It is common for background documents and a photograph to be shown to the persons involved before scheduling an omiai. People can go through several omiai before finding a partner. Needless to say, many younger Japanese refuse to participate in omiai and prefer to take a chance on romance.

A Mrs. Ichinose still tries to get Kyoko to consider an omiai several times in *Maison Ikkoku: Ronin Blues* (ep. 2). • An omiai party is arranged for Lum without her knowledge in *Urusei Yatsura* (TV tp. 6, ep. 22, sts. 43–44). • Rumors of an omiai complicate things in *You're Under Arrest* (OVA 3). • Ms. Ayumi attends an omiai in *Project A-Ko 4*.

ONI (DEMON)

 Often oni are often portrayed with horns and wearing animal, usually tiger, skins. Oni are not always evil and are sometimes protective.

M Two oni are Zenki from the *Zenki* series and Lum from *Urusei Yatsura*. • The *Ogre Slayer* stories involve an oni who has been hunting down and killing other oni for centuries in the belief that if he kills all the others he will become human.

ONIGOKKO (TAG)

 The Japanese name for tag means "demon-game." The first **oni** (demon) is often the person who loses in **jan-ken**. Whoever is tagged becomes the oni.

M The most famous game of tag has to be that between Ataru and Lum (*Urusei Yatsura*, TV ep. 1; *Lum Urusei Yatsura: Perfect Collection*, p. 9).

WETNESS

The Japanese refer to themselves as "wet" and Americans as "dry." This is the Japanese way of saying that they place a high value on feelings while Americans place a high value on reason. In anime, wetness and feelings often are in the form of tears, which may be revealed by only a subtle glistening look in the eye. In humorous anime the stray trickle becomes a flowing stream, gushing from the eyes in arcs. In *All Purpose Cultural Cat Girl Nuku Nuku* Akiko's pain at being separated from her son, Ryuunosuke, is expressed in fountains of tears pouring from her eyes; no one would accuse her of placing a high value on reason.

Then there is the nose; not only does it tend to bleed in sexual contexts, but snot may appear as bubbles when a character is sleeping, or may flow when someone has a cold or is crying.

Then there is sweat. Not just the droplets caused by exertion or heat but large single drops when a character is nervous or embarrassed.

And finally sex, a very wet activity. Until recently, under Japanese censorship laws genitals could not be shown shown in graphic works like anime and manga. Artists have employed a variety of ways to deal with this restriction, including positioning the bodies so that the genitals are not visible, or using large dots or computer-generated pixels to obscure the view and fluids. Again, there are abnormally large splashes of vaginal fluids and sperm—kinda hard to see the details with all that wetness in the way.

ONOMICHI

 Located in southeastern Hiroshima Prefecture on the coast of the Inland Sea, Onomichi has been a port since the 12th century. The major industry is shipbuilding.

A *Wandering Days* takes place in Onomichi. • The noted fried rock fish of Onomichi is mentioned in *Urusei Yatsura* (TV tp. 15, ep. 55, st. 78).

THE EYES! THE EYES!

Why do they have Caucasian eyes?

They don't!

No race has eyes as big as those sported by many anime and manga characters!

Then why are their eyes so big?

The credit, or blame, for this is often laid at the feet of Disney studios since they were so greatly admired by Tezuka Osamu, the man who did so much to make manga and anime widely accepted in Japan. But actually if you look at other U.S. and European animation from the early days you will see similarities in eye size in such characters as Betty Boop and Felix the Cat. Big eyes are simply part of the history of animated stories.

But why does it continue to be so?

Well, not all anime employs large eyes. *Ghost in the Shell*, *Sanctuary*, *Hakkenden*, and *Tale of Genji*, just to mention a few, use smaller eyes. Many other anime may have some characters with large eyes and others who have smaller eyes. In these cases the large eyes are usually there to express innocence. Compared to their parents and to Kuno, Akane and Ranma are very innocent, and in the case of Kuno the lack of innocence is even dangerous. Cuteness is also a factor. After all would Lum-chan and Nuku Nuku be as adorable if they had "normal" eyes? Of course, even the very existence of large eyes gets poked fun at in *Urusei Yatsura* in the "Terror of Girly-Eyes Measles" OVA.

Then there is the comment my friend Suzette made about some people's comments on the size of the eyes: "It's just damn cartoons for God's sake!"

Kind of sums it up.

ONSEN (HOT SPRING)

Hot springs are found throughout volcanically active Japan. A convenient source of hot water for Japanese-style baths, they are often part of an inn (**ryokan**), which provides food and lodging to those taking the waters. The men's area of an onsen is usually larger than the women's, since until recently customers were primarily male. (Mixed bathing facilities can still be found.) Onsen waters are considered to have many therapeutic qualities. Onsen are also put to other uses such as generating electricity, heating buildings and greenhouses, and processing sake or miso. Tokyo even has a famous onsen within the city, the **Azabu Jūban**.

🅐 A hot springs bath is seen in *Zenki* (tp. 1, ep. 1).

• Both the women's and men's areas of an onsen are seen in *Tenchi Muyo!* (OVA 4) and *Neon Genesis Evangelion* (Genesis 0:5, ep. 10).

OSAKA

The capital of Osaka Prefecture in central **Honshu** and the third largest city in Japan (only Tokyo and Yokohama are larger). As early as the 7th century Osaka was a port for trade with China. Today it is a major center for manufacturing and trade. The traditional greeting of Osakans is *Mōkari makka* or "Making money?"

🅐 Osaka is mentioned in Nagumo Shinobu's lecture in *Patlabor 2*.

Ⓜ Akogiville in *Caravan Kid* (vol. 1, p. 224) is an extremely thinly disguised Osaka, right down to the **Tsūtenkaku** tower, castle, and **Dotonbori** neighborhood.

OSECHI-RYŌRI (NEW YEAR'S FOODS)

Certain foods with symbolic meanings are often eaten during the New Year celebrations. This custom began in the **Heian period** with seasonal parties in the imperial court. These traditionally include salted herring roe, symbolic of a large number of offspring; black soybeans, as black is considered a charm against evil; chestnuts, symbolic of wealth for their golden color; and shrimp, the bent back of a shrimp resembling the bent back of someone who is very old and thus representing hope for a long and healthy life. All the food is made in advance and preserved so that there is no need to cook on the day it is eaten. A traditional way of presenting osechi-ryōri is in stacked lacquered boxes (**jūbako**) Today there is usually a serving of **toso** (spiced sake) before the meal and a type of soup known as **zōni**.

🎅 Lum and Ataru's family are getting ready for the New Year's meal in *Urusei Yatsura*; notice the soup bowls, sake cups, flasks, and jūbako in *Return of Lum: Trouble Times Ten* (p. 40).

OSERO ("OTHELLO")

 This game was invented in 1972 and is played on a board of 64 squares with pieces that have one side black and one side white. Four pieces are placed in the center, two white and two black, with the matching colors diagonal to each other. Pieces are placed so that one or more pieces of the opponent's color are between the new piece and another piece; when "captured" the opponent's pieces are flipped to one's own color. When the board is full the person with the largest number of pieces face up wins. An International Othello Championship has been held since 1977. The game is easily obtainable in stores around the world.

🅰 Othello is mentioned in *Roujin Z*. • Kyoko and Godai play Othello in *Maison Ikkoku: Welcome to Maison Ikkoku* (ep. 2).

OTAKU

 The use of the term otaku has an interesting history. Literally, the word is written as a combination of the character for "house" and the honorific prefix *o-* and can be translated as "your house." The word can also be used for "you" as a very polite way of addressing another person in conversation. For many of the shy, socially inept young males who are anime and manga fans in Japan, such a safe way of speaking is common. Then in June 1983 along comes Nakamori Akio, who starts to write a column called "Otaku no Kenkyū" (Studies in Otaku) in *Manga Burikko*, a magazine devoted to **rorikon** manga, where he pro-

poses that the term "otaku" be applied to the fans. The word sticks and is used by the media and fans to describe anyone obsessed with a particular subject. Today there are fans all over the world who call themselves "otaku" with pride. Meanwhile discussions (arguments) by non-Japanese on Usenet continue over the meaning of the word.

🅰 We see military otaku in *Otaku no Video*, including an interview (pt. 1, 4th interview), and in *801 TTS Airbats* (pt. 1); the subtitles use the term "fanboys," but the word "otaku" is what is used by Isurugi, and of course Isurugi is an otaku himself, as we see when he is playing with his model collection. • Noriko is praised as being quite an otaku by Amano at a lecture episode in *GunBuster* (OVA 3). • In *Key the Metal Idol* (tp. 1, ep. 2) Tataki identifies himself as a martial arts otaku. • The ultimate otaku are seen throughout the *Otaku no Video* anime. The term is first used to address Kubo in the elevator in *Otaku no Video* (pt. 1, 1st anim. seq.), and later a drunk takes offense at being addressed in such a formal manner (pt. 1, 6th anim. seq.).

ŌTOMO NO YAKAMOCHI

 718?–85. Believed to be the compiler of **Man'yōshū**, which includes 479 of his poems. Yakamochi's father was also an important poet, and the boy grew up surrounded by other noted poets of his time. He spent most of his adult life in government positions and apparently wrote very little poetry late in his life.

🅰 Mendou recites a poem by Ōtomo no Yakamochi in *Urusei Yatsura* (TV tp. 5, ep. 20, st. 40).

OZAKI SHIRŌ

1898–1964. A novelist who was born in **Aichi** Prefecture and studied at Waseda University. Before the war his work reflected an interest in socialism. During the war he was a nationalist, and this resulted in his being banned from publication between 1948 and 1950.

🅰 Ozaki Shirō is the author of *Jinsei Gekijō*, which is available as *Theater of Life*.

Godai and Sakamoto in Maison Ikkoku *kill some time at a local* **pachinko** *parlor.*

PACHINKO

I have heard pachinko called "vertical pinball," and this is not a bad description. Both pinball and pachinko originated from the Corinthian Game, which was developed in the United States in the early 20th century. Pachinko parlors are found all over Japan, and in them you will find rows of players lining the aisles. The balls launched into play are kept in an open tray at the bottom that fills up as you win or empties as you lose. Some pachinko machines have a slot-machine window display in the middle that when the numbers line up right results in more winnings. If you win enough balls you can trade them in for prizes, which are at times illegally exchanged for money. Pachinko parlors have a rather rough reputation in the eyes of some Japanese.

M In *Maison Ikkoku* (*Spring Wasabi*, ep. 1; vol. 3, pp. 22, 181, 213ff) we see several scenes of the interior or exterior of pachinko parlors.

A A pachinko machine is part of a computer in *Urusei Yatsura* (TV tp. 4, ep. 14, st. 28).

M We see inside a pachinko parlor and get a good look at the machines, and a couple tough-looking customers, in *Mai the Psychic Girl* (vol. 1, pp. 218–24).

PINKKU BIRA ("PINK LEAFLETS")

Stickers often placed in phone booths. These usually are advertisements for sexual services such as **sōpurando**, date clubs, or telephone services. Some of these have photographs of attractive women on them; some have manga-style artwork. The word *pinkku* ("pink") has a pornographic connotation in Japan.

A A *pinkku bira* gets used as scratch paper to write down a phone number in *Here Is Greenwood* (tp. 3, ep. 6). • Pinkku bira are seen in a phone booth in *Bubblegum Crisis* (OVA 1) and in *Kimagure Orange Road: I Want to Return to That Day.*

POKE-BERU (BEEPER)

Literally, "pocket bell," very popular among business people and even school children, especially high school girls. Until recently beepers only displayed numbers, but creative minds went to work and developed simple messages which could be displayed in numbers that

Kazuya and Mitsuru are barely visible through the **pinkku bira**-*covered glass of a phone booth in* Here Is Greenwood.

when spoken out loud would sound like words. Several books of these codes were published. For example 0840 can be pronounced as O-HA-YO-O (meaning "good morning").

A Pagers are used by Ayaka in *Phantom Quest Corp.* (tp. 1, ep. 2) and several characters in *Blue Seed* (tp. 2, ep. 4).

RABU HOTERU (LOVE HOTEL)

Hotels for couples to rent rooms by the hour or night. In 1993 there were 30,000 love hotels in Japan, each with an average of 20 rooms occupied by two or three couples per day. Love hotels are not cheap, shoddy places for a quickie but often have richly decorated rooms designed for a variety of romantic and erotic moods. The outside can be flashy—purple neon signs are standard—and exotic motifs like Western castles, palaces, or even churches are common. Married couples living together with their children (and possibly with their elderly parents) in a small apartment also go to love hotels to get some privacy.

A We see many of the details of a love hotel in the "Our Karuizawa" episode of *Patlabor: New Files* (vol. 4, ep. 12), including **beer** and **eiyō drinks** in a small refrigerator.

M Godai almost goes into a love hotel with a young woman in *Maison Ikkoku* (vol. 5, p. 67). • In *Oh My Goddess!* (OVA 1) Urd tries to make Keiichi's room look like one from a love hotel; near the end of the

same volume we see the exotically named "Motel d'Amour."

RAIJIN (GOD OF THUNDER)

Raijin is portrayed as having a circle of drums (*taiko*) attached to his back that he beats to make the sound of thunder.

M We see Lum portrayed as the god of thunder with the circle of drums in *Lum Urusei Yatsura: Perfect Collection* (p. 329) and in *Urusei Yatsura* (TV tp. 3, ep. 9, st. 18).

RĀMEN (NOODLES)

A popular noodle dish. Originally from China, it is still served in Chinese bowls. Rāmen can be made at home, ordered at rāmen shops, or packaged as dried "instant" rāmen with flavorings included. The Japanese often slurp their hot rāmen noodles to cool them (see **noodle slurping**).

A In *Urusei Yatsura* (TV tp. 2, ep. 5, st. 9) Ataru is eating rāmen in a restaurant while watching TV. • In *Oh My Goddess!* (OVA 1), Keiichi's second takeout order attempt is for rāmen. • Rāmen and pot stickers are being eaten by Ken when Miyuki introduces herself at the station in *You're Under Arrest* (OVA 1). • In *Neon Genesis Evangelion* Misato often eats instant rāmen, one of the few foods she knows how to prepare. • In *Phantom Quest Corp.* (tp. 2, ep. 4) Ayaka is eating instant cup rāmen when Mamoru answers the phone.

M Godai gives rāmen to Kyoko in *Maison Ikkoku* (vol. 2, p. 14); note the Chinese-style bowl he uses. • In *Ranma 1/2* (vol. 5, p. 158ff) during the martial arts takeout contest Ranma delivers rāmen.

RANMA (TRANSOM)

Not to be confused with the title character of *Ranma 1/2*. A ranma is an architectural element, an open grating near the ceiling of traditional rooms to allow air and light in. Often ranma are very complex and attractive wood carvings.

M In *Lum Urusei Yatsura: Perfect Collection* (p. 183)

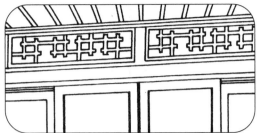

Sometimes carved from a single piece of wood, openwork **ranma** *are an excellent device for allowing air to circulate.*

we see a ranma in a room in a traditional Japanese inn (**ryokan**) where Ataru's parents are staying.

RED TRIANGLE

Red triangles are placed outside some windows and doors as indicators of places for firemen to enter a building.

▲ We see such a red triangle through the glass as Keiichi is washing windows in *Oh My Goddess!* (OVA 5) and on Clancy's apartment window in *Patlabor: Original Series* (tp. 2, ep. 5).

RENRAKU-SEN (FERRYBOAT)

Ferries are essential in an island nation like Japan, especially with the mountainous nature of the country making road construction difficult. Most of the modern ferry traffic is oriented to commuters, goods, and businesses. Japan Railways (**Jē Āru**) operates several major ferry routes, and there are international ferries to nearby countries like Russia, Korea, and China. Ferries are also popular with tourists, as are car ferries for drivers who want to avoid driving long distances (especially popular with honeymooners).

▲ Long-distance ferries play a part in *Patlabor: Original Series* (tp. 3, ep. 6).

RENTING

In Japan, home, apartment, and small office rentals are generally handled by a real estate agent and not the landlord. Part of

the cost of moving in thus includes a fee to the agent as well as a deposit and "key money." Deposits are refundable, minus property damages, but key money—which may amount to several months' rent—is not, since it represents the tenant's payment to the landlord for agreeing to the lease. Sometimes the landlord may request additional key money for a good location or for the right to sublease the property.

Ⓜ In *Maison Ikkoku* we see Yusaku looking at the ads in a real estate office window (vol. 3, p. 158) and later in the office (p. 180).

RŌNIN

Literally, "person cast on the waves." Originally rōnin were farmers who left home in search of employment; many ended up in the military. Then the term came to mean being a warrior without a master. During the **Muromachi period** the defeat of an army would leave many warriors as rōnin; after the decisive Battle of Sekigahara that effectively ended the feudal wars as many as 400,000 rōnin existed in Japan. During the **Edo period** attempts were made to find employment for rōnin and their numbers greatly decreased. Today the term is applied to students who have failed their college, or even high school, entrance examinations and are spending a year or two studying for the next round.

Ⓜ Early in *Maison Ikkoku* Godai is an example of a student rōnin.

▲ Most of the main characters in *Hakkenden* are rōnin.

Ⓜ There is a rōnin who has been trying to get into college for three years in *Domu: A Child's Dream.*

ROPPONGI

After WWII the Roppongi district of Minato Ward of Tokyo was the location of a U.S. Army base, and this naturally resulted in the growth of many businesses to serve the GIs. Today Roppongi is still a major entertainment area with discos, bars, clubs, and restaurants. The many embassies in this area contribute to its international flavor.

M *Sanctuary* opens in Roppongi (vol. 1, p. 6).

RORIKON ("LOLITA COMPLEX")

 A Japanese-made word for a sexual obsession with young girls (also transliterated as "lolicon"). Fred Schodt in *Dreamland Japan* speculates that this genre in manga and anime could have been the result of the government's prohibitions against showing pubic hair or adult genitalia in photos and drawings.

A Rorikon is mentioned in *Urusei Yatsura* (TV tp. 4, ep. 16, st. 31) and in the first interview in *Otaku no Video* (pt. 1). • Dracula is shown as having a Lolita complex in *Urusei Yatsura* (TV tp. 8, ep. 27, st. 50). • In *All Purpose Cultural Cat Girl Nuku Nuku* ("Phase 0I") Mishima Akiko accuses Natsume Kyusaku of making his android Nuku Nuku in the form of a teenager as his vision of a perfect woman, implying that he has a Lolita complex; later he is accused of rorikon by several customers of a restaurant where Nuku Nuku is working ("Phase 0V").

RYOKAN (JAPANESE INN)

 There are over 80,000 ryokan in Japan. Lodging includes two meals, usually traditional food dishes. Instead of numbers, rooms have names. Guests always take their shoes off before entering a ryokan and then use slippers to access their rooms. Ryokan often have a Japanese-style common bath. In ryokan you almost always use a futon and sit and sleep on tatami.

A Shino stays in a ryokan in *Hakkenden* (tp. 2, ep. 4). • A ryokan that goes up hillsides with long covered walkways is in *Patlabor: New Files* (tp. 3, ep. 9). • We see several details of a ryokan and hear the pine room mentioned by a maid in *Rupan III: The Fuma Conspiracy.*

M In *Mai the Psychic Girl* (vol. 1, p. 55) Mai is waiting for her father in the Crimson Foliage room. • In *Lum Urusei Yatsura: Perfect Collection* (p. 183) Ataru's parents are "enjoying" a stay at a ryokan.

SAIFUKU

 A formal white costume made of silk that is worn by **Shintō** priests during religious ceremonies.

A The priest at the wedding in *Rupan III: The Fuma Conspiracy* is wearing this kind of garb.

SAIGŌ TAKAMORI

 1827–77. A political leader credited with bringing down the **Tokugawa** shogunate. A bronze statue of him with a dog is located in Ueno Park (**Ueno Kōen**), near Ueno Train Station (**Ueno Eki**) in Tokyo.

A Early in *Mermaid Forest* we see the statue shortly after seeing the train station. • The statue also appears in the opening sequence of *Patlabor: New Files* (tp. 5, ep. 14). • Near the end of *Dagger of Kamui* Jiro is introduced to Saigō Takamori.

M In *Mai the Psychic Girl: Perfect Collection* (vol. 1, p. 65) we see the statue of Saigō Takamori above a crowd in the park.

SAIGYŌ

1118–90. A famous poet and priest of the Shingon sect of esoteric Buddhism. He spent a large portion of his life on Mt. Kōya (**Kōya-san**). Legend has it that he tried to use magic to recreate a deceased friend but with an imperfect result.

M In *Mermaid's Scar* (p. 272) a story is told about Saigyō on Mt. Kōya.

PANTIES

The more anime you watch, the more you see circumstances where panties are the object of attention. This can be simply an innocent cute flash, as when Sasami's skirt goes up in the opening of the *Pretty Sammy* OVAs, or something more lecherous.

More commonly, situations with panties are for humorous effect, such as when a male character's motives are misunderstood.

Hikaru, for example, is found picking up some undies he accidentally knocked over while waiting for Minmay in a woman's clothing store (*Robotech Perfect Collection: Macross*, tp. 3, ep. 6). In *801 TTS Airbats* Takuya is found clutching a pair that he accidentally grabbed while falling down.

In the *Blue Seed* TV series panty jokes are part of a running series of gags, with Momiji being teased by Kusanagi for wearing girlish panties with animal decorations. I don't even want to think why Yaegashi tested his prediction software by having it predict which animal would be on Momiji's panties (tp. 3, ep. 6) or why he happened to have a pair in his brief case with "I Love You" written on them (*Blue Seed: Rebirth*, ep. 13).

Then there are the out and out extreme panty-loving perverts such as Happosai, with his large-scale theft of women's underwear in *Ranma 1/2*, and Yuji in *Burn-Up W*, who probably would be satisfied with just one pair of Rio's dainties.

SAIKORO (DICE)

 Also called *sai*. The Japanese die has a red dot for the one spot, a 20th-century embellishment.

🅰 We see a dice game with the—anachronistic—red spot in *Hakkenden* (tp. 4, ep. 7).

Ⓜ A giant die with the large red spot visible is seen in *Ranma 1/2* (vol. 8, p. 33, lower right).

SAILOR FUKU (SAILOR SUIT)

A common style of girls' uniform for middle school and high school students. The design comes from European sailor uniforms and was introduced in the early 20th century. Almost any manga or anime with school scenes, especially *Urusei Yatsura*, will have girls wearing their sailor uniforms. Some translations of more pornographic anime and manga will occasionally have "college" students in uniforms; in the original Japanese these are actually middle or high school students.

🅰 In *Rupan III: The Fuma Conspiracy* you see sailor fuku in a flashback to the earlier relations of two of the characters. • Kodachi wears a sailor fuku in *Ranma* (TV sub tp. 4, dub tp. 6, ep. 11). • In *Blue Seed* (tp. 1, ep. 1) we see Momiji and the other school girls in sailor fuku; note that when she later changes schools she no longer wears sailor fuku but a different style of uniform. • In *Otaku no Video* (1st interview) sailor fuku is mentioned as an interest of a student club; one is later shown on the wall (3rd anim. seq.).

Ⓜ In *Maison Ikkoku* (vol. 2, p. 167) Kyoko's father is looking at several photos including one with her in a sailor fuku.

Nuku Nuku in All Purpose Cultural Cat Girl Nuku Nuku *looks very* kawaii *in her **sailor fuku** on her first day at school.*

©1992 MOVIC / KING RECORDS / YŪZŌ TAKADA / FUTABA SHA

SAISEN (MONEY OFFERING)

 Small amounts of money tossed into a box called a *saisen-bako* at the temple or shrine or in a portable version at a procession.

A In *You're Under Arrest* (OVA 1) you see Natsumi toss a coin in a saisen-bako.

SAKAZUKI (SAKE CUP)

 These special cups are made from lacquered wood and are very expensive. They are used for drinking sake at weddings and on New Year's Day and other special occasions. You sometimes see a stack of several sizes, with the largest on the bottom. Sometimes this word is used to refer to **choko**.

M Sakazuki are seen at a wedding in *Ranma 1/2: Fowl Play* (ep. 2, vol. 9, p. 32).

SAKE

 The most well-known of Japanese alcoholic beverages, sake is made from fermented rice. Sake dates back to the 3rd century and was primarily associated with shrines, the nobility, and festivals. Large-scale brewing began around the 12th century. In stories taking place in the past you often see unrefined sake that is a milky white color. This *nigorizake* is traditionally drunk chilled and is a favorite of mine. Refined sake is *seishu* or *nihonshu*. Drinking sake warm was originally a custom for the cold winter months, but as people realized that poor-quality sake tasted better heated they started drinking warm sake year round. Sake is traditionally heated in a small bottle called a *tokkuri* placed in hot water. (I have found that 1 to 1½ minutes in a microwave works well.) Heated sake should not be so hot that it burns the mouth, but true connoisseurs drink their premium sake slightly chilled. Sake can be packaged in traditional wooden casks (opened by splitting the lid with a mallet), bottles, or small glasses of "cup sake" dispensed warm from vending machines. The word "sake" can also refer to alcoholic beverages in general. (Gee, I wonder why the sake entry is so long!)

*A sturdy **saisen** box sits at the top of the stairs in front of a temple (**jiin**) in* YOU'RE UNDER ARREST.

A When the teacher in *El-Hazard*, either the OVA or TV series, refers to sake he is often referring to anything with alcohol in it. • In *Oh My Goddess!* (OVA 1) when the former dormmates arrive for a housewarming celebration we see the tall blond one with a large bottle of sake. • In *You're Under Arrest* (OVA 3) we see Natsumi holding "cup sake" in her hand; at first she holds one with a blue and white label that indicates it is Ozeki's One Cup brand; the second has a red and white label that I have not been able to identify. • One Cup is also seen in *Blue Seed: When Gods Walk the Earth* (ep. 17) and *Hyperdoll* (Act 2).

M We see cup sake in *Maison Ikkoku* (vol. 1, p. 47).

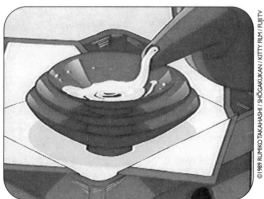

***Sake** poured into red **sakazuki** at a wedding in the* RANMA *1/2 TV show . . . but whose?*

ANIME CLUBS

Anime clubs are a great way to enjoy anime with others as well as a way to expose others to anime. If there are no clubs in your area consider starting one with a few friends. Check to see if your school or local library has a room with equipment that you can use. Reserve the space, choose some titles to show, print up some fliers, and you're on your way to having an established club. At first you can probably get by with tapes from your own collections. Don't forget to ask for permission from the companies to show their titles. Not only is this a legal issue but it is good manners. Some companies may even send you goodies to give away as door prizes. Later, if your club grows you may want to set up a more formal structure with officers, dues (showings should always be free), and a newsletter. At this point you should also consider joining the Anime Club Officers electronic mail list; this is a great way to keep in touch with officers at other clubs and establish contacts that you can deepen by meeting up at conventions. One word of advice: all of this can be a lot of work, so spread the chores around and ask people at the showings to consider becoming officers in your club. That way if someone flakes off it is easier to get someone else to pick up the ball, plus more people means more good ideas and people to carry them out.

And don't forget, have fun.

SAKURA (CHERRY BLOSSOMS)

Cherry blossom viewing parties, **hanami**, are popular every spring when groups of people drink, eat, and entertain themselves under cherry trees. Sometimes the blossoms fall so thickly that they can easily be mistaken for snow. Sakura are a symbol of a short life and so have a tragic significance along with their springtime association.

🅐 In *Oh My Goddess!* (OVA 1), sakura are most visible in the final scene. • The early *Ranma* TV episodes often have stray cherry blossoms blowing in the wind, cluing us in that it is spring, the beginning of the school year. • We see sakura in the memories Makoto gives Ifurita in *El-Hazard* ("Seventh Night"). • Cherry blossoms fall in *Tenchi Muyo in Love* as Achika says she will live her life with Nobuyuki to the fullest.

Ⓜ In *Mai the Psychic Girl: Perfect Collection* (vol. 1, p. 59) Mai is at an inn (**ryokan**) where she sees many cherry blossoms. • We see by the profusion of cherry blossoms that the story in *Maison Ikkoku* (vol. 1, p. 44) begins in the springtime.

SAMURAI

Literally, "one who serves." Early samurai were administrative officials in the provinces. Many were surplus offspring of imperial ancestry who were deprived of any royal status and given new names as the **Taira** family and the **Minamoto** family. Over time these families came into conflict, and this led to the eventual defeat of the Taira (see **Dannoura no Tatakai**) and the establishment of the **Kamakura** shogunate. Samurai played a major role in the Warring States period (**Sengoku jidai**). During the peaceful **Edo period** the samurai became administrators or simply lived on stipends. The Bushidō ("Way of the Warrior") code was developed during this time when there was little need for warriors. Some of the depictions of samurai in anime and manga owe more to film than to historical record.

🅐 We see Taira samurai flee from the Minamoto armies in *Zenki* (tp. 5, ep. 11). • The classic Samurai Trilogy film series is parodied in *Urusei Yatsura* (TV tp. 15, ep. 55, st. 78). • We find out that Mendou in the *Urusei Yatsura* TV series is of samurai ancestry (tp. 10, ep. 36, st. 59).

SANDO-GASA (HAT)

 A bowl-shaped hat made from sedge. 🅼 In *Urusei Yatsura* the character Cherry often wears a sando-gasa.

SANGI (YIN-YANG DIVINATION BLOCKS)

 Sangi are used to produce the trigrams that make up the hexagrams of the ancient Chinese book *I Ching*.
🅰 The *Phantom Quest Corp.* insert for tape 1 mentions that Ayaka 's family had a yin-yang fortune-telling business.

SAPPORO

 Capital of **Hokkaido**. Established in 1869 when the Japanese government began heavily promoting development of this northern island, Sapporo is famous for the ice sculptures of the February Snow Festival.
🅼 In *Sanctuary* (vol. 4, p. 201) we see a street scene in Sapporo.

SARARĪMAN ("SALARIED-MAN")

 One of many loanwords (**gairaigo**) common in Japanese. The sararīman is a white-collared salaried wage earner. By reputation he puts in long hours devoting his life to the company and has little contact with his family.
🅼 One of the most famous examples of a sararīman is Ataru's father in *Urusei Yatsura*.

Worn by monks or travelers, **sando-gasa** *are an efficient way to keep the sun off the head.*

🅰 The two main male characters in *Incident in the Bedroom Suburb* are sararīman.

SARU (MONKEY)

 Japanese monkeys, specifically a macaque, have short tails and are medium sized, about 2 feet from head to tail, with brown fur, red buttock pads, and a hairless face. In Japan's cold winter climate monkeys will sometimes sit in hot springs to stay warm. There is a folk belief that monkeys can prevent diseases in horses, so at times monkeys have been kept in stables. Trained monkey shows (**saru mawashi**) still exist in Japan.
🅼 Princess Kurama shares a hot spring with monkeys in *Lum Urusei Yatsura: Perfect Collection* (p. 385).

SARU MAWASHI (MONKEY SHOW)

 Training monkeys to perform tricks began in the **Kamakura period**, apparently due to a Chinese belief that horses who saw monkeys perform would have good health. In the **Edo period** traveling monkeys shows would visit samurai homes to give performances in the stables. Later the shows became a popular entertainment.
🅰 Kojirō (Mendou) does a trained monkey show in *Urusei Yatsura* (TV tp. 15, ep. 55, st. 78). • We also see a trained circus monkey in *Ranma 1/2: Fowl Play* (ep. 1).
🅼 An irritated circus monkey bites Mouse in *Ranma 1/2* (vol. 8, p. 187).

SATSUMAIMO (SWEET POTATO)

The sweet potato was introduced to Japan in the 17th century. Because it could be grown in a variety of conditions, large areas of Japan otherwise untillable were converted to sweet potato production. One way of cooking sweet potatoes outdoors is to roast them in a burning pile of leaves.
🅰 We see a **yatai** with stone roasted sweet potatoes and hear the chant of the seller in *Ranma 1/2: Goodbye Girl-Type* (ep. 1). • Baked sweet potatoes appear

OTAKU QUIZ
ARE YOU SAMURAI SAVVY?

Without looking at any entry in this book identify six of the following items that are in this picture of a samurai.

yukata	nihontō
obi	shinai
ōgi	mon
naginata	hakama
kimono	

ANSWERS

nihontō, mon, ōgi, hakama, obi, kimono

in *Urusei Yatsura* (TV tp. 14, ep. 51, st. 74). • Ryo-Ohki jumps into a leaf pile and steals a sweet potato in the opening sequence of the *Tenchi Universe* TV series.

 Ataru's mother serves sweet potatoes in *Lum Urusei Yatsura: Perfect Collection* (p. 119).

SEI BARENTAIN NO SHUKUJITSU (VALENTINE'S DAY)

February 14 is celebrated as Valentine's Day in Japan, but it is women who give chocolates to men. This may be an act of affection or, in the case of candies given to another worker, it may be "duty chocolate" (*giri-choco*).

 We learn that Mitsuru got 47 boxes from admirers in *Here Is Greenwood* (tp. 1, ep. 2). • Makoto gets lots of chocolate from girls at school in *The Wanderers: El-Hazard* (tp. 1, ep. 1). • Takeuchi gives Kunikida some chocolate in *Blue Seed: When Gods Walk the Earth* (Omake Theater).

Ⓜ Kozue gives chocolate to Godai in *Maison Ikkoku* (vol. 4, p. 127).

SEIDŌKYŌ (BRONZE MIRROR)

In ancient Japan bronze mirrors had ritual significance. Originally brought from China, the Japanese started making them in the 3rd century. One of the three traditional treasures of the Imperial Family is a bronze mirror. When you see a seidōkyō on an altar you know you are looking at a **Shintō** altar.

Ⓐ In *Blue Seed* (tp. 1, ep. 1) the cave in which Momiji purifies herself has an altar with a mirror and food offerings on it.

Ⓜ In *Lum Urusei Yatsura: Perfect Collection* (p. 82) we see a Shintō altar with a mirror as well as paper slips on the wall (**senja-fuda**) and statues of a **tanuki** and a fox (**kitsune**).

SEMI (CICADA)

The semi is often not seen but heard in anime and manga. This noisy insect is a symbol of summer, since its distinctive sound is common at that time of year.

Ⓐ We hear this sound at the beginning of the first

Tenchi Muyo! OVA and in *Hakkenden* (tp. 3, ep. 6), *Theater of Life*, and *You're Under Arrest* (OVA 1). • Semi are seen in *Ranma 1/2: One Grew over the Kuno's Nest* (3rd music video after ending credits) and in *Blue Seed: Fate and Destiny* (ep. 20).

Ⓜ We "see" the sound of the semi in *Ranma 1/2* (vol. 5, p. 22).

SENBAZURU (ORIGAMI PAPER CRANE)

 Folded paper cranes made in different colors are strung together and hung, often as part of a prayer offering at temples or shrines. Sometimes they are given to someone enduring hardship. The Hiroshima Park memorials often have senbazuru hung on them.

Ⓐ A bundle of senbazuru are given to Amano by students as she leaves for her last mission in *Gun-Buster* (OVA 6).

SENBEI (RICE CRACKER)

Rice crackers come in a variety of shapes and sizes. They are usually shaped in a mold, oven dried, grilled over a low fire, and basted with soy sauce. At times they are wrapped in seaweed (**nori**) or sprinkled with sugar.

Ⓐ We see senbei in *Tenchi Muyo! Mihoshi Special*. • Akemi tosses senbei to Soichiro in *Maison Ikkoku: Welcome to Maison Ikkoku* (ep. 2). • A cracker is rejected by Fin in *Dragon Half* (pt. 2).

Ⓜ Kyoko and Godai share senbei in *Maison Ikkoku* (vol. 2, p. 76). • Senbei with pieces of nori wrapped around them are seen in *Rumic Theater* (chapt. 6, p. 182).

SENGOKU JIDAI

The Warring States period of 1467–1568, beginning with the outbreak of the Ōnin War and ending with the entrance of Oda Nobunaga into Kyoto. This was one of the bloodiest periods in Japan's history, with local officials establishing their own rule over areas and then fighting

for power among each other. At the same time it was a period of economic and cultural growth with increased contact with the rest of Asia and Europe. During this time knowledge spread of, among other things, classical Chinese poetry, the tea ceremony (**cha-no-yu**), Zen Buddhism, and Confucian (**Jukyō**) teachings.

Ⓐ *Hakkenden* and *Fire Tripper* take place during the Warring States period.

Ⓜ The "Ash Princess" (*Mermaid's Scar*) also partly takes place at the end of the Warring States period.

SENJA-FUDA (SHRINE CARD)

 Slips of paper pasted to walls and pillars of temples and shrines. A literal translation of the term would be "one thousand shrine card." Senja-fuda are an expression of devotion placed by pilgrims as they travel from religious site to site. They contain the address of the worshiper or their group and information about them.

Ⓐ Senja-fuda are on the temple gates in Maebashi in *Patlabor: New Files* (tp. 5, ep. 16) and in *Hakkenden* (tp. 3, ep. 6).

Ⓜ In *Lum Urusei Yatsura: Perfect Collection* (p. 82) we see a **Shintō** altar in the first panel with **torii**, mirror (**seidōkyō**), fox (**kitsune**) statue, **tanuki** statue, and senja-fuda.

*A **semi** clings to a tree trunk in* PROJECT A-KO. *These critters are noisy in summer!*

*This **senbei** in* DRAGON HALF *has a strip of **nori** wrapped around part of it.*

SENKŌ-HANABI (SPARKLER)

 Literally, "incense fire flower." The cheapest and most common kind of fireworks (**hanabi**) in Japan is the senkō-hanabi. Unlike the Western sparkler it is not made with a wire but is more like a twisted string of paper and held downward. You must be sure to hold the right end so it will not burn your fingers. Like the **sakura** it has a short bloom and is very pretty.

🅐 A senkō-hanabi is used by the goblin in *Urusei Yatsura* (TV tp. 11, ep. 40, st. 63). • Sparklers are played with in *Growing Up* and in *Ranma 1/2: One Grew over the Kuno's Nest* (1st music video after ending credits). • In *Blue Seed: Fate and Destiny* (ep. 20) Momiji and her mother play with sparklers, and when the mother's starts to go out Momiji moves hers over to keep it lit.

Ⓜ We see Akane with a sparkler in *Ranma 1/2* (vol. 8, p. 166). • In *Return of Lum: Lum in the Sun* (p. 216) the sadness of the sparkler's short duration is commented upon in a highly sentimental manner.

SENPAI (SENIOR)

 Generally a senpai is someone with greater seniority in a particular situation. Often the word is used in reference to an upperclassman in school, but it can also refer to a mentor who has taken someone under their wing, such as a coworker with greater seniority helping a newer worker. The person who is the junior in this relationship is called the *kōhai*.

🅐 In *Oh My Goddess!* and *Ranma 1/2* the term is often used to indicate an upperclassman. In *Ranma 1/2* Kuno is sometimes called Kuno-senpai. • In the *Macross* TV series Hikaru calls Lieutenant Commander Fokker "senpai"; note that the translators have given the term as "brother," a meaning the word does not have. • Since she has been at the TAC longer Momiji refers to Kome as "senpai" in *Blue Seed* (tp. 2).

SENSEI (TEACHER, MASTER)

Titles are important when addressing people in Japan. The title "sensei" is most commonly used for doctors and teachers, no matter what their actual rank is within their particular profession.

🅐 In *Ranma 1/2* (TV sub tp. 3, dub tp. 5, ep. 9) Akane refers to Dr. Tofu as Tofu-sensei. • In *Urusei Yatsura* (TV tp. 2, ep. 5, st. 10) Sakura as school nurse is called Sakura-sensei.

SENSŌJI

A famous Buddhist temple in the **Asakusa** area of Tokyo, the grounds of which are entered by the **Kaminarimon** gate. It was

Senkō hanabi, like this one from BLUE SEED, *will burn better if you twist them tighter. A simple but pleasant way to pass the time on a summer evening.*

established in the 7th century to house a statue of the **bosatsu** Kannon found by two fishermen. Inside the gate is the Nakamise shopping arcade that leads to the main hall. The temple grounds also contain **Asakusa Jinja**, a shrine in honor of the souls of the temple's founders. Sensōji is very popular and has many visitors.

▲ We see Momiji and Kome at **Sensōji** (identified erroneously as Kaminarimon Shrine) in *Blue Seed* (tp. 2, ep. 4). In this episode we see Kaminarimon Gate, Nakamise Shopping Street, and then the Hondō or Main Hall. At this temple Momiji and Kome use **mikuji** to have their fortune told. • *Tenchi Muyo in Love* has a long sequence that takes place on these grounds.

SENTŌ (PUBLIC BATH)

 Public baths are more than a place to get clean. They serve a social role as gathering places for conversation, gossip, and general neighborhood interaction. Public baths are divided into two sections, one for women and one for men. When going to a public bath you bring your own soap, shampoo, hand towel, and a small wash bowl. Murals of **Fuji-san** are popular decorations in sentō. Sentō can often be recognized by their large smokestacks, since many are still wood heated.

▲ In *All Purpose Cultural Cat Girl Nuku Nuku* ("Phase OIV") both men's and women's sides of the bathhouse are shown. • In *Ranma 1/2* (TV tp. 1, ep. 3) the fathers go to the public bath when the plumbing is out of order in the Tendo house.

Ⓜ We see Godai and Kentaro meeting as they leave the public bath in *Maison Ikkoku* (vol. 1, p. 152). Note that they have their wash bowls with them. • In *Ranma 1/2* (vol. 2, p. 198) Ranma-chan goes to a public bath to change back into Ranma-kun.

SEPPUKU (RITUAL SUICIDE)

 Commonly known in the West by the cruder word *harakiri* ("belly slicing"). As ritual suicide, seppuku was largely limited

WHAT IS IT WITH ALL THE MONEY-HUNGRY WOMEN?

Nanami in *El-Hazard*, Nabiki in *Ranma 1/2*, Akiko in *All Purpose Cultural Cat Girl Nuku Nuku*, Sakura in *Key the Metal Idol*, Lina in *Slayers*, and, well, not Ayaka in *Phantom Quest Corp.*

In Japan the woman holds the household purse strings. On payday hubby gets home and hands over the cash—and I mean cash, as companies give out envelopes of cash, not checks, in low-crime Japan.

The husband may get an allowance to spend on snacks and drinks, but the wife determines where the bulk of the money goes.

Such an arrangement has a long history, or you can be sure that men in a male-dominated society like Japan would not put up with it. Women are as a result expected to be more practical about money than men and so are more likely to show an interest in cash flow, and to be teased for doing so, or for not doing so.

to the samurai. It could be done to preserve honor or imposed as a punishment. As a punishment, seppuku allowed the guilty man to preserve some honor in what would otherwise be a shameful situation. The act of seppuku was very structured, with strict procedures for the number of witnesses and the use of an assistant (**kaishakunin**) to lop off the person's head before he died. (One variant has the person committing seppuku cutting his own throat after cutting his stomach.)

Ⓜ Mendou is preparing to commit seppuku after his defeat by Ataru in *Urusei Yatsura* (TV tp. 4, ep. 14, st. 27) and *Return of Lum Urusei Yatsura* (p. 24).

▲ We see a dramatic use of seppuku to preserve honor in *Hakkenden* (tp. 1, ep. 2).

SETSUBUN

 Setsubun is the 3rd or 4th of February, which according to the old calendar is the end of winter. On this day you scatter roasted soybeans (*daizu*) outside the house while chanting *Oni wa soto, fuku wa uchi* ("Out with bad luck, in with good") to drive out **oni**. Scattering the soybeans is called *mame-maki*. (There is a pun here in that the word *mame* can be written with characters that can mean "evil eye" or "evil diminishing.") Often the father of the house wears an oni mask and is chased out of the house by the kids throwing the beans at him. Part of the tradition is to eat one bean for each year of your age. At shrines you can see celebrities throwing beans at the crowds.

A Ataru and Shinobu plan to chase Lum and Ten, who are of course oni, away by throwing soybeans at them in *Urusei Yatsura* (TV tp. 4, ep. 15, st. 30).

M Ataru is the target of soybean throwing in *Lum Urusei Yatsura: Perfect Collection* (p. 172).

SHABU-SHABU

 A popular meat dish consisting of very thin slices of beef dipped in a boiling kelp (*konbu*) stock and eaten with sauces. Vegetables, mushrooms, and tofu are also cooked in the stock. Shabu-shabu is cooked right at the table, with each person dipping their own meat into the stock.

A Shabu shabu is one of the Earth foods listed by Ataru in *Urusei Yatsura* (TV tp. 8, ep. 29, st. 52).

SHACHIHOKO (DOLPHIN ROOF ORNAMENT)

 Many old buildings have dolphin-shaped ornaments on their roofs and gates. The dolphin holds its tail over its head and has its fins outstretched. Traditionally shachihoko are seen as a charm against fire and are placed in pairs, one at each end of a rooftop ridge.

A Shachihoko are visible on the roof of the treasure house in *Rupan III: The Fuma Conspiracy*.

*The **shakuhachi** is carved from a single length of bamboo. Here, one of a special pair is played in* HAKKENDEN.

SHAKUHACHI (BAMBOO FLUTE)

 The shakuhachi entered Japan from China in the late 7th century and became modified into the form we have today, a length of bamboo with carved holes that is held vertically. At one time the shakuhachi was the instrument of begging *komusō*, or priests of the Fuke school of Zen, who played it as a spiritual exercise. In the 17th century the government ordered that only *komusō* could play the shakuhachi. The robed priests wore a straw hat so deep that it completely covered the head, looking much like an upside-down basket, and they carried an extra shakuhachi in their belts. In the **Edo period**, fugitives and **rōnin** would at times hide in Fuke temples and wear the garb of a Fuke priest when venturing outdoors; spies would also use the same disguise. During the **Meiji period** the Fuke sect was disbanded, but the costume continued to be worn by those asking for alms. Playing of the shakuhachi was carried on by those whose interest was in the music.

A A pair of shakuhachi play a major role in part of *Hakkenden* (tp. 5, ep. 8).

SHAMISEN

 A three-stringed musical instrument that entered Japan around the end of the 16th century from the Ryūkyū Islands. Unlike the Ryūkyū version, which is made of snakeskin and played with a bow, the Japanese shamisen is covered with cat or dog skin and plucked. The shamisen is played in theaters, tea houses, folk festivals, almost any place or occasion where music is called for, and its song accompaniments can be very crude or highly refined. In the Kyoto–Osaka area it is called a *samisen,* and when used in classical chamber music it is called a *sangen.*

🅐 A shamisen is seen in *Tale of Shunkin* • Several shamisen are played by old women in one of Godai's dreams in *Maison Ikkoku: Spring Wasabi* (ep. 1).

*This line of elderly **shamisen** players in* Maison Ikkoku *is only one example of what one finds in Godai's dreams.*

SHATAKU (COMPANY HOUSING)

 Some companies offer their married workers discounted housing. With the cost of living in urban areas so high this can be an important incentive for an employee to hire on. Such housing is not the same as the university-style dormitories (*ryō*) that are provided for single employees.

🅐 The Mikami family moves to company housing in *Voice from Heaven.*

SHICHIFUKU-JIN (SEVEN DEITIES OF GOOD FORTUNE)

Also called the Seven Lucky Gods: **Ebisu, Daikokuten** (aka Daikoku), **Fukurokuju** (Jurōjin), Kisshōten, **Hotei, Bishamon, Benten** (Benzaiten). The origins of these deities lie in various traditions, including Buddhism, **Shintō,** Taoism, and Hinduism.

🅜 We meet the Shichifuku-jin in Takahashi Rumiko's story "Golden God of Poverty" in *Rumic World Trilogy* (vol. 2). • The Shichifuku-jin are parodied in *Lum Urusei Yatsura: Perfect Collection* (p. 159).

SHICHI-GO-SAN (7-5-3 FESTIVAL)

On November 15 boys who are 3 and 5, and girls who are 3 and 7 are taken to shrines to be presented to the local **kami**

(*uji-gami*). Prayers (**inori**) are offered to prevent misfortune and to insure the good health of the children, who are dressed in their best clothes for this occasion. Shrines sell talismans and stick-shaped, pink-and-white "thousand year candy" (*chitose-ame;* see also **aka to shiro**).

🅐 We see a photo of Ataru as a child at the Shichi-go-san Festival in *Urusei Yatsura* (TV tp. 8, ep. 28, st. 51).

🅜 Ikuko shows Godai her photos, including one of her at the festival in *Maison Ikkoku* (vol. 1, p. 83).

SHICHIRIN (CERAMIC BRAZIER)

Small enough to be portable, this brazier is handy for cooking outdoors.

🅜 The character Cherry in *Urusei Yatsura* often uses a shichirin to cook in the empty lot he camps in. In OVA 4 (pt. 2) he uses one to heat **sake**.

🅐 Tenchi's father uses a shichirin indoors to create smoke to add to the atmosphere of a ghost story in *Tenchi Muyo!* (OVA 9).

SHIKA (DEER)

Cervus nippon. This species of deer, found naturally throughout East Asia, has been introduced to many parts of the world including the United Kingdom, New Zealand, and North America. It has a chestnut color with white

Some surume *is cooked over a* **shichirin** *as the coals are fanned with an* **uchiwa** *in* TENCHI UNIVERSE.

spots in the summer. Many craft items are made from the antlers. Nara Park is famous for shika so tame that people can feed them by hand.

Ⓜ We see the tame deer of Nara in *Urusei Yatsura* (TV tp. 6, Spring Special 2; *Return of Lum: Sweet Revenge*, p. 74).

Ⓐ Japanese deer are in *Blue Seed: Rebirth* (ep. 14).

SHIKEN JIGOKU (EXAMINATION HELL)

 The term was coined by the press as a label for the rigors of attempting to pass entrance exams in Japan These exams are not just for colleges and universities but for high schools and even grade schools and prestigious kindergartens. There are only so many openings in the schools, and only those with the higher scores gain access. What school you go to affects your job opportunities, so competition is fierce. Every year the media publish reports of student breakdowns and suicides.

Ⓜ Godai in the earlier parts of *Maison Ikkoku* is going through Examination Hell, with of course the help of his fellow lodgers.

Ⓐ The plot of *Student Days* centers around characters going through Examination Hell, as does in part *Kimagure Orange Road: I Want to Return to That Day*.

SHIMANE KEN

 A prefecture in western **Honshu** with Hiroshima Prefecture to the south, Tottori Prefecture to the east, and the Sea of Japan to the north. The territories of the ancient provinces of Izumo (**Izumo no Kuni**), Iwami, and Oki are contained in Shimane Prefecture.

Ⓐ Momiji in *Blue Seed* (tp. 1, ep. 1) is from the Izumo portion of Shimane Prefecture.

SHIMENAWA (SACRED ROPE)

A cord or rope made of rice straw used to mark a place as sacred. Shimenawa are often hung on **torii**, **shinboku**, around rocks, before altars, etc. They often have **gohei** attached. Shimenawa can also be used like protective amulets, such as when they are hung at home during New Year's.

Ⓐ Shimenawa are seen in the first *Zenki* episode, hung across a path, around the stone pillars at the top of the stairway, on torii, around the fire altar, and also around shinboku and across the entrance to the forbidden area. • Shimenawa are around some rocks in *Hakkenden*, particularly the one near the old tree that is the background for so many important encounters.

Ⓜ In *Mai the Psychic Girl: Perfect Collection* (vol. 1, p. 88) we see a gate with a shimenawa over the entryway.

Here a large stone in BLUE SEED, *probably a* **shintai**, *has a* **shimenawa** *wrapped around it to mark it as sacred.*

SHINAI (BAMBOO SWORD)

 This sword is used in **kendō** practice.
Ⓜ Akane uses a shinai on Ranma after he
makes a comment on the proportions of
her clothes in *Ranma 1/2* (TV sub tp. 3, dub tp. 4,
ep. 7; vol. 1, p. 210).
Ⓐ We see the bamboo sword used by Kodachi in
Ranma 1/2 (TV sub tp. 4, dub tp. 6, ep. 12). • The
coach in *Metal Fighters Miku* (tp. 3, ep. 6) carries
such a sword, without its ties holding the bamboo
together, in the gym.

SHINBOKU (SACRED TREE)

 Shinboku are often identified by a **shimenawa** placed around them. These trees
may be **shintai** of a **kami**. Some shrines
may have an entire grove of shinboku.
Ⓐ In *My Neighbor Totoro* we see that the camphor
tree is a shinboku. • There is a shinboku in *Tenchi
Muyo!* (OVA 1).

SHINBUN (NEWSPAPER)

There are 5 daily national newspapers in
Japan: *Asahi, Mainichi, Yomiuri, Sankei*,
and *Nihon Keizai*. If you add in the prefec-
tural papers you end up with 82 newspapers plus
sports papers, some of which are dailies. In 1991
newspaper circulation was over 52 million daily.
Competition for readers is fierce, and attempts are
always being made to get people to change their
subscription. Deliveries are usually made by boys
on bikes. There are even English-language papers,
with the *Asahi Evening News, Mainichi Daily News,
Daily Yomiuri*, and *Japan Times* being the largest.
Ⓐ A newspaper is delivered through the mail slot in
Incident in the Bedroom Suburb. • The *Mainichi
Daily News* is read by a guy in a white suit at the
pool in *Project A-Ko 2*.
Ⓜ Kei has his newspaper delivery job interrupted in
"Those Selfish Aliens" in *Rumic World Trilogy* (vol.
1, p. 6). • Godai is mistaken for a subscription sell-
er in *Maison Ikkoku* (vol. 3, p. 183).

*The **shimenawa** identifies this sacred tree as a **shinboku**
. . . perhaps there is a **tengu** nearby guarding it.*

SHINJŪ (DOUBLE OR GROUP SUICIDE)

Suicide in desperate circumstances is a
well-established tradition in Japan, unfortunately romanticized. Shinjū is suicide involving more than one person, and there are several
classifications. *Jōshi* is double suicide committed by
lovers. Chikamatsu Monzaemon, the famous puppet theater playwright, wrote many works on this
theme that have been adapted for kabuki and film.
Ikka shinjū involves members of the same family,
often a mother and children. *Gōi shinjū* is suicide by
mutual consent. *Muri shinjū* is suicide without mutual consent, i.e., murder-suicide.
Ⓐ Asuka remembers her mother wanting them to
die together when she was a child in *Neon Genesis
Evangelion* (tp. 11, ep. 22). In *Irresponsible Captain
Tylor* (tp. 1, ep. 2) the ugly terrorist is so overjoyed
at meeting others who seem to understand him that
he wants them all to die together as he sets off a
bomb, not their intention when they showed him
sympathy.
Ⓜ In jealous anger Lum attempts shinjū, actually
muri shinjū, in *Lum Urusei Yatsura: Perfect Collection* (p. 106).

OTAKU QUIZ
IDENTIFY THAT COMPOSER!

Match the person who wrote the music to the anime.

ANIME

Blue Seed
Ghost in the Shell
GunBuster
Irresponsible Captain Tylor
Macross Plus
Mermaid Forest
Mighty Space Miners (1995)
Moldiver
Patlabor 2
Tenchi Muyo in Love
Vampire Princess Miyu OVAs

COMPOSERS

Asagiri Priss
Christopher Franke
Kawai Kenji
Kijima Sario
Sakamoto Ryūichi
Tanaka Kōhei
Wakakusa Kei

ANSWERS

Asagiri Priss: Macross Plus, Ghost in the Shell, Irresponsible Captain Tylor, Blue Seed, Mermaid Forest, Mighty Space Miners (1995)
Kawai Kenji: Vampire Princess Miyu OVAs, Patlabor 2, Macross
Christopher Franke: Tenchi Muyo in Love
Wakakusa Kei: Moldiver
Tanaka Kōhei: Gunbuster

SHINJUKU

This Tokyo ward is a major administrative and commercial area. Many of Tokyo's skyscrapers are found here, as are the of-fices of the metropolitan government (**Tōkyō Tochōsha**). The Shinjuku train station is the busiest in Japan; nearby is a major entertainment area.

Ⓐ Shinjuku is where Phantom Quest Corp. is head-quartered (*Phantom Quest Corp.*, tp. 1, insert).

Ⓜ The Shinjuku office of the Sagara Alliance **yakuza** group is attacked in *Sanctuary* (vol. 5, p. 248).

SHINKANSEN (NEW TRUNK LINE, BULLET TRAIN)

This is the famous high-speed "Bullet Train" of Japan that started service be-tween Tokyo and **Osaka** in October 1964 to coincide with the Tokyo Olympics. These electric-powered trains have very comfortable accommoda-tions for passengers; some include dining cars. The first line to open was the Tōkaidō Line that runs south from Tokyo to **Osaka** and has a great view of Mt. Fuji (**Fuji-san**). Later the San'yō Line to Hakata was added; total travel time between Tokyo and Hakata is 5 hours 51 minutes at speeds of up to 168 mph. The trains leave Tokyo approximately every seven minutes between 6 A.M. and 12 P.M. Today other Bullet Trains connect to other parts of Japan, and newer lines are being designed and built.

Ⓜ In *Sanctuary* (vol. 4, p. 163) we see Mt. Fuji from the Tōkaidō line.

SHINKŌ SHŪKYŌ (NEW RELIGIONS)

Since the early 19th century many new re-ligions have sprung up in Japan. Some of them are cultlike, and many have their roots in populist forms of **Shintō** and Buddhism. Be-fore WWII some founders and adherents were per-secuted by the authorities and even imprisoned. After the war, with the new constitution (**Nihon-koku Kenpō**) granting freedom of religion, there was a dramatic increase in the number of new reli-gions and a revival of some suppressed movements like **Shugendō**.

Ⓐ Key meets the somewhat rude but interesting leader of one of these religions in *Key the Metal Idol* (tp. 2, ep. 5).

SHINRAN

1173–1263. Founder of the Jōdo Shin sect of Pure Land Buddhism, which emphasizes being reborn into Paradise through faith. Shinran became a monk at the age of 8 and lived at the temple Enryakuji on Mt. Hiei until 1201, when he became a disciple of Hōnen. Conflicts with the government resulted in a four-year exile to the province of Echigo. During exile he became the first Buddhist priest in Japan to openly marry and began to raise a large family. After his exile he gathered disciples and spread his teachings.

◮ The principal in *Urusei Yatsura: Beautiful Dreamer* quotes Shinran.

SHINTAI ("KAMI-BODY")

Literally, "body of the divine." A difficult term to translate. A shintai is where a **kami** resides (or enters into) and serves as the object of ritual worship. It can be a mountain, well, waterfall, tree, or rock, or even a small manmade object. In many shrines no one knows what the shintai looks like as it has been kept stored away for so many generations. When a branch shrine is established a mirror will often be sent from the main shrine to function as a shintai.

◮ A watermelon is a shintai in *Urusei Yatsura* (TV tp. 11, ep. 40, st. 63).

SHINTŌ

The indigenous religion of Japan. Shintō does not have a single holy book like Christianity, Judaism, and Islam. While there are written works that are of importance in Shintō there are various traditions that are of equal or greater importance. Shintō may not even have had a name until after Buddhism (**Bukkyō**) was introduced into Japan. The word Shintō is written with two Chinese characters (**kanji**) which mean **kami** (*shin*) and way (*tō* or *dō*), or the "way of the kami." Shintō worship of the kami by local communities plays a role in ordering the lives in the community. Worship can consist of individuals praying (**inori**), priests performing rituals, or communities participating in **matsuri**. Since Shintō does not have a central body of dogma but rather a focus on ritual purity and accepting life joyously it can be hard for Westerners to understand. Much of Shintō is a very loosely organized body of local practices particular to regions or specific shrines, but it is also closely associated with the structuring of the whole of Japanese society, with the imperial family playing a religious role. Given Japan's long tradition as an agricultural society, the rituals of Shintō often have strong connections with the seasons and the natural cycles of planting and harvest. Today Shintō is at times seen as linked to the promotion of harmony between humanity and nature. Even in urban Japan these connections to nature remain strong for many in a variety of subtle ways.

◮ *Blue Seed* incorporates many Shintō legends and practices. • When you see a **matsuri** you are looking at a Shintō festival.

SHIN TŌKYŌ KOKUSAI KŪKŌ (NEW TOKYO INTERNATIONAL AIRPORT)

Commonly referred to as Narita Airport. Located 30 miles or so east of Tokyo, it opened in May 1978 and replaced the older Haneda Airport as the major international airport for the metropolitan area. The development of Narita Airport in the late 1960s and 1970s was opposed by many of the local farmers, who had obtained this very poor quality land at the end of WWII and made it productive farmland. With the help of radical students strong protests continued for many years.

◮ Narita Airport is mentioned in *Patlabor 2*.

SHINZEN KEKKON (SHINTŌ WEDDING)

In Japan weddings are usually **Shintō** rituals, but Buddhist- and Christian-style weddings are also common. Historically weddings were performed in the home without a Shintō priest playing a role, but this changed in the **Meiji period**. The first wedding held in a Shintō

WHAT'S THAT FOOD?

One of my pet peeves in reading manga and anime (remember I'm a sub fan) translations is the way food names get translated. OK, maybe it's because I grew up in a California farm town and live in the San Francisco Bay Area and have eaten Asian food since I was a child. But why call **okonomiyaki** pizza or pancake or call **takoyaki** dumplings when a small line of type at the bottom of a page or screen or in an insert could define it for the reader? Why plaster signs that say **sukiyaki** all over the front of a restaurant in a manga translation to show characters eating from **donburi** inside?

Thank God that **rāmen** is now a well-known word or who knows what it would be called. For that matter, why look for a familiar term when we are obviously dealing with a different culture? Why do we have to "Americanize" the translations at all? At least AnimEigo gives you the original name and footnotes their anime on screen or in their excellent liner notes.

shrine, in 1900, was that of the Crown Prince, who later became the Taishō emperor.

🅐 In the beginning of *Rupan III: The Fuma Conspiracy* the bride wears a **tsunokakushi** and we see the Shintō priest shaking *harae-gushi* (see **gohei**) as part of a purification ritual.

SHIRITORI (WORD GAME)

 A game in which you take the last syllable of a word said by another player and say another word that begins with that syllable. Words can only be used once.

🅐 We hear voices playing this game in *Urusei Yatsura* (TV tp. 14, ep. 53, st. 76).

SHIRO (CASTLE)

 Many of the major developments in castle building took place during the Warring States period (**Sengoku jidai**). Earlier castles were mainly wooden fortifications, intended only for use until the war was over. Later the more extensive use of stone made the castles more permanent. The main structure is usually a large central wooden tower with a tile roof that is surrounded by concentric stone walls, fortifications, and moats. The courts and walls were organized as to almost make a maze to the central tower, and this would make an attack extremely difficult to pull off.

🅐 A castle is on a mountain in *Botchan* (pt. 1). • Osaka Castle is seen as Ryoga travels in *Ranma 1/2: The Breaking Point* (ep. 1). • Himeji with its castle is seen in *Urusei Yatsura* (TV tp. 15, ep. 55, st. 78).

SHIRUKO

 Often, *oshiruko*. A soup made from red *azuki* beans and sugar with either grilled mochi or a dumpling added. Shiruko originated in the late **Edo period**.

🅐 In *Urusei Yatsura* (OVA "Catch the Heart") Ten asks some girls if they like **anmitsu** or *oshiruko*.

Ⓜ We see "oshiruko" written on the noren of a restaurant in *Maison Ikkoku* (vol. 8, p. 225).

SHISHIODOSHI (DEER SCARE)

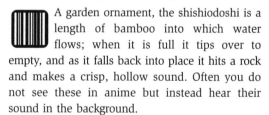 A garden ornament, the shishiodoshi is a length of bamboo into which water flows; when it is full it tips over to empty, and as it falls back into place it hits a rock and makes a crisp, hollow sound. Often you do not see these in anime but instead hear their sound in the background.

🅐 We see a shishiodoshi in *Urusei Yatsura* (TV tp. 3, ep. 9, st. 17) and during the **omiai** for Ayumi-**sensei** in *Project A-Ko 4*. • We hear one in *Vampire Princess Miyu* (tp. 1, ep. 1) as Himiko is taken to the girl.

SHŌGI (JAPANESE "CHESS")

 Shōgi is played on a chess-style board with pieces representing different ranks. The game involves considerable strategy. The object is to checkmate the opponent. Shōgi probably came to Japan from China. As shōgi evolved in Japan the pieces became wedge shaped; a new rule allowed captured pieces to be returned to the board on the side of the player who had captured them. Today there is an official shōgi federation that administers rankings and tournaments, as well as numerous amateur associations.

Ⓜ In *Ranma 1/2* (TV sub tp. 3, dub tp. 4, ep. 7; vol. 5, p. 153) we see the fathers playing a game of shōgi.
Ⓐ Shōgi is played by the coach in *One Pound Gospel* and by Tenchi's father and grandfather in *Tenchi Universe* (tp. 6, ep. 18).

SHŌGUN

 The abbreviation of *seii tai shōgun*, "barbarian subduing generalissimo." The original shōgun were Nara-period generals assigned the task of subduing the Ezo tribes of northeastern **Honshu**. Four hundred years later the title was adopted by Minamoto no Yoshinaka after a victory over the **Taira** forces; after his death his

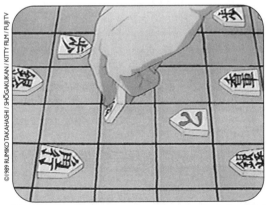

Placed on the board with a crisp snapping sound, the **shōgi** *pieces advance in the* RANMA 1/2 *TV show.*

This **shōji***'s wooden frame in* TENCHI MUYO IN LOVE *has simple clean lines, while the paper glued to the other side allows light to pass through.*

cousin Minamoto no Yoritomo was given the title by the emperor, resulting in the founding of the **Kamakura** shogunate (1185–1333). Other shogunates in Japanese history were the **Muromachi** (1333–1568), and the **Tokugawa** (1603–1867). The shōgun never claimed to usurp the emperor's role, but held de facto power by demanding the loyalties of feudal lords throughout the land.
Ⓐ A highly decadent Ashikaga shōgun (Muromachi period) is in *Hakkenden* (tp. 2, ep. 4).

SHŌJI

 A sliding screen that acts as a door to a room, usually to the veranda (**engawa**), or as a window covering. Shōji are made from a light wood frame covered with rice paper on one side. The paper allows light in while preserving privacy. For ventilation there may be **ranma** above the shōji. The easiest way to clean a shōji is to replace the paper after cleaning the frame. Shōji are common in older homes and some newer ones. An interior sliding door, usually heavier and opaque, is a **fusuma**.
Ⓐ Mitsuru uses an unusual method to begin the removal of paper from a shōji in *Here Is Greenwood* (tp. 3, ep. 6).
Ⓜ A shōji is used as an interior door between rooms in Oniko's mountain cabin in *Lum Urusei Yatsura: Perfect Collection* (p. 395).

SHOKUHIN SANPURU (FOOD MODEL)

 If you have ever walked by a Japanese restaurant you may have seen replicas of foods in its window that are so realistic they can be mistaken for the real thing. In the late 19th century many foreign dishes were introduced to Japanese restaurants, and displays were used to allow passers-by to see what these new foods looked like. With the heat of the Japanese summer—plus flies, dogs, cats etc.—this food did not maintain an appetizing appearance for long. In 1951 food models were produced with painted wax, but this did not solve the problem of deterioration in the summer heat. Nowadays plastics are used, but the manufacturing resembles that of a more traditional craft, with a system of master and apprentice. I once saw a TV show that showed how a head of cabbage was made leaf by leaf and then cut in half. It looked like you could use it in a soup.

🅰 In the *Macross* TV series (*Robotech Perfect Collection*, tp. 8, ep. 16) some very hungry Zentradi spies try to steal and eat food models.

Ⓜ We see food models displayed under glass outside a restaurant in *Maison Ikkoku* (vol. 3, p. 237).

SHŌYO (BONUS)

 Many businesses pay permanent workers bonuses twice a year, in June and December. In some cases, in a very profitable year for example, the bonus can be several months' pay, though usually it is between one and two months' pay. Bonus amounts are often the subject of union negotiations.

🅰 In *Urusei Yatsura* (TV tp. 2, ep. 7, st. 14) Ataru's mother comments on her husband's bonus helping them, since his income is so low.

SHŌYU (SOY SAUCE)

 Made from fermented wheat, soybeans, salt, and water. Shōyu is used in a variety of ways in a variety of dishes. Foods may be cooked in a broth containing shōyu, dipped in a shōyu-based sauce, or have shōyu poured over them. There are many types of shōyu, including tamari, that are made without wheat.

🅰 Nanami ends up in El-Hazard confused and holding a bottle of shōyu in *Wanderers: El-Hazard* (tp. 1, ep. 2).

SHŪGAKU RYOKŌ (SCHOOL TRIP)

 During the final, i.e., third, year of junior and senior high school, students take organized trips to famous places or even to other countries to gain exposure to different cultures. The outings usually last several days. Hotels in some major cities specialize in housing groups of students.

🅰 The Eva pilots have to stay behind while their classmates take a trip to Okinawa in *Neon Genesis Evangelion* (Genesis 0:5, ep. 10). • The climax of *Tenchi Muyo in Love* takes place during a shūgaku ryokō to Tokyo.

SHŪGAKUZEN KYŌIKU (PRESCHOOL EDUCATION)

 The education of children before entering elementary school falls into two categories, kindergartens and day-care centers. Many of these schools are privately owned. Over 60% of all 5 year olds are in a kindergarten.

🅰 The students of the Wakaba preschool appear in *You're Under Arrest* (OVA 2).

SHUGENDŌ

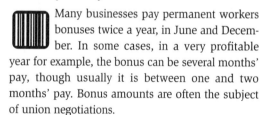 A Buddhist tradition that performs ascetic practices on mountains to obtain holy magical powers to benefit the community. Its members wear a distinctive garb and are called **yamabushi**. Tradition says that **En no Gyōja** is the founder of this movement.

🅰 An example of a Shugendō practitioner is Rokkon of *Phantom Quest Corp.*

SŌPURANDO ("SOAPLAND")

What are called massage parlors in America. In the past these were called "Turkish Baths," but complaints in the 1980s from the Turkish community resulted in a name change. Soaplands provide a steam bath, washing, and massage by young women. The experienced customer knows what to ask for and may receive a series of extra services, commonly including what some places call a "Hormone Massage," or masturbation. Ⓜ Godai finds out that Ayako works at a massage parlor in *Maison Ikkoku* (vol. 3, p. 192); in the original Japanese she says "Toruko" ("Turkish").

SOTOBA

Tall wooden tablets with Buddhist texts on them. These are set up behind tombstones on special anniversaries (*hōyō*) of the death of a person. The texts vary by sect, but generally include the posthumous name (**kaimyō**) of the deceased.
Ⓐ Sotoba are seen in the graveyard during Asuma and Noa's visit in *Patlabor: New Files* (tp. 5, ep. 16).
• An excellent view of sotoba and the writing on them is in the graveyard in *Here Is Greenwood* (tp. 3, ep. 6). • Sotoba are seen in the opening credits of *Rupan III: The Fuma Conspiracy*.

© 1992 HEADGEAR / EMOTION / TFC

Sotoba are clearly seen next to a memorial stone in a grave-yard in Patlabor New Files.

WHAT IS THAT LANGUAGE IN *WINGS OF HONNEAMISE*?

Ever wonder what language the citizens of Rimadan speak in *Wings of Honneamise*?

Someone asked the director, Yamaga Hiroyuki, about this at Fanime Con '97 and the answer was this: They wrote the actual dialogue in Japanese, then rewrote it in nonstandard Japanese dialects, transliterated it into the Roman alphabet, and then had non-Japanese actors perform the parts.

Small wonder it sounds like a real language but can't be understood.

Ⓜ The graveyard scenes in *Adolf: Days of Infamy* (p. 20) and *Maison Ikkoku* (vol. 1, p. 59) include sotoba.

STUDENTS CLEANING SCHOOL

In Japan the cleaning of homerooms and school grounds is the duty of the students.
Ⓜ In *Lum Urusei Yatsura: Perfect Collection* (p. 308) and *Urusei Yatsura* (TV tp. 3, ep. 9, st. 18) we see some of the students cleaning their classroom and complaining about Ataru skipping out on his part.
Ⓐ We see Noriko and Kimiko talking instead of cleaning the school grounds in *GunBuster* (OVA 1).
• A-ko is punished by being made to clean the classroom by herself in *Project A-Ko*. • In *Grave of the Wild Chrysanthemum*, we see the students cleaning the dorm. • In *Shonan Bakusozoku* several students are knocking a can around instead of cleaning the grounds.

WHY SO MANY TRAINS?

Trains are familiar to non-Japanese, but why are they seen and heard so often in anime and manga? Well, because trains are everywhere in Japan. Japan has a high population density, approximately 125 million people in a nation with the land mass of California. Most of the land is too steep to build on, and the result is crowded cities with scarce real estate.

Why spend money on cars when there is little or no place to park them and all petroleum is imported and fuel is expensive?

Why build lots of wide roads when people need the space for housing and work?

Neighborhood shopping areas are common, and if you need to go farther away you can simply take the local mass transit, which in many cases means a train. If a story takes place in a large city like Tokyo or Osaka, and many do, the odds are good that some event will take place on, in sight of, or within earshot of a moving train.

SUDARE (HANGING BLINDS)

 Sudare are made of split bamboo or reeds and are hung in the summer where a home's outer **shōji** or **amado** would be in the winter. These allow privacy and block sunlight but at the same time let in air to help ventilate the building. Expensive sudare have tassels and silk borders. There is a special kind, called *misu*, that are used for privacy at sacred sites and palaces.

A We see sudare along the **engawa** in *Tenchi Muyo!* (OVA 13), *Vampire Princess Miyu* (tp. 1, ep. 2), *Ranma 1/2* (OVA "Shampoo's Sudden Switch!"), and *Suikoden Demon Century*.

M Godai's grandmother hangs up some sudare in his window in *Maison Ikkoku* (vol. 5, p. 134).

SUIKA-WARI (WATERMELON GAME)

 A game played at the beach where one person is blindfolded and tries to break open a watermelon with a stick.

A An explanation of this game, using Ataru's head and an aluminum baseball bat, is in *Urusei Yatsura* (TV tp. 11, ep. 40, st. 63).

M In *Ranma 1/2* (vol. 4, p. 184) we see an interesting variant on this game, without blindfolds, as a martial arts competition.

SUKĪ (SKIING)

 Skiing in Japan dates back to 1911 when Major Theodor von Lerch, the Austrian military attaché, taught skiing to soldiers of the Takada 58th Infantry Regiment in Niigata Prefecture. The first Japanese ski club was also formed that year. Today skiing is quite popular, and resorts have hot baths for relaxing after a day's activity on the slopes. The snow in **Honshu** is heavier than that in more northern **Hokkaidō**.

A A martial arts skiing competition with wooden swords (**bokken**) takes place in *Ranma 1/2: Breaking Point* (ep. 1). • The major characters visit Kyosuke's grandparents in the winter and have a dangerous skiing experience in *Kimagure Orange Road* (tp. 2, ep. 1).

SUKIYAKI

 A food dish made of meat, tofu, and vegetables, cooked in a broth in a shallow iron pan. Sukiyaki dates from the **Meiji period**. The price of meat in Japan makes the dish a special treat for many households. There are many regional varieties.

A Sukiyaki appears in *Wandering Days, Urusei Yatsura* (TV tp. 4, ep. 15, st. 29), *Ranma 1/2* (TV tp. 12, ep. 29), and *Tenchi Universe* (tp. 1, ep. 3).

M In *Lum Urusei Yatsura: Perfect Collection* we see a sukiyaki restaurant (p. 134), and Ataru's parents who are ready to cook sukiyaki (p. 161). The translation on pages 134 and following is inaccurate, as in the original this is not a sukiyaki place but a restaurant specializing in **gyūdon**.

SUMI (INK)

To write with a brush (*fude*) you need ink (*sumi*). Carrying or storing fluid ink in the past was a problem. It was easier to carry a dry ink stink and to prepare ink as needed by rubbing it on a wet ink stone.

A Kuno is first seen using an ink stick and stone for writing a message in *Ranma 1/2* (TV tp. 2, ep. 4). • Ink and a brush is used to paint sutras in *Ghost Story*.

SUMŌ

Sumō, considered by many to be the national sport of Japan, is an ancient contest requiring great strength and skill. Two hefty wrestlers face each other in a ring and then collide, each trying to topple the other or push him out. Whoever touches the ground outside the ring first or has any part other than his feet touch the ground inside the ring loses the match. Over time sumō has developed into a professional sport watched by millions, with a large body of tradition in dress, training, ritual, etiquette, and even food.

A In *Ranma 1/2* (TV sub tp. 1, dub tp. 2, ep. 3) Akane fights a high school sumō wrestler, among others. • Ataru is in such a hurry to get a drink of water that he pushes a sumō wrestler some distance in *Urusei Yatsura* (TV tp. 6, ep. 21, st. 41). • In the first *Patlabor* movie we see a sumō doll in a glass case; the doll is in the posture and costume of the ring-entering ceremony.

M We see a sumō match in *Lum Urusei Yatsura: Perfect Collection* (p. 100).

SURGICAL MASKS WORN IN PUBLIC

You often see ordinary Japanese wearing white surgical masks on the train or at work. Sick people wear them to prevent spreading their illness in public, and healthy people wear them to avoid getting sick. This is important given the close quarters in mass transit and the population density of many cities. In the wintertime the masks help keep your face warm. In spring and fall they help hay fever sufferers filter out pollen and dust.

M We see Ataru wearing a mask as part of a disguise in *Urusei Yatsura* (TV tp. 2, ep. 5, st. 9) and in *Lum Urusei Yatsura: Perfect Collection* (p. 71).

A In *Shonan Bakusozoku* some gang members are wearing masks to help hide their identities. • In *Urusei Yatsura* (TV tp. 2, ep. 5, st. 10) we see a whole classroom full of sick students with masks on.

SUSANOO-NO-MIKOTO

The **kami** of many things, including storms, the underworld, agriculture, water, and disease, as well as the younger brother of **Amaterasu Ōmikami**, the kami of the sun. After being incredibly rude to his older sister and the other kami he is forced to make restitution, has his hair cut and his fingernails and toenails pulled out, and is banished from the High Celestial Plain (**Takamagahara**). Susanoo then descends to the mountain Torikamiyama in **Izumo no Kuni** where he meets an old couple weeping. They tell him that every year an eight-headed and -tailed serpent, Yamato-no-Orochi, comes and eats one of their daughters, and that the last one, Kushinada Hime, shall be devoured soon. Susanoo has them make eight barrels of sake and leaves them for the serpent. After it empties the barrels the serpent falls into a drunken stupor and Susanoo slays it by cutting off all of its heads. In one of the tails he finds a sword that he presents to his sister; later this sword shall be known as the Kusanagi and become one of the items of the Imperial Regalia.

A The story of Susanoo-no-Mikoto's slaying of Yamato-no-Orochi, mis-transliterated as Orochi-no-Orochi, and rescuing Kushinada Hime is told in *Blue Seed* (tp. 1, ep. 1). Note that one of the characters in *Blue Seed* is named Kusanagi. • A version of the sacrifice of a girl and a beast with seven peach heads is seen in *Urusei Yatsura* (TV tp. 18, ep. 67, st. 90).

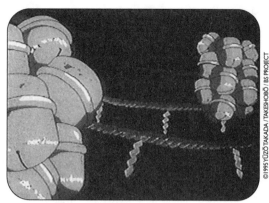

Suzu in clusters, like these in BLUE SEED, are sometimes used in **Shintō** rituals.

🅼 A rather fanciful Susanoo-no-Mikoto is in *Orion*.

SUSHI

 Many Westerners make the mistake of confusing sushi with raw fish. Sushi is sweetened rice; it might be combined with raw or cooked seafood, but it might be used plain or with vegetables alone. The forms of sushi known best in the West are *nigirizushi* (also known as *edo-maezushi*), which is hand-molded sushi with a topping added to it, and *makizushi*, sushi and ingredients rolled in a sheet of **nori** (seaweed). Other varieties include *oshizushi*, where seafood and rice are pressed into a mold then sliced, and *chirashizushi*, where ingredients are, in the Tokyo style, scattered on top of a bowl of rice or, in the Osaka style, mixed into the rice. Sushi has its origin in a Chinese method for preserving fish. Fish, salt, and rice would be packed together and fermented for two months to a year. Originally the rice was discarded and the fish eaten. In time the rice was eaten along with the fish. In the late **Edo period** the pickling process was discarded in favor of using seasoned rice with fresh fish toppings.

🅰 We see a variety of sushi being eaten by the deck officers after the lens-cleaning scene in *GunBuster* (OVA 3). • *Makizushi* is in *Urusei Yatsura* (TV tp. 9, ep. 34, st. 57). • Sushi is served when Kenji shows

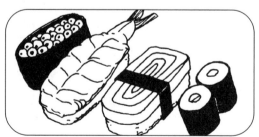

Sushi, yum yum. Fresh ingredients shaped by hand . . . the original fast food. Itadakimasu!

up in *Student Days*. • Nabiki tries to order a deluxe sushi plate but Soun Tendo stops her in *Ranma 1/2* (OVA "Tendo Family Christmas Scramble"), as this would be quite expensive.

🅼 We see takeout *makizushi* in a tray in *Maison Ikkoku* (vol. 3, p. 162) and later Kyoko rolls some to take with her (vol. 7, p. 174). • In *Rumic Theater*, "One Hundred Years of Love" (chapt. 5, p. 151) Takanezawa and some friends go out for sushi.

SUSU-HARAI (END-OF-YEAR HOUSECLEANING)

 Starting on the 13th day of the last month, the Japanese have traditionally begun housecleaning in preparation for the New Year. The idea is to have the home completely cleansed for the arrival of the **kami**. People may delay the cleaning for vacations or other reasons, but it generally still gets done. Temples and shrines also get a thorough cleaning in preparation for the throngs of New Year visitors.

🅰 Kazuya helps Mitsuru's family with their New Year's house and temple grounds cleaning in *Here Is Greenwood* (tp. 3, ep. 6). • We see Chiaki, her grandmother, and Zenki cleaning the shrine in *Zenki* (tp. 6, ep. 12).

SUZU (ROUND BELLS)

Suzu can be very small bells, with a pellet inside or small clapper, such as a bell worn on a cat's collar, or very large like the bells at **Shintō** shrines. Over the offering box (see **saisen**) at a shrine will be a rope attached to a small clapperless bell that the worshiper can shake to attract the attention of the kami. Suzu may also be attached in clusters to handles and shaken in dances performed at shrines by **miko**.

🅰 In *You're Under Arrest* (OVA 3) we see Ken and Natsumi at a mountain shrine shaking the suzu rope before praying. • Tenchi pulls on the suzu rope while sitting on the offering box in *Tenchi Muyo in Love*. • Clusters of suzu in a cave are in *Blue Seed: Fate and Destiny* (ep. 19).

TABI (SPLIT-TOED SOCK)

The split between the big toe and other toes allows you to wear sandals (**zōri**) with tabi. Originally tabi were made of deer or monkey skin and had no separation between the toes. Cloth replaced skin after the 17th century due to a scarcity of hides. White tabi are worn with kimono for formal occasions; solid colors are for ordinary wear. *Jika-tabi* are tabi-like foot coverings with soles that can be worn without sandals; they are often seen on day laborers.

🅰 Okoto wears tabi in *Tale of Shunkin*, as do Momiji's grandmother in *Blue Seed: Sacrifice* (ep. 21) and

Tenchi's grandfather in *Tenchi Universe* (tp. 1, ep. 1).

TACHIMONO (SOMETHING ABSTAINED FROM)

Literally, "that which is cut off." Priests or worshipers sometimes choose to abstain from a particular food as a religious offering, often in preparation for a ritual or to fulfill a vow.

🅰 In *Blue Seed: Rebirth* (ep. 14) Kome describes asking for something in prayer and promising something in exchange, like not drinking for a year. • There is no temple or shrine around when the coach swears to not drink until Miku beats Aquamarine in *Metal Fighters Miku* (tp. 5, ep. 10), but he tells his promise to Miku.

TACHISHŌBEN (PEEING IN THE STREET)

It is not unheard of for Japanese men and children to urinate in the street. While this is not as common for adults (unless they are drunk) children have fewer social inhibitions. The activity is at times spoken of as being closer to nature, something that Japanese aesthetics surely values. Note that one would not urinate in a garden since that is a private space to be respected, while a city street is a public space much like a roadside in the country.

*The straps of **tabi**, like these in* BLUE SEED, *are designed to fit comfortably between the toes.*

129

At the beginning of *All Purpose Cultural Cat Girl Nuku Nuku* Ryuunosuke is putting his plumbing to one of its intended uses in an alley.

TAIFŪ (TYPHOON)

 The Asian Pacific equivalent of the hurricane. These occur in late summer and early autumn. The typhoons that in 1274 and 1281 destroyed the fleets of the Mongols and saved Japan from invasion were named *kamikaze*, "divine winds." The weather services in Japan take great pains to accurately track and predict the behavior of typhoons.

 In *Urusei Yatsura* (TV tp. 11, ep. 41, st. 64) you hear that Ataru as a child liked typhoons • Typhoons are seen in *Patlabor: New Files* (tp. 4, ep. 12); in both the first *Patlabor* movie and *You're Under Arrest* (OVA 2) typhoons play a major role.

TAIKO (LARGE DRUM)

 There are several types of *taiko* drum: *dadaiko*, an enormous laced drum; *tsuridaiko*, a nailed drum; *ninaidaiko*, a laced drum carried on a pole; *shimedaiko*, a barrel-shaped laced drum; *ōdaiko*, a large nailed drum; *hirazuridaiko*, a thin barrel-shaped drum on a stand. Some of these drums are used in court music, noh drama, and kabuki. Taiko are also used in festivals (**matsuri**).

 We see a taiko drum on a cart in *Grave of the Wild Chrysanthemum*.

 We see a taiko drum used by the supporters of Tobimaro in *Return of Lum: Lum in the Sun* (p. 101).

TAIRA

 One of the four great families of Japanese history. Also known by the alternative pronunciations of the characters for "Taira" (*hei*) and "family" (*shi* or *ke*) = Heishi or Heike. The Taira were an offshoot of the imperial family. They defeated the **Minamoto** family in 1160 but were later defeated themselves at the Battle of Dan-

noura (**Dannoura no Tatakai**) by the Minamoto under the leadership of **Minamoto no Yoshitsune**. The war between the families is the frequent subject of Japanese literature and art.

 The Battle of Dannoura is shown in the beginning of *Ghost Story*. • We also hear of the Heike clan and Ushiwakamaru's plan to destroy them in *Urusei Yatsura* (TV tp. 3, ep. 12, st. 24).

TAI-YAKI

 A confection of *azuki* beans inside a small fish-shaped pastry. The fish design represents a sea bream, a symbol of good luck.

 Kosaku buys tai-yaki in *One Pound Gospel* and Noa gives Asuma some in *Patlabor: New Files* (tp. 5, ep. 14).

 In *Maison Ikkoku* (vol. 2, p. 13) two of the lodgers bring Kyoko a gift of tai-yaki.

TAKAMAGAHARA (PLAIN OF HIGH HEAVEN)

Also seen as Takamanohara. It is the dwelling place of the celestial **kami** above this world in the sacred hierarchy of **Shintō**.

 That the kami **Susanoo-no-Mikoto** was banished

*With such a booming sound, who can avoid getting excited when the **taiko** is beat?*

Even though she has been told to avoid snacks, Nuku Nuku in ALL PURPOSE CULTURAL CAT GIRL NUKU NUKU *can't resist a little **tai-yaki** on the sly.*

from Takamagahara is mentioned in *Blue Seed* (tp. 1, ep. 1).

TAKARAZUKA KAGEKIDAN (TAKARAZUKA OPERA COMPANY)

 An all-female musical theater troupe famous for extravagant productions in a large variety of styles, including musical adaptations of several **manga**, such as the *Rose of Versailles*. The company was founded in 1913 as an attraction for the resort area at Takarazuka near Osaka. All performers undergo at least two years of training at the Takarazuka Music School before they appear on stage.

M Tezuka Osamu was a fan of the Takarazuka Opera Company; in *Adolf: The Half-Aryan* (p. 275) a murdered **geisha** was once an applicant of the Takarazuka school.

TAKENOKAWA (BAMBOO SHEATH)

 As sprouts of bamboo grow they are protected by leafy sheaths that can be up to 1 foot wide and 2 feet long. These sheaths are harvested and used to wrap foods, either for storage or as packaging. Rice balls (**nigirimeshi**), for example, are often wrapped in takenokawa. The sheaths can be torn into strips and woven into san-

dals or used like string. Flat hats woven of takenokawa are used by farmers, A round flat pad covered with takenokawa is used to rub down woodblock prints. Household items made of this material have a rustic charm.

A Akane unpacks nigirimeshi wrapped in takenokawa in *Ranma 1/2: An Akane to Remember* (pt. 2) as does the aunt in *Grave of the Fireflies*.

TAKEUMA (BAMBOO HORSE OR STILTS)

 As early as the 12th century, a takeuma was a toy horse with reins at one end and a small wheel at the other, or just a plain bamboo pole that children would place between their legs while pretending they were on horseback. In time a head of cloth or papier mâché was added with a mane of yarn or string. These were especially popular in the **Edo period**. Later the name takeuma was applied to stilts in the form of two poles with elevated footholds.

A We see takeuma (stilts) used by Cherry in *Urusei Yatsura* (OVA 2, pt. 2).

TAKO (OCTOPUS)

 There are about 50 species of octopus in Japan, but three common species make up most of what is captured for food. Octopus is used in a variety of dishes and is always cooked, even when it is used on **sushi**. A popular image of the tako is with a spouting mouth and **hachimaki** tied around its red head.

A Cherry mentions octopus as a food in *Urusei Yatsura* (TV tp. 10, ep. 36, st. 59), and an octopus-shaped balloon is among the stuff in Azusa's room in *Ranma 1/2: Darling Charlotte* (ep. 2).

M In *Return of Lum Urusei Yatsura* (p. 6) Mendou is holding an **inrō** with his family crest, which shows a tako, most appropriate for a wealthy industrial family. • Octopus-shaped balloons are seen in *Maison Ikkoku* (vol. 6, p. 4). • A tako-shaped face mask is in *Rumic World Trilogy* (vol. 3, p. 167). • An actual octopus with a spouting mouth is depicted in *Return of Lum: Lum in the Sun* (p. 153).

OTAKU QUIZ
MECHA MATCH!

Match these mecha to the show and to the designer.

MECHA	SHOW	DESIGNER
7B/2B Brocken	*GunBuster*	Akitaka Mika
Aestivalis	*Macross Plus*	Izubuchi Yutaka
General Galaxy YF-21 Omega One	*Martian Successor Nadesico*	Kawamori Shōji
Gratan	*Mobile Police Patlabor*	Masuo Shōichi
Machine Weapon RX-7	*The Secret of Blue Water*	Ohata Kōichi

ANSWERS

DESIGNER	SHOW	MECHA
Ohata Kōichi	*GunBuster*	Machine Weapon RX-7
Masuo Shōichi	*The Secret of Blue Water*	Gratan
Kawamori Shōji	*Macross Plus*	General Galaxy YF-21 Omega One
Akitaka Mika	*Martian Successor Nadesico*	Aestivalis
Izubuchi Yutaka	*Mobile Police Patlabor*	7B/2B Brocken

TAKO-AGE (KITE FLYING)

 The origins of kite flying in Japan go back as far as the 10th century. Kites are not merely children's toys but can be very large and complex, requiring the strength of several adults, sometimes as many as 50 men, to get up and control. There are stories of kites so large that they could carry a person aloft. Many kites are painted with intricate designs and are impressive works of art. Kites are often flown during **Kodomo no Hi**.

A We see a public-service announcement on kite flying safety tips in *Urusei Yatsura* (TV tp. 6, Spring Special 1). • Kites are flying right after New Year's in *Grave of the Wild Chrysanthemum* and *Zenki* (tp. 6, ep. 13).

TAKOYAKI

 Golfball-size snacks made of small pieces of boiled octopus, scallions, pickled ginger, and a wheat-flour batter. Seasoned with a brown sauce and seaweed (**nori**) and eaten with a toothpick, takoyaki are often served from food carts (**yatai**) on the street.

A Eating takoyaki in seaweed is one of the items on Natsumi's list of things undone that summer in *You're Under Arrest* (OVA 2). • Ataru and Megane share takoyaki in *Urusei Yatsura* (TV tp. 17, ep. 64, st. 87).

M Kyoko is treated to takoyaki in *Maison Ikkoku* (vol. 2, p. 13). • In *Caravan Kid* (vol. 1, p. 235) some very impressive takoyaki are sold by Babo with impressive profits and some impressive side effects.

TAKUSHĪ (TAXI)

You can get a taxi at a taxi stand or simply by raising your hand in the street. The doors are controlled by the driver and open automatically. Given the complexity of Japanese street addresses you should be able to provide directions. Cab drivers in Japan have a reputation for good manners (and, with Japan's low crime rate, there is no glass between the passenger and cab driver).

🅐 In *Ranma 1/2* (TV sub tp. 5, dub tp. 7, ep. 14) Dr. Tofu's mother chews out a driver who is impatient about finding the clinic. • We see a cab door open and close in *Kimagure Orange Road* (OVA 3, ep. 1) and in *Blue Seed* (tp. 4, ep. 8).

TANABATA

A festival that originated in the traditional Chinese tale of the Weaver Star (Vega) being separated from her lover, the Cowherd Star (Altair). In Japan this story was mixed with that of Tanabatatsume, a celestial weaving maiden. Tanabata is celebrated on July or August 7 with feasting and offerings to the stars; poems written on oblong sheets of paper called **tanzaku** are attached to bamboo branches planted in gardens and fields. The festival shares some features with the **Bon** Festival, which is celebrated around the same time. Tanabata was traditionally popular with girls due to the romantic nature of the story and the association of weaving with women.

🅐 We see Kimiko and her daughter celebrating Tanabata in *GunBuster* (OVA 6).

🅜 Lum watches a TV dramatization of the story of the cowherd and the weaver in *Return of Lum: Lum in the Sun* (p. 24).

TANIZAKI JUN'ICHIRŌ

1886–1965. Born in the **Nihonbashi** district of Tokyo, Tanizaki left Tokyo after the Great Tokyo Earthquake of 1923 and moved to the Kansai (Kyoto–Osaka) area. Many of his works focus on the struggles for happiness of men and women.

🅐 Tanizaki is the author of *Shunkinshō* (1933), available as *Tale of Shunkin*.

TANUKI

A mammal of the Canidae family, the tanuki resembles the raccoon in its facial features. It is thought to have supernatural abilities but, unlike the fox (**kitsune**), is usually seen as amusing. Large ceramic statues of male tanuki with large testicles, wearing a straw hat and holding a gourd (**hisago**) bottle of sake are sometimes displayed outside shops as decorations.

🅐 One of the children plays a tanuki in a performance of the play "Rocky Mountain," which we are told is put on by the preschoolers in *You're Under Arrest* (OVA 4). • Ayaka is carrying a ceramic tanuki in *Phantom Quest Corp.* (tp. 1, case 1) as she follows a suspect. • In *Urusei Yatsura: Beautiful Dreamer* we see a giant tanuki statue being moved at the school.

🅜 In *Ranma 1/2* (vol. 4, p. 43) we see a ceramic tanuki used in a booby trap. • In *Lum Urusei Yatsura: Perfect Collection* (p. 82) we see a **Shintō** altar with a mirror (**seidōkyō**) as well as paper slips on the wall (**senja-fuda**) and statues of a tanuki and a fox (**kitsune**).

*In front of the Tendo **dōjō** in* RANMA 1/2 *stands a gift of a ceramic **tanuki**.*

TANZAKU

 A strip of paper on which poems, and sometimes prayers, are written. These are hung during the **Tanabata** Festival, along with other ornaments, on a branch of bamboo in the garden in hope of a better future. They can also be attached to **fūrin** to catch the breeze.

A We see Kimiko and her daughter attaching tanzaku to bamboo during the Tanabata Festival in *GunBuster* (OVA 6).

TATAMI

 Floor mats made of straw with a rush surface and cloth border that measure approximately 6 x 3 feet. The mats are laid side by side to create the "floor" of a room, whose size is frequently measured by the number of standard tatami it contains. You never step on tatami unless you are in stockings or bare feet. After vacuuming or sweeping tatami you wipe them down with a slightly damp cloth.

M Tatami are often seen in historical settings and in many scenes in more traditional houses such as in *Ranma 1/2*.

TEIKOKU DAIGAKU (IMPERIAL UNIVERSITIES)

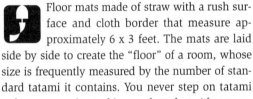 The universities established by the Imperial University Order of 1886. These were founded in several cities in the following order: Tokyo (**Tōkyō Daigaku**) 1886, **Kyoto** 1897, Sendai 1907, Fukuoka 1910, **Sapporo** 1918, Osaka 1931, and Nagoya 1939. The imperial universities were abolished as such after WWII, and the schools were reorganized into national universities.

A The imperial university is mentioned in Sanshiro the Judoist (pt. 1).

M In *Mermaid's Scar* (p. 55) Yuta speaks to Nae about her fiancé, an imperial university student.

TEMIZUYA

 A roofed basin with running water and ladles where you ritually cleanse your hands and rinse your mouth upon entering the grounds of a **Shintō** shrine. (For other forms of purification by water see **misogi, mizugori**.)

A We see temizuya examples at the shrine in the beginning of *Student Days*, behind the wedding party as they walk up the stairs in *Rupan III: The Fuma Conspiracy*, and after Ryo-Ohki is caught eating carrots in *Tenchi Universe* (tp. 2, ep. 7). • There is water flowing out of a temizuya and a closeup of the ladles in *Blue Seed* (tp. 5, ep. 10); in this case it is at a Buddhist temple rather than a Shintō shrine.

TENGU (MOUNTAIN SPIRIT)

A supernatural being, sometimes depicted as a human body with a bird's head and wings. Tengu are also depicted as being more humanlike, with a red face and long nose. Tengu can wear the garb of a **yamabushi** and carry a feather fan. Traditionally they live in trees and often protect certain mountains.

M In *Urusei Yatsura* (TV tp. 3, ep. 9, st. 17) and *Lum Urusei Yatsura: Perfect Collection* (p. 287) we see alien tengu wearing garb similar to yamabushi.

A Tengu are mentioned in *Blue Seed* (tp. 2, ep. 3) where the term is translated "long nosed goblins."

*Ladles in BLUE SEED are ready for visitors as water flows through this **temizuya**.*

©1995 YŪZŌ TAKADA /TAKESHOBŌ / BS PROJECT

Tengu are often associated with mountains, trees, and alien princesses.

TENISU (TENNIS)

 Tennis was introduced to Japan in 1878. Since equipment was difficult to come by a Japanese-style tennis evolved, with a softer ball. "Japanese" tennis is still played, but so is the more conventional variety, which is taken very seriously indeed. Space in tennis courts is scarce and may need to be reserved a month or more ahead of time. One thing you will notice in anime and manga is that almost everyone playing tennis is properly dressed in whites—as you would expect in Japan.

Ⓜ In *Maison Ikkoku* (vol. 1, p. 112ff) Kyoko starts attending the local housewives' tennis club. • Kyosuke and Madoka meet for tennis in *Kimagure Orange Road* (tp. 1, ep. 2). • Kubo plays at a tennis club in *Otaku no Video* (pt. 1, 1st anim. seq.).

TENNYO (HEAVENLY MAIDEN, NYMPH, ANGEL)

 Tennyo wear *hagoromo* ("wing-robes"), which enable them to fly. In the noh play *Hagoromo* a young fisherman finds one of these robes while a tennyo is bathing and takes it.

The tennyo asks for it back and the young man agrees, if she dances for him. Variants of this tale exist that have the man marrying the tennyo; in some cases they stay together for life, in others the tennyo gets the robe back and flees back to heaven. Some say that tennyo wives should not be allowed to see their robe until they have had three children, since a tennyo can only carry away two.

Ⓐ In *Urusei Yatsura* (TV tp. 14, ep. 54, st. 77), as a group of tennyo bathe in the sea, Ataru clutches to his face a wrap that he has found; but the wrap turns out, to his disgust, to be a loincloth (**fundoshi**).

Ⓜ The cover of *Return of Lum: Feudal Furor* depicts Lum as a tennyo.

TENSHŌ KEN'Ō SHISETSU

 On February 20, 1582 four Japanese boys left as emissaries to the courts of Philip II of Spain and Pope Gregory XIII. Their mission was part of an attempt by the Jesuits to publicize their work in Asia and to obtain an official monopoly on missionary work in Japan. The boys were Itō Mancio, Chijiwa Miguel, Nakaura Juliāo, and Hara Martinho; they were students of the Jesuit seminary and between 12 and 23 years old when they left. They were well received in Europe and were given many gifts to bring back with them. But when they returned in July 1590 they found that **Toyotomi Hideyoshi** had banned Christianity in Japan, and the young men were unable to publicly speak on what they had seen in Europe.

Ⓐ Kanuka challenges Takeo to name the emissaries of Tenshō in *Patlabor: New Files* (vol. 3, ep. 9).

TEPPŌ (FIREARMS)

Guns were first introduced into Japan in 1543 by shipwrecked Portuguese. That firearms were not introduced from China, in spite of the proximity of Japan and China, illustrates how isolated Japan was at that time. The military potential of the Portuguese harquebuses was quickly recognized by the Japanese, who began to learn the manufacturing techniques as fast as they could. The innovative military leader Oda Nobunaga bought 500 matchlocks in 1549 and established a firearms brigade in his army during the Warring States period (**Sengoku jidai**). Firearms were completely banned in the **Edo period**. Japan's Firearms and Sword Possession Control Law is the strictest weapons control law in the world. Police officers are not even allowed to carry firearms unless they are on duty, and many police never even draw their weapon during their entire career, much less ever fire their gun. A survey done in the late 1970s indicated that only 5.3 of all homicides in Japan involved guns and 0.8% of robberies. In 1979 there were 48 handgun murders in Japan and 9,848 in the United States. More than 90% of the guns in Japan are hunting rifles, including powerful air guns used mainly for target shooting or killing harmful animals. Permit owners are required to pass tests to prove they can properly use their weapons; every five years they must get their permits renewed and have their guns inspected for safety. More casual gun owners can buy excellent quality replicas of real guns that cannot fire real ammunition or that can only fire small pellets.

🅜 Many of the characters in *Sanctuary* obviously do not have permits for their weapons.

🅐 We see matchlock rifles used in *Hakkenden* (tp. 1, ep. 11) and found by Jigen in *Rupan III: The Fuma Conspiracy*. • Some members of TAC are allowed to carry firearms in *Blue Seed*. • Clancy's keeping a gun at home is highly illegal in *Patlabor: Original Series* (tp. 2, ep. 5). • We hear that the police did not even carry guns until after WWII in *Patlabor: Original Series* (tp. 2, ep. 4). • In *Here Is Greenwood* (tp. 1, ep. 2) a pellet gun is used by Shinobu and a high-quality rifle replica is owned by Nagisa. • Examples of model and pellet guns are a model gun shop in *Blue Seed* (tp. 2, ep. 4), the pellet firing guns in *Otaku no Video* (pt. 1, 4th anim. seq.), in *Urusei Yatsura* (TV tp. 15, ep. 56, st. 79), and in *Patlabor: New Files* (tp. 3, ep. 8).

TERUTERU BŌZU (RAIN DOLL)

 Small doll-like charms made with a ball or wad of stuffing and a piece of white cloth or paper tied just below. These are hung from the eaves of a house as a charm to invite good weather. If the weather is good a face may be added to the teruteru bōzu. In some rural areas farmers make them with black heads in the hope of getting some rain.

🅐 Dancing teruteru bōzu are seen during the rainy part of the ending animation to the first *Tenchi Muyo!* OVA series. • A teruteru bōzu with Kusanagi's face on it is in *Blue Seed* (tp. 5, Omake Theater). • A bag full of teruteru bōzu is given to Lum by Cherry in *Urusei Yatsura* (TV tp. 8, ep. 30, st. 53); Cherry is mistaken for a large teruteru bōzu in the same story.

TOBUKURO (POCKET DOOR)

 A boxlike structure for storing storm doors (**amado**), often built right into the outer wall adjoining the **engawa** or windows. While these often exist close to the ground at the end of the engawa, in older buildings they are usually seen in anime and manga near second-story windows since lower windows are often obscured by bushes or fences.

🅐 A tobukuro is seen as Sanshiro Sugata and Hansuke Murai talk in *Sanshiro the Judoist* (pt. 3).

*Kusanagi's visage on the **teruteru bozu** in BLUE SEED may have been enough to keep the rain away.*

TOKKURI (SAKE FLASK)

 Tokkuri come in a variety of sizes and shapes, but the most common is rather small and white. The tokkuri is filled with **sake** and then placed in boiling water (or these days, a microwave). While some drink directly from the tokkuri it is considered proper to pour the sake into a ceramic cup (**choko**), lacquered cup (**sakazuki**), or square wooden cup (**masu**).

A Yotsuya demonstrates his party skills by balancing several tokkuri on top of one in his mouth in *Maison Ikkoku: Welcome to Maison Ikkoku* (ep. 1). • Lord Awayuki drinks straight from a tokkuri in *Hakkenden* (tp. 6, ep. 10). • A tokkuri and two choko float in a wooden tray in an **onsen** in *Zenki* (tp. 4, ep. 9). • Choko and tokkuri are also seen in *Tenchi Muyo! Mihoshi Special*, in *Suikoden Demon Century*, and in the cat's flashback in *Urusei Yatsura* (TV tp. 14, ep. 51, st. 74).

M We see a kamikaze pilot drinking from a tokkuri in *Barefoot Gen* (p. 147).

TOKONOMA (DECORATIVE ALCOVE)

 The tokonoma is used in traditional Japanese rooms for the display of art such as a hanging scroll and a flower arrangement, or sometimes an incense burner. (In ryokan, the tokonoma is where the TV is often placed.) The floor of the tokonoma is raised a few inches higher than the floor of the room.

M A tokonoma can be seen behind Ataru's father in *Urusei Yatsura* (TV tp. 19, ep. 73, st. 96) and in *Lum Urusei Yatsura: Perfect Collection*, p. 183).

A A tokonoma is behind the grandmother during the meeting in *Blue Seed* (tp. 1, ep. 1) and behind the head of the Suminawa during his talk with Goemon in *Rupan III: The Fuma Conspiracy*.

TOKUGAWA

 The Tokugawa family ruled Japan during the **Edo period** (1603–1867). In 1600 Tokugawa Ieyasu defeated the heir of **Toyotomi Hideyoshi** and thereby gained military control

WHY'S EVERYONE LEFT-HANDED IN THIS MANGA?

Ever notice the number of southpaws in manga translations? Or the side of the car Rally's steering wheel is on in *Gunsmith Cats*? The steering wheel location may not be that noticeable to an American for a story that takes place in drive-on-the-left Tokyo, such as *Sanctuary*, but when the story is set in drive-on-the-right Chicago it looks a little strange.

In Japan as well as several other Asian nations, if you place a book rightside up the spine is on the right and the pages open left to right. But for the Western market manga images are usually flipped so that the books can be opened right to left. When the art is flipped right-handed characters become left-handed, steering wheels change sides, and cars go down the other side of the road. Some Japanese artists don't like flipping because it disrupts the design structure of the panels. In fact, some series may never be published in translation because the artists refuse to allow the pages to be reversed.

Some manga that have been published in their original format like *Ironfist*, *Comics Underground Japan*, and the "Special Collector's Edition" of *Neon Genesis Evangelion* seem to sell well enough, so perhaps more publishers will start issuing unflipped manga translations.

Note: Studio Proteus deserves credit for the many panels in *Gunsmith Cats* manga that have the steering wheel on the correct side of the vehicle and for its excellent work in adapting complex panel designs without flipping in the manga *Blade of the Immortal*.

of Japan; in 1603 the imperial court gave him the title of **shōgun**. The Tokugawa maintained total control of Japan until their removal from power in 1868. Today several branches of the family survive and some descendants have distinguished themselves in public service.

M The defeat of the Toyotomi by the Tokugawa clan is mentioned in *Mermaid's Scar* (p. 241).

TŌKYŌ DAIGAKU (TOKYO UNIVERSITY)

Established in 1877, Tōdai, as it is called, is the most prestigious university in Japan. At one time Tokyo University was part of the Imperial University system (**Teikoku Daigaku**). Ⓜ In *Sanctuary* (vol. 2, p. 104) a meeting takes place at Tokyo University; the main tower, a symbol of the campus, is clearly shown.

TŌKYŌ DŌMU

Japan's first indoor baseball stadium, it was completed in 1988. Located in Bunkyō Ward in the middle of Tokyo, it is the home of two professional baseball teams, the Yomiuri Giants of the Central League and the Nippon Ham Fighters of the Pacific League. Tōkyō Dome seats 56,000 people and is also used for concerts, exhibitions, and trade shows. Ⓐ We see "Tokyo Big Dome" in *Metal Fighters Miku* (tp. 1, ep. 2); in *Blue Seed* (tp. 2, ep. 4), where part of the Dome is damaged; and in *Otaku no Video* (pt. 2, 5th anim. seq.).

TŌKYŌ EKI (TOKYO STATION)

The city's major terminus. Originally built with steel-reinforced red brick and white stone, it was finished in 1914. The Marunouchi (western) side was modeled on the central station in Amsterdam. During WWII it suffered major damage, but it has since been restored to its original style. The building faces the Imperial Palace, and before WWII the main entrance was reserved for the imperial family. Today there is a second wing on the Yaesu (eastern) side of glass and steel built in 1968. Ⓐ Miyuki uses the old entrance when she enters the station in *You're Under Arrest* (OVA 3). • We also get a good view of many aspects of the station when the students arrive and when Tenchi gets ready to go to **Tōkyō Tawā** in *Tenchi Muyo in Love*. Ⓜ Yoshio catches a train at Tokyo Station in *Adolf: Days of Infamy* (p. 14).

The European style of the Marunouchi side of **Tōkyō Eki**, seen here in YOU'RE UNDER ARREST, is a famous landmark.

TŌKYŌ KOKUSAI KŪKŌ

Also known as Haneda Airport. It opened in 1931; in 1952, after being decommissioned as a U.S. military facility, it became Tokyo International Airport. Since the 1978 opening of the New Tokyo International Airport, **Shin Tōkyō Kokusai Kūkō**, in Narita, Haneda has mostly handled domestic flights. A monorail connects the airport to Hamamatsuchō Station on the Japan Railways (**Jē Āru**) Yamanote line. Ⓐ Noa and Asuma fly into Haneda Airport in *Patlabor: Original Series* (vol. 3, ep. 6).

TŌKYŌ TAWĀ (TOKYO TOWER)

Built in 1958 in Minato Ward as a broadcast tower, Tokyo Tower is the tallest structure in Tokyo, with a height of 1,090 feet (100 feet higher than Paris's Eiffel Tower, which it strongly resembles) and two observation decks that are popular with tourists and offer a wonderful view of the central city. Ⓐ Tokyo Tower was used in the fourth lecture in *GunBuster* to indicate the relative size of other objects. • Tokyo Tower is seen in the sequence with the monster Pyogora's attack on Tokyo in *801 TTS Airbats* (pt. 1). • In *Phantom Quest Corp.* (tp. 1, ep. 1) the higher observation deck (250 meters from the

In PATLABOR: NEW FILES *we get a view of the lower observation deck of* Tōkyō Tawā.

ground) is the location of the battle with the vampire. • In *Urusei Yatsura* (tp. 1, ep. 2, st. 4) Tokyo Tower becomes the nesting site for a swallow. • Tokyo Tower is the location of the climax in *Tenchi Muyo in Love*.

Ⓜ In *Sanctuary* (vol. 1, p. 32) a meeting takes place at Tokyo Tower.

TŌKYŌ TOCHŌSHA (TOKYO METROPOLITAN GOVERNMENT OFFICES)

 Located in **Shinjuku** Ward in western Tokyo, the metro government's offices are housed in three buildings for some 13,000 employees. The distinctive shape of the twin towers of Office Building Number One, with the helicopter pad atop one of the towers, is now a famous Tokyo landmark.

Ⓐ At the beginning of *Bubblegum Crisis* (OVA 1) we see the old, damaged Office Building Number One of the future being demolished; we see a similar scene in *Metal Fighters Miku* (tp. 5, ep. 10). • The twin towers of Office Building Number One are seen in the opening sequence of *Blue Seed* (tp. 1, ep. 1). • In *Patlabor: Original Series* we see the building as Asuka walks to the toilet (tp. 1, ep. 2); in *Patlabor: New Files* (tp. 3, ep. 10) the building is seen many times. • The towers are seen among skyscrapers early on in *Suikoden Demon Century*.

TORII (SHRINE GATE)

 Torii are tall archlike gates or archlike structures traditionally placed at the entrance to a **Shintō** shrine or (rarely) a Buddhist temple. They come in a variety of designs and materials. Torii are often painted red. The most primitive torii is two upright posts with a **shimenawa** tied between them. If you see a row of torii forming a tunnel you know you are at an **Inari** shrine.

Ⓐ At the beginning of *Rupan III: The Fuma Conspiracy* you see a scene with red torii and stairs. • Torii appear in *Kimagure Orange Road: I Want to Return to That Day*, *Blue Seed* (tp. 1, ep. 1), and *Vampire Princess Miyu* (tp. 1, ep. 1). • A crude wooden torii is near the ferryman's hut in *Hakkenden* (tp. 3, ep. 6); a concrete torii is in *Blue Seed* (tp. 1, ep. 1).

Ⓜ In *Mai the Psychic Girl: Perfect Collection* (vol. 1, p. 87) we see a torii in the *myōjin* style.

TOSO

 A drink made of **sake** and medicinal spices commonly drunk at New Year's. Toso came from China and was adopted by the court during the **Heian period**.

Ⓜ Lum and Ataru's family are getting ready for their New Year's meal in *Return of Lum: Trouble Times Ten* (p. 40). Notice the soup bowls, sake cups and flasks, and the lacquered boxes (**jūbako**).

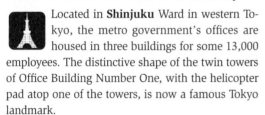

Asuma's hunt for a toilet in PATLABOR: ORIGINAL SERIES *gives us a clear view of the* Tōkyō Tochōsha *buildings.*

*This **torii** in Blue Seed spans a wide concrete road.*

TOYOTOMI HIDEYOSHI

1537–98. Hideyoshi, the son of a farmer, in 1558 entered the service of the warlord Oda Nobunaga, who gave him the nickname Saru ("monkey") because of his looks. Quickly he demonstrated his skills and rose up the ranks to general. After Nobunaga was assassinated by Akechi Mitsuhide in 1582, Hideyoshi quickly defeated the armies of Mitsuhide to gain control over several key provinces. After a series of battles he was able to make peace in 1584 with a rival, **Tokugawa** Ieyasu, and acquire more power. After Hideyoshi's death in 1598 his son Toyotomi Hideyori held power for a short period of time until his armies were defeated by Ieyasu in 1600, which led to the Tokugawa shogunate in 1603. Toyotomi Hideyori lived in Osaka Castle until conflict again broke out, resulting in his final defeat and suicide in 1615.

🅜 The defeat of the Toyotomi clan is mentioned in *Mermaid's Scar* (p. 241).

TSUKEMONO (PICKLE)

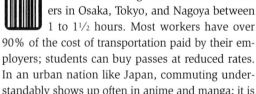

An essential part of traditional Japanese meals or drinking. There are many types of pickles in Japan as well as pickling methods. Most pickles are made with vegetables, but some use seafood or meat. Some pickling methods take very little time, only two or three hours,

while others take months. The most common methods include using salt (*shiozuke*), which is the method used to make **umeboshi**; vinegar (*suzuke*), which is intended for quick consumption; rice bran (*nukazuke*); **sake** lees (*kasuzuke*); **miso** (*miso-zuke*); rice mold (*kōjizuke*); and soy sauce (**shōyu**) mixed with mirin (*shōyuzuke*). *Nukazuke* is unique to Japan and involves placing vegetables in a rice bran and salt water mixture that has been kneaded until it looks and feels like miso.

🅐 Ranma and Genma fight over an eggplant pickle in *Ranma 1/2: It's Fast or It's Free* (ep. 2). • Mitsuru steals Hasukawa's pickle in the second breakfast (**chōshoku**) scene in *Here Is Greenwood* (tp. 1, ep. 1).

TSUKIMONO OTOSHI (EXORCISM)

In Japan exorcism is performed by someone with the proper training, often a **yamabushi**. There are several types of spirits that can possess a person, and only someone with the proper training and the right techniques can drive them out. Generally this involves forcing the spirit to state its reason for possessing an individual and then negotiating terms for its departure.

🅜 Sakura in *Urusei Yatsura* (TV tp. 2, ep. 5, st. 9; *Lum Urusei Yatsura: Perfect Collection*, pp. 80–88) attempts to exorcise the spirits associated with Ataru.

🅐 Rokkon in *Phantom Quest Corp.* has among his skills the ability to perform exorcisms.

TSŪKIN (COMMUTING)

In 1990 commuting took 40% of the workers in Osaka, Tokyo, and Nagoya between 1 to 1½ hours. Most workers have over 90% of the cost of transportation paid by their employers; students can buy passes at reduced rates. In an urban nation like Japan, commuting understandably shows up often in anime and manga; it is most evident in the proliferation of busses and trains depicted. Characters are also heard to comment on the length of their commute.

A Tenchi's father, Nobuyuki, complains of having such a long commute home in *Tenchi Universe* (tp. 1, ep. 1); later, in *Tenchi Muyo in Love*, we see Tenchi's mother as a high school girl making the same complaint.

TSUNOKAKUSHI (HEADDRESS)

Sometimes worn by brides at weddings, this (literally, "horn-hiding") headdress is supposed to suppress and hide the feminine "horn of jealousy."

M Note the jealousy of the horned Lum in *Urusei Yatsura*.

A The headdress can be seen at the beginning of *Rupan III: The Fuma Conspiracy*.

TSURI-DŌRŌ (HANGING LANTERN)

Most commonly made of bronze, these are pierced and sometimes have paper linings inside. Famous tsuri-dōrō include the massive, 13-foot one at Tōdaiji, a Buddhist temple in Nara, and the over 1,000 examples at Kasuga Shrine, also in Nara.

A We see a single tsuri-dōrō at the early shrine scene in *Blue Seed* (tp. 2, ep. 3); later in the series (*Rebirth*, ep. 14) we see a single lantern with a pattern on its paper insert, and then we see a row of them. • Tsuri-dōrō are also seen in *Tale of Genji*.

TSURU (CRANE)

Seven species of cranes are found in Japan. It is considered an auspicious bird and a symbol of a long life. The expression "the voice of the crane" is sometimes used to refer to the breaking of deadlocks in decision making by a higher authority.

A A flying crane is seen as Goto returns to Division 2 by boat in *Patlabor 2*. • The crane and turtle are spoken of as good luck symbols in *Urusei Yatsura* (TV tp. 9, ep. 31, st. 54); Ten reads a book with a crane on the cover (TV tp. 14, ep. 52, st. 75).

BLOODY NOSES AND SEX

The bloody nose, which turns up again and again, is one of those cultural details that seems not to have been covered in any of the secondary literature I have read. So I asked a few Japanese and got a variety of pseudoscientific, and occasionally embarrassed, explanations about humidity and blood pressure.

But the best response I got was from one fellow who simply recounted that when he was a child he was told by his mother that if he stared at a pretty woman he would get a bloody nose. So the bloody nose in manga and anime is associated almost exclusively with men looking at scantily clad and undressed women. Whether they are extremely lustful idiots like Ataru in *Urusei Yatsura* or shy gentle fellows like Hasukawa, whom Sumire hugs in *Here Is Greenwood*, blood flows.

This device can be useful for writers who want to add humor to their work, and that is how it is used again and again.

You even see Ohta in *Patlabor* get a nosebleed just by looking at a really big gun (*Original Series*, OVA 6)—but then Ohta has a thing for firearms.

TSŪSHŌ SANGYŌ SHŌ (MINISTRY OF INTERNATIONAL TRADE AND INDUSTRY)

Commonly known in the West as MITI, the Ministry of International Trade and Industry is responsible for formulating and implementing trade and industrial policy. Much of Japan's growth and development as an industrialized nation is considered a result of MITI's planning and guidance. There is no parallel body to this ministry in any other industrialized nation.

M In *Sanctuary* (vol. 3, p. 7) mention is made of MITI.

TSŪTENKAKU (OSAKA TOWER)

 Commonly known as **Osaka** Tower. Built in 1956, this 335-foot tower with its observation deck is a symbol of the city of Osaka. It is in the Shinsekai ("New World") entertainment district.

A The tower is briefly seen in *Blue Seed* (tp. 10, ep. 20).

M Akogiville has a not so strangely similar tower in *Caravan Kid* (vol. 1, p. 224).

Tsūtenkaku, as seen in Blue Seed, *stands against the Osaka nighttime sky.*

UCC COFFEE

A popular brand of canned coffee sold in tall slender cans in Japan. I have recently seen this beverage in regular aluminum cans in California.

A A UCC can is among other trash after the assembly in *GunBuster* (OVA 1). • In *Oh My Goddess!* (tp. 1) Keiichi trips over a UCC can while getting up to help Belldandy make tea. • Toward the end of *Neon Genesis Evangelion* (tp. 12, ep. 23) Misato switches to UCC coffee as her beverage of choice. After this episode aired on TV the manufacturer of UCC coffee sold cans with characters from the series printed on them.

UCHIWA (NON-FOLDING FAN)

 The round, flat fan was probably introduced into Japan from China or Korea in the Nara period. These stiff fans are made of bamboo ribs covered in paper or cloth. Military commanders would carry iron fans called *gunbai uchiwa*.

A A non-folding fan is packed by the dorm mates early in *Oh My Goddess!* (OVA 1). • An uchiwa is used to fan a flame by the grandfather in *Tenchi Universe* (tp. 6, ep. 17).

UENO

 This north-central district in Taitō Ward in Tokyo originally was a temple town for the temple Kan'eiji.

M Mai and her father stay at a **ryokan** in this area in *Mai the Psychic Girl: Perfect Collection* (vol. 1, p. 55).

UENO DŌBUTSUEN (UENO ZOO)

The first and most famous of Japan's zoos. It was founded in 1882 in the **Ueno** district of Tokyo and in 1924 was taken over by the Tokyo Metropolitan Government. The zoo functions both as a recreational and research facility.

A Ueno Zoo is mentioned by Tofu's mother in *Ranma 1/2* (TV sub tp. 5, dub tp. 7, ep. 14).

UENO EKI (UENO TRAIN STATION)

 Built in 1883, this station is one of Japan's major transportation centers and the departure point for trains heading north to the Tōhoku region.

 In *Mai the Psychic Girl: Perfect Collection* (vol. 1, p. 62) Mai and her father catch a train here.

UENO KŌEN (UENO PARK)

This Tokyo park opened to the public in 1873 and has a zoo (**Ueno Dōbutsuen**), the temple Kan'eiji, a nearby shopping area, and several art and science museums. Ueno Kōen is the location of a famous statue of **Saigō Takamori**.

The conclusion of a *Patlabor: Original Series* story (tp. 1, ep. 1) takes place here.

Mai and her father go through Ueno Kōen in *Mai the Psychic Girl: Perfect Collection* (vol. 1, p. 65).

UMA-YAKU

Kabuki actors who play horses. A kabuki horse has a papier-mâché head and cloth body on a wooden frame. The "horse" contains two men in tight trousers, one in front of the other, who carry another actor on their back. The actors need great skill to work together on

*A can of **UCC coffee** in* OH MY GODDESS! *sits on the floor; notice how slender it is compared to most aluminum soda cans.*

© 1993 KOUSUKE FUJISHIMA / KŌDANSHA / TBS / KSS

stage. *Uma-no-ashi*, "horse's leg," is a popular term for uma-yaku.

We see uma-yaku in *Urusei Yatsura* (TV tp. 13, ep. 50, st. 73) with the sounds of hooves made by coconut shells.

UME

 Prunus mume or *Armeniaca mume*. Japanese apricot or Japanese plum is the most common translation of this early summer fruit's name. It is eaten fresh but mainly used to make **umeboshi** pickles and **umeshu**, or plum wine. It is in these two forms that ume generally shows up in anime and manga.

UMEBOSHI (SALTED JAPANESE APRICOT)

 Sometimes improperly referred to as a plum. This is probably the best known of Japanese pickled fruit. **Ume** are packed in salt and colored red with *akajiso* (red beefsteak plant) leaves. The flavor is salty and sour. Eating umeboshi every day is said to keep you healthy, so umeboshi are often seen in the middle of the rice in the school lunch **bentō** that mothers make for their children. There is also a tradition of placing an umeboshi in your tea on the morning of the first day of the New Year to insure good health for the coming year.

Much to the disadvantage of everyone else Lum and Ten discover the joys of eating umeboshi in *Urusei Yatsura* (TV tp. 11, ep. 42, st. 65).

UMESHU (PLUM "WINE")

 "Plum wine" is the usual translation, but this is not the overly sweet stuff made from ripe plums you find in some liquor stores. Umeshu is a mixture of sweet and tart that is hard to define. You can be sure you are getting the right stuff if there is a green ume at the bottom of the bottle. Many families prefer to make their own at home. Umeshu is very good for sore throats.

Ataru and Megane try to drink Onsen Mark's umeshu in *Urusei Yatsura* (TV tp. 19, ep. 74, st. 97).

Godai's grandmother drinks, and shares, her homemade umeshu in *Maison Ikkoku* (vol. 5, p. 133).

UNAGI (EEL)

 Eels are considered a good food for building stamina and for this reason are traditionally eaten on the hottest days of the year. A common way of cooking them is to baste them with a sauce and serve them on top of rice. This dish is called *unajū* and is often served in a lacquer box.

 Unagi are ordered for Sakura and Cherry, and how expensive it is is pointed out in *Urusei Yatsura* (TV tp. 14, ep. 51, st. 74).

 In *Ranma 1/2* (vol. 5, p. 27) Tofu-**sensei** gives Ranma an eel to deliver to Mr. Tendo.

URASHIMA TARŌ

 Urashima Tarō is a fisherman who saved and set free a turtle that was being abused. There are several variants of this story, but the common feature is that the man rode the turtle to Ryūgū-jō, or Dragon's Palace. He was welcomed and lived there for some time but eventually decided he wanted to go home. He was given a box as a parting gift by the princess of the palace with instructions never to open it. When he got back home he found that his village had greatly changed and no one knew who he was. Eventually he decided to open the box to see if it contained anything that could help him. Instantly he was turned into an old man; it had been 300 years since he had left his home.

 Onsen Mark thinks he is Urashima Tarō in *Urusei Yatsura* (TV tp. 14, ep. 54, st. 77), and the story is discussed in *Urusei Yatsura: Beautiful Dreamer*. • Reference to the story is made in *Blue Seed* (tp. 8, ep. 16).

UTA KARUTA (POEM CARD)

 Traditionally played at New Year's is a card game involving 100 poems by 100 famous poets. On one set of cards is the full poem; on a second set is the last two lines. The second set is divided up among the players and laid out face up on the floor. A reader, who does not play the game, slowly begins to read a poem from the first deck. Each player tries to be the first to pick up the card showing the second half of the poem. If you win the card that is in front of another player you get to give them a card. The first player to get rid of all of their cards wins. Sometime the game is played by groups. Uta-karuta is sometimes referred to as *karuta hajime* or *hyakunin isshu*, which is also the title of the 13th-century book the poems come from.

 This game is being played in *Urusei Yatsura* (TV tp. 3, ep. 11, sts. 21–22) and in *Return of Lum: Trouble Times Ten* (p. 49).

WASEDA DAIGAKU (WASEDA UNIVERSITY)

 Founded in 1882 by Ōkuma Shigenobu, Waseda is one of the major private universities of Tokyo. It regularly sends graduates to major corporations and is thus frequently the goal of those who endure Examination Hell (**shiken jigoku**).

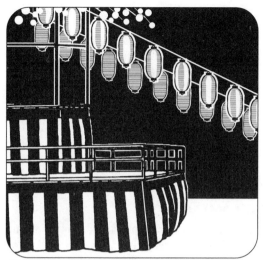

*With lanterns strung, all that is needed on the **yagura** is the **Bon** musicians and dancers.*

 Hyokichi decides to go to Waseda Daigaku in *Theater of Life*.

WATER HOLDING AS PUNISHMENT

Holding water in the hallway is a punishment sometimes used in Japanese schools. There is a story about the writer **Miyazawa Kenji** as a child thoughtfully drinking some of the water from a heavy bowl that a friend of his was holding in the school hallway.

Ⓜ Ranma, Akane, and Kuno are all punished at school by being made to hold buckets in the hallway in *Ranma 1/2* (TV tp. 1, ep. 2; vol. 1, p. 91).

WHITE DAY

 March 14. **Sei Barentain no shukujitsu** in Japan has traditionally been a day for women to give chocolate, so the confectioners wanted to get men to give their products to women. Their promotion of White Day did not quite go as planned, as men started giving other types of gifts as well, like lingerie.

Ⓐ Ten is misinformed about the meaning of White Day by both Ataru and Lum in *Urusei Yatsura* (TV tp. 16, ep. 59, st. 82).

YAGURA (STAGE)

 Elevated temporary stages for drummers and other musicians. They are often erected for community celebrations like the summertime **Bon** Festival.

Ⓜ In *Maison Ikkoku* we see a yagura under construction (vol. 3, p. 114) and then people dancing around it (vol. 3, pp. 114, 124).

YAKISOBA (NOODLES)

Steamed **rāmen**—not soba—noodles mixed on a hot plate with vegetables, meat, and sauce. It is served with a type of *benishōga* (pickled ginger) and seaweed flakes. A quick and simple food, it is sometimes served on the street from **yatai**.

Ⓐ Yakisoba is cooked at the **ennichi** in *Kimagure Orange Road* (tp. 1, ep. 1), by Shampoo's great grandmother in *Ranma 1/2: Fowl Play* (ep . 2), by

*Yakisoba is turned with **ichimonji** on a hot griddle in the* Tenchi Universe *TV series.*

145

Kiyone in *Tenchi Universe* (tp. 2, ep. 7), and by Ryuunosuke in *Urusei Yatsura* (OVA 5, pt. 1). • Yakisoba is used to bribe Cherry in *Urusei Yatsura* (TV tp. 12, ep. 46, st. 69). • Keiichi's first takeout order attempt is for Shanghai Yakisoba in *Oh My Goddess!* (OVA 1).

Ⓜ Ukyo uses yakisoba as a weapon in *Ranma 1/2* (vol. 8, p. 29), yet another example of the martial arts resourcefulness of Takahashi's characters.

YAKITORI

 Small bits of chicken or other bird meat and organs with vegetables, skewered on bamboo and grilled over charcoal. This is an inexpensive food frequently enjoyed by salarymen (**sararīman**) stopping off for a few drinks and a little to eat on the way home.

Ⓐ We hear yakitori mentioned in *Urusei Yatsura* (OVA 2, pt. 1). • Kosaku breaks his diet and buys five sticks of yakitori for ¥500 in *One Pound Gospel*.

YAKUZA (GANGSTER)

 "Yakuza" is translated as gangster, gambler, good-for-nothing but literally means "8, 9, 3," a losing hand from a popular card game of the **Edo period**. Usually the term refers to persons involved in organized crime. Yakuza are often associated with right-wing politics and have taken part in attacks on protesters. They are also famous for their tattoos (**irezumi**) and elaborate codes of honor and behavior. In 1990 the majority of arrests of yakuza involved stimulant drugs, infliction of bodily injury, blackmail, and gambling.

Ⓜ *Sanctuary* heavily involves yakuza.

Ⓐ Yakuza are mentioned when Miyoshi is introduced in *Otaku no Video* (pt. 1, 3rd anim. seq.). • A yakuza with a large tattoo appears in the **sentō** in *Patlabor: New Files* (tp. 2, ep. 7).

YAMABUSHI (MOUNTAIN ASCETIC)

 Originally this term was applied to those ascetics who practice austerities in the mountains to gain magical powers and holy abilities. It has also come to be used to refer to members of the **Shugendō** order. The traditional garb of a yamabushi includes, among other things, a small cap (*tokin*), baggy trousers (*suzukake*), a collar with colored tufts (*yuigesa*), a Buddhist rosary (*nenju*), and a staff with rings (*shakujō*).

Ⓐ In the first episode of *Zenki* we see two corrupt yamabushi break into a building on the shrine grounds, with bad results. • The character Rokkon in *Phantom Quest Corp.* (tp. 1, ep. 2) is in the garb of a yamabushi.

YANAGI (WILLOW)

 Many species of willow grow in Japan. The weeping willow, *shidareyanagi* or *itoyanagi*, originally came from China. Willow wood is used to make **geta**, match sticks, cutting boards, and drawing boards.

Ⓐ We see a willow when Okoto trips in *Tale of Shunkin*. • In the beginning of *Growing Up* we see willows at the entrance to the Yoshiwara district.

YANKĪ ("YANKEE," JUVENILE DELINQUENT)

 The origin of the term is open to discussion, but it comes from a corruption of **yakuza** or some association with American vulgarity. Yankī are junior high and senior high school kids whose main activities seem to be hanging around streets on weekend nights and occasionally getting into trouble. Fashions change, but the Yankī styles common in the '80s are easy to recognize in several anime and manga. Yankī boys have hair that is permed in a wave or combed straight back. Occasionally the hair is bleached or dyed. The stereotypical Yankī attire is a modified school uniform with baggy high-waist pants, longer jacket hems, and a correspondingly higher collar. The jackets often have colorful linings with flowers or dragon designs. Other signs include shaved temples, sunglasses with sharply angled lenses, aloha shirts, clothing in primary colors, and women's sandals with thin heels (remember we are talking about boys' clothing here). Yankī girls have heavy make-up, curl and bleach or dye their hair, wear knit cardigans in primary colors, and like tank tops, women's sandals with thin heels, miniskirts, and black net stockings. If they are wearing school uniforms their skirts may be longer than the standard set by the schools they attend. Yankī who graduate from hanging out on the street, often in their school uniforms after hours, may join the **bōsōzoku**, considered the elite of Yankī youth. Some of the Yankī styles have blended into the general population, so simply having dyed hair or slightly unusual clothing is not enough to identify someone as a Yankī.

 The main characters in *Shonan Bakusozoku* were Yankī before they were members of bōsōzoku groups.

YATAI (OUTDOOR STALL)

Mobile outdoor stalls or carts where inexpensive food is cooked and served. While their numbers have declined yatai are still seen in Japanese cities. Sometimes they have **noren** and a small area with benches or stools for customers. A yatai will usually specialize in one food or style of food. Many serve alcoholic beverages and can be identified by the red lantern (**aka-chōchin**) hung out front.

 In *Urusei Yatsura* (tp. 1, ep. 3, st. 6) we see a yatai in the park. • A yatai with red noren serving **rāmen** is in *Neon Genesis Evangelion* (tp. 6, ep. 12). ◩ In *Lum Urusei Yatsura: Perfect Collection* (p. 145) we see an *ishiyaki-imo-ya* (sweet potato seller) yatai stand and another selling corn on the cob in a park. • In *Sanctuary* (vol. 4, p. 201) we see a yatai on a street in **Sapporo** with stools for the customers. • Kyoko's dad and Godai have a few drinks together at a yatai in *Maison Ikkoku* (vol. 3, p. 48).

YOBIKŌ (CRAM SCHOOL)

Special schools for students preparing for college entrance exams. The attendees are usually high school graduates who have yet to pass an entrance exam or high school stu-

IS IT LUPIN OR RUPAN OR WOLF?

The master thief Lupin was the main character of the crime story series by the French writer Maurice LeBlanc at the turn of the century. When the manga artist Monkey Punch decided to do a few stories with a Lupin III character in honor of these works he did not expect the stories to be so popular that he would still be doing them 30 years later. He also did not expect trademark problems to arise from taking the name of a character from writings by a long-dead author. In fact the artist intended his work to be an homage to the French stories he had greatly enjoyed.

But the LeBlanc family thought otherwise (years later by the way), for when they found out about Lupin III they raised an international stink. I think they should have just taken advantage of the situation and pushed for more translations of the original stories. But the complaint presented a problem for U.S. companies that wanted to put out the Lupin anime in America. So Streamline changed Lupin's name to Wolf, a literal translation, and AnimEigo used an alternative transliteration of the Japanese pronunciation and called him Rupan. The name changes are apparently no longer necessary, since the trademark has reportedly expired. Lupin can now use his real name when appearing on video in the U.S. Unfortunately it has been too many years since the last U.S. release of a Lupin III anime.

dents who are hoping to improve their chances of entering a good college. Some cram schools are for even younger students hoping to get into a better high school after they graduate from middle school.

 Ataru is followed by Lum and Cherry to what he has claimed is a cram school in *Urusei Yatsura* (TV tp. 3, ep. 9, st. 18). • Cram school is mentioned in *Student Days*.

GESTURES

The meanings of hand gestures vary worldwide according to culture. Gestures in Japan don't necessarily have the same meaning as elsewhere.

1. In Japan something that looks like what we would call waving, palm down, fingers moving up and down, means "come here." This can be seen in *Metal Fighters Miku* (tp. 2, ep. 4), in *Ranma 1/2* (OVA 1, "Shampoo's Sudden Switch! The Curse of the Contrary Jewel"), as well as in several other anime. Ataru uses this come-here gesture to Lum before giving her the yellow ribbon in *Urusei Yatsura* (TV tp. 2, ep. 7, st. 13).

2. When you hold up your little finger you are referring to a girlfriend or mistress. This is seen in *Oh My Goddess!* (tp. 1) when Keiichi and Belldandy are looking for a place to stay. In *Ranma 1/2* (sub tp. 5, dub tp. 7, ep. 14), when Dr. Tofu's mother is first talking with Kasumi, she holds up her little finger. Sakamoto uses his little finger gesture to hint that Godai has arrived at a bad time in *Maison Ikkoku* (vol. 3, p. 255). Tokai in *Sanctuary* (vol. 3, p. 19) uses this gesture when talking about Japanese girls.

3. Holding a hand flat in front of the face and waving it back and forth is very similar to the Western shaking of the head in disagreement. Mink's friend Lufa waves her hand in front of her face in *Dragon Half* (pt. 1).

4. When the Japanese refer to themselves they do not point at their chest but at their face. We see this in the meeting after the suit accident in *Metal Fighters Miku* (tp. 2, ep. 4). Urd uses this gesture in *Oh My Goddess!* (tp. 4).

5. Mimicking the tipping of a sake cup is a gesture used to invite one to have a drink. This is done by Ryuichi in *Voice from Heaven*. A woman makes this gesture to Sasuke in *Tale of Shunkin*.

6. Children hook little fingers together to seal a promise. This is called *yubi-kiri* ("finger cutting"). We can see this gesture in *Friendship* and *Urusei Yatsura* (TV tp. 8, ep. 30, st. 53).

YOPPARAI (A DRUNK)

Alcohol has long played a role in Japanese society. **Sake** is among the traditional religious offerings to the **kami** and is drunk at weddings and other ceremonial occasions. In a highly structured society like Japan, alcohol serves as a social lubricator. Being drunk also allows you to act in ways that would not be tolerated in other circumstances. Japan in fact is called a paradise for drunks, for it treats the inebriated (except drunk drivers) with great indulgence. Late-night trains are full of tipsy commuters on their way home, and entertainment districts are accustomed to public retching and urination (see **tachishōben**). Most Japanese show a distinct "alcohol flush" (red face) when drinking.

A In *Patlabor: New Files* (tp. 3, ep. 9) several members of Unit Two on leave drink a great deal in an uncomfortable situation to avoid responsibility for their actions. • We see a drunk salaryman on his way home with a box of snacks in *Urusei Yatsura* (TV tp. 12, ep. 44, st. 67). • In two scenes in *El-Hazard* (tp. 3, "Fifth Night") we see Jinnai's and Shayla-Shayla's faces getting red from drinking, Miyuki and Natsumi are red-faced in *You're Under Arrest* (OVA 3), and Akane's and her friends' faces are flushed in *Kimagure Orange Road* (OVA 4, ep. 1).

M To cover up a red face, makeup is applied to Yoshi's face before he performs a wedding ceremony in *Rumic Theater* (p. 39). • In *Maison Ikkoku* (vol. 3, p. 109) Godai says that Kyoko is blushing from embarrassment, but Mrs. Ichinose accuses her of being drunk.

YŌSHI (ADOPTION)

In Japan adoption is primarily concerned with the continuity of the household. Historically adoptions have also been used to strengthen political alliances between families. The person adopted is usually a relative or from a family well known to the new parents. In the practice known as *muko yōshi*, a couple with no male heir adopts their son-in-law to continue the family name. In *fūfu yōshi* a married couple is adopted. Rarely, a son judged unworthy to carry on the family traditions will be supplanted by a more qualified adopted male.

A At the beginning of *Ranma 1/2* (tp. 1, ep. 1) Soun Tendo is explaining to his daughters that one of them will be engaged to Ranma so that the family tradition can continue. • In *Rupan III: The Fuma Conspiracy* Goemon is told as part of his wedding ceremony that he is going to become a member of the Suminawa clan.

YUINŌ (BETROTHAL GIFT)

A ceremonial exchange of cash and gifts that takes place between families when a couple becomes engaged. In some areas it is simply a gift from the groom's side, but in the Kantō (Tokyo) region the bride's family presents a gift worth about half that of the groom's. Today this exchange is less traditional and may take place in a hotel or restaurant with an exchange of keepsakes. Some of the traditional gifts include symbols of good luck such as abalone (*awabi*), dried squid (*surume*), dried kelp (*konbu*), and linen thread (*tomoshiraga*).

A Yuinō can be seen in *Ranma 1/2: Nihao My Concubine*.

YUKATA (LIGHTWEIGHT KIMONO)

A type of informal, unlined **kimono** made of light cotton. Yukata are strictly seasonal or indoor wear, as they offer no protection from cold weather. They are commonly worn at festivals in the summer, by guests staying at inns (**ryokan**), and when going to and coming from a public bath house (**sentō**). Women's and men's yukata are very similar, but women's yukata sometimes have more feminine patterns, such as flowers or leaves.

A Yukata and **haori** are worn by SV2 members on the walkways of a ryokan in *Patlabor: New Files* (tp. 3, ep. 9). • The girls wear yukata at an inn in *Metal Fighters Miku* (tp. 6, ep. 12). • Kome wears a yukata in the summer in *Blue Seed* (tp. 7, Omake Theater).

YŪREI (GHOST)

In Japan a ghost is a spirit of a dead person, though this is sometimes confused with *yōkai* (**bakemono**). A ghost appears in the form of a person and has a reason for staying behind; it manifests itself to family or intimate acquaintances. Persons who have died unnatural or violent deaths are more likely to become ghosts. Vengeful ghosts who haunt someone are called **goryō**; another kind of harmful spirit is the *mononoke*, which can cause illness or death. Sometimes ghosts, or other preternatural beings, will be accompanied by or manifested as floating lights or flames (**hitodama**).

A Several yūrei that haunt men include Maiko in *Urusei Yatsura* (OVA 4, pt. 1), Nagisa in *Urusei Yatsura* (OVA 5, pt. 1), and Misako in *Here Is Greenwood* (tp. 2, ep. 4). • In *Phantom Quest Corp.* (tp. 2, ep. 3, "Love Me Tender") we see a male ghost staying behind to protect his love.

You wouldn't guess that these three young women wearing **yukata** in METAL FIGHTERS MIKU are pro-wrestlers, would you?

ZABUTON (FLOOR CUSHION)

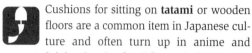

Cushions for sitting on **tatami** or wooden floors are a common item in Japanese culture and often turn up in anime and manga. Originating in the **Edo period**, zabuton were at first used only in the cold seasons but now are used year round.

Ⓐ In *Urusei Yatsura* (TV tp. 1, ep. 4, st. 1) several characters sit on zabuton. • Momiji's mother sits on a zabuton in *Blue Seed* (tp. 1, ep. 1). • In *Ranma* (TV tp. 1, ep. 1) Soun Tendo is sitting on one of these when he is speaking to his daughters about Ranma.

Ⓜ Princess Kurama is on two zabuton in *Lum Urusei Yatsura: Perfect Collection* (p. 301). • In *Maison Ikkoku* (vol. 1, p. 54) Godai offers Ikuko a zabuton to sit on.

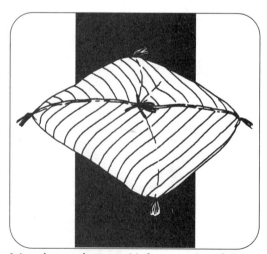

It is an honor to have you visit; here, come in and sit on a **zabuton**.

ZASHIKI WARASHI

A household god said to live in the homes of old and wealthy families in northern **Honshu**. He is said to be a red-faced mischievous boy with long shoulder-length hair.

Ⓜ When Princess Kurama calls Shinobu "jailbait" in *Urusei Yatsura* (tp. 3, ep. 9, st. 17) and the "legendary ghost boy" in *Lum Urusei Yatsura: Perfect Collection* (p. 296), the original Japanese in both cases is "zashiki warashi."

Ⓐ In *Patlabor: New Files* (tp. 3, ep. 9) Asuma says Noa looks like a zashiki warashi, but being from **Hokkaidō** she does not know what he means.

ZENKI

One of the two demon attendants of **En no Gyōja**. A village at the base of Mt. Omine proudly claims descent from, and is named after, Zenki.

Ⓐ Zenki is of course the title character of the *Zenki* TV series.

ZŌKI ISHIOKU (ORGAN TRANSPLANT)

The Japanese legal definition of brain death is such that there is a shortage of suitable organs for transplant; this is a source of tremendous controversy. Recently Japanese law has been changed so that transplants are easier than in the past and a system for donor registration has been set up.

Ⓐ In *Phantom Quest Corp.* (tp. 1, ep. 2) there is a hospital director who takes unusual means to obtain organs for transplant, a most profitable operation.

ZŌNI

A simple soup traditionally consumed with the New Year's meal (**osechi-ryōri**) to bring good luck. This custom is believed to have started in the 15th century as part of a ritual offering of food to the **kami**. Grilled mochi (rice cake) is the main ingredient.

☒ In *Return of Lum: Trouble Times Ten* (p. 40) Lum and Ataru's family are getting ready for the New Year's meal. Notice the soup bowls, sake cups and flasks, and the lacquered **jūbako** boxes.

ZŌRI (THONGED SANDALS)

Traditionally zōri were made with a bamboo sole and woven from bamboo or grass. Modern zōri are cork soled with leather, plastic, or cloth. Raised heels are common on women's zōri. Zōri are often worn with **kimono** and split-toed socks called **tabi**. Zōri worn by men are called *setta*. Cruder straw sandals called *waraji* were commonly worn on long journeys.

☒ Shogoro Yano is wearing setta when he is first seen in *Sanshiro the Judoist* (pt. 1). • Tenchi's grandfather usually wears setta in *Tenchi Universe* (tp. 1, ep. 1).

Setta or *zōri*, woven or cloth covered, are a comfortable way to protect the feet.

ENGLISH-JAPANESE REVERSE LOOKUP GLOSSARY

abstinence: **tachimono**
acupuncture: **hari**
address: **atena**
adoption: **yōshi**
Air Self Defense Force: **jieitai**
alcove: **tokonoma**
altar, family, Buddhist: **butsudan**
altar, family, Shintō: **kamidana**
altar, memorial, Buddhist: **butsudan**
altar on wall: **kamidana**
amulet: **ofuda, omamori**
anniversary of death: **meinichi**
annual events: **matsuri to nenchū gyōji**
Aoyama Cemetery: **Aoyama Reien**
apparition: **bakemono**
apprentice geisha: **maiko**
apricot: **ume, umeboshi**
apron: **kappōgi**
archery: **kyūdō**
arranged marriage: **kon'in**
arranged marriage meeting: **omiai**
arrows, New Year's: **hamaya**
Asakusa Shrine: **Asakusa Jinja**
ascetic practice: **Shugendō, tachimono, yamabushi**
Awa Dance: **Awa Odori**

badger: **tanuki**
balls of floating fire: **hitodama**
bamboo flute: **shakuhachi**
bamboo pipe (garden decoration): **shishiodoshi**
bamboo sheath: **takenokawa**
bamboo sword: **shinai**
banners and standards: **hata, fū-rin-ka-zan, koinobori, matoi, nobori**
banquet: **enkai**
bar girl: **hosutesu**
baseball, high school: **kōkō yakyū**
basin at Shintō shrine: **temizuya**
bath, public: **sentō**
bath, public, at hot spring: **onsen**
bath in home: **furo**
Battle of Dannoura: **Dannoura no Tatakai**

battledore: **hagoita**
battledore market: **hagoita ichi**
beads: **magatama**
beckoning: **jesuchā**
beckoning cat: **manekineko**
bedding: **futon**
"beef bowl": **gyūdon**
beeper: **poke-beru**
beer: **bīru**
bell on rope at shrine: **suzu**
bell ringing at New Year's: **Joya no kane**
bell used in Buddhist service: **kei**
bell: **bonshō, kei, suzu**
belly: **hara**
belt: **obi**
betrothal gift: **yuinō**
bikers: **bōsōzoku**
blinds: **sudare**
blood type: **ketsueki-gata**
bloomers: **burūmā**
bodhisattva: **bosatsu, Jizō**
Bon dance: **Bon Odori**
bonfire: **okuribi**
bonus: **shōyo**
bow: **ojigi**
bowl: **chawan, donburi**
box lunch: **bentō**
Boys' Day: **Kodomo no Hi**
Boys' Festival: **Kodomo no Hi**
brain death: **zōki ishioku**
brazier: **shichirin**
breakfast: **chōshoku**
bride's headdress: **tsunokakushi**
bronze mirror: **seidōkyo**
Buddhism: **bukkyō**
Buddhist family altar: **butsudan**
Buddhist memorial altar: **butsudan**
Buddhist practice: **en no gyōja**
Buddhist prayer: **nenbutsu**
Buddhist rosary: **juzu**
Buddhist temple: **jiin**
Buddhist temple bell: **bonshō**
Bullet Train: **Shinkansen**
business card: **meishi**
business crest: **mon**

buying gifts on vacation: **miyage**

cabaret girl: **hosutesu**
calling card: **meishi**
card games: **hanafuda, uta karuta**
carp streamer: **koinobori**
carp: **koi**
carrying cloth: **furoshiki**
castle: **shiro**
cat: **neko**
censorship: **ken'etsu**
characters, Chinese: **kanji**
charm, Shintō: **ofuda, omamori**
cherry blossom: **sakura**
cherry blossom viewing: **hanami**
chess: **shōgi**; see also **go**
Children's Day: **Kodomo no Hi**
chop: **hanko**
chopsticks: **hashi**
Christianity: **Kirisutokyō**
Christmas: **Kurisumasu**
chrysanthemum: **kiku**
cicada sound: **semi**
Civil War period: **Sengoku jidai**
clapping hands: **kashiwade**
class number, homeroom: **homurūmu**
cleaning classroom: **school students cleaning classroom and grounds**
clothing. See "Clothing" in section "Entries Arranged by Category"
coffeehouse: **kissaten**
coffee shop: **kissaten**
colored cords on envelope or gift: **mizuhiki**
comb: **kushi**
comic books: **manga**
comic market: **Komiketto**
Communist Party of Japan: **Nihon Kyōsantō**
commuting: **tsūkin**
company housing: **shataku**
Confucianism: **Jukyō**
Constitution: **Nihonkoku Kenpō**
cooking apron: **kappōgi**
cowherd and weaver story: **Tanabata**

crab with face pattern: **heikegani**
cracker, rice: **senbei**
cram school: **yobikō**
crane: **tsuru**
cranes, a thousand: **senbazuru**
cremation: **kasō**
crest: **mon**
crow: **karasu**
cucumber: **kyūri**
cup and ball toy: **kendama**
curry rice: **karē raisu**
curtain: **noren**
cushion for sitting: **zabuton**
cuttlefish: **ika**

dance: **Awa Odori, Bon Odori**
death, legal definition of: **zōki ishi-oku**
death anniversary: **meinichi**
death fire: **hitodama**
decorative alcove: **tokonoma**
deer: **shika**
Democratic Socialist Party: **Minshatō**
demon: **oni, tengu**
department store: **depāto**
devil's tongue jelly: **konnyaku**
dice: **saikoro**
Diet or Parliament: **Kokkai**
directions to addresses: **atena**
divination: **sangi, mikuji, zeichiku**
doll display: **Hina Matsuri**
Doll Festival: **Hina Matsuri**
door: **fusuma, shōji**
dowry: **yuinō**
dream eater: **baku**
drink. See "Food and Drink" in section "Entries Arranged by Category"
drinks, mixing Japanese and Western: **chanpon**
drum: **taiko**
drunkard: **yopparai**
DSP: **Minshatō**
dumpling: **manjū**
duster: **hataki**

ear cleaning tool: **mimikaki**
ear scoop: **mimikaki**
earthquake: **jishin**

Economic Planning Agency: **Keizai Kikaku Chō**
eel: **unagi**
eggplant: **nasu**
electric rice cooker: **denki-gama**
emissary, imperial: **Tenshō Ken'ō Shisetsu**
engagement gift: **yuinō**
entryway where you remove shoes: **genkan**
EPA: **Keizai Kikaku Chō**
etiquette: **noodle slurping**
European mission: **Tenshō Ken'ō Shisetsu**
examination hell: **shiken jigoku**
exorcism: **tsukimono otoshi**

fair day: **ennichi**
fairy: **tennyo**
family altar, Shintō: **kamidana**
family crest: **mon**
fan: **ōgi** (folding), **uchiwa** (non-folding)
fanzine: **dōjinshi**
fart: **he**
feast day: **ennichi**
feng shui: **kasō**
ferryboat: **renraku-sen**
festival: **Bon, Hina Matsuri, Kodomo no Hi, matsuri to nenchū gyōji**
field trip: **shūgaku ryokō**
fire brigade standard: **matoi**
fire: **okuribi**
firearm: **teppō**
firefly: **hotaru**
fire pit: **irori**
fireworks: **firecrackers in the sky, hanabi**
fish cake: **tai-yaki**
fish ornaments on roof: **shachihoko**
fish paste swirl: **naruto**
fish-shaped percussion instrument: **mokugyo**
fish, goby: **haze**
flag: **fū-rin-ka-zan, koinobori, matoi, nobori**
flint and steel: **hiuchi-ishi**
floating balls of fire: **hitodama**

floor covering: **tatami**
floor cushion: **zabuton**
flower viewing: **hanami**
flute, bamboo: **shakuhachi**
food cart/mobile stall: **yatai**
food container: **donburi**
food model: **shokuhin sanpuru**
food. See "Food and Drink" in section "Entries Arranged by Category"
foods to not be eaten together: **mis-matched foods**
football, Japanese: **kemari**
foreigner: **gaijin**
form: **kata**
formal banquet: **enkai**
fortune stick: **mikuji**
fortunetelling: **mikuji, sangi, ze-ichiku**
fox: **Inari, kitsune**
fried noodles: **yakisoba**
funeral tablet, name on: **kaimyō**

game, Othello: **Osero**
games and sports. See "Entertainment/Game" and "Sport/Activity" in section "Entries Arranged by Category"
gangster: **yakuza**
garden decoration: **shishiodoshi**
gate pine: **kadomatsu**
gate: **torii**
geisha, apprentice: **maiko**
Genji family: **Minamoto**
geomancy: **kasō**
gesture: **inzō, jesuchā**
ghost: **yūrei**
ghost fire: **hitodama**
giant lantern float: **Nebuta Matsuri**
Gion temple bell: **Heike Monogatari**
Girls' Day: **Hina Matsuri**
globe fish: **fugu**
goby: **haze**
god: **kami**
goddess of the river: **Benten**
god of happiness, wealth, long life: **Jurōjin Fukurokuju**
god of thunder: **Raijin**
god vehicle: **shintai**

Goemon: **Ishikawa Goemon**
Golden Pavilion: **Kinkakuji**
goldfish: **kingyo**
goldfish dipping: **kingyo-sukui**
gourd: **hisago**
gravesite visit: **hakamairi**
graveyard, wooden stake in: **sotoba**
Great Wisdom Kings: **Fudō-Myōō**
Ground Self Defense Force: **Jieitai**
guardian gods: **jūni jinshō**
gun: **teppō**
gym shorts: **burūmā**

hairpin: **hana-kanzashi**
halberd: **naginata**
hand gesture: **inzō, jesuchā, kuji**
handkerchief: **hankachi**
Haneda Airport: **Tōkyō Kokusai Kūkō**
hanging scroll: **kakemono**
hat: **sando-gasa**
haunting: **goryō**
headband: **hachimaki**
Health and Welfare Ministry: **Kōseishō**
health drink: **eiyō drink**
Hearn, Lafcadio: **Koizumi Yakumo**
hearth: **irori**
heavenly maiden: **tennyo**
Heike family: **Taira**
Hida Mountains: **Hida Sanmyaku**
high school baseball: **kōkō yakyū**
historical period: **jidai**
holiday: **bon, ennichi, hina matsuri, kurismasu, Kodomo no Hi, nebuta matsuri, setsubun**
homeroom: **homurūmu**
horse's leg: **uma-yaku**
hostess: **hosutesu**
hot rodders: **bōsōzoku**
hot spring: **onsen**
hot spring, Azabu Number Ten: **Azabu Jūban**
hot tea over rice: **chazuke**
housecleaning: **susu-harai**
housing, company: **shataku**
hydrangea: **ajisai**

Ibaraki Prefecture: **Ibaraki Ken**
"idol" singer: **aidoru**
Imperial University: **Teikoku Daigaku**
indigenous Japanese: **Ainu**
inebriation: **yopparai**
ink: **sumi**
ink on face: **hanetsuki**
inn: **ryokan**
instrument: **biwa, shamisen**
Iris Festival: **Kodomo no Hi**
Izumo Province: **Izumo no kuni**
Izumo Shrine: **Izumo Taisha**

jacket worn over kimono: **haori**
Japan Broadcasting Corporation: **Nippon Hōsō Kyōkai**
Japan Communist Party: **Nihon Kyōsantō**
Japanese chess: **shōgi**
Japanese Industrial Standards: **Nihon Kōgyō Kikaku**
Japanese inn: **ryokan**
Japanese-style banquet: **enkai**
Japanese sword: **nihontō**
Japan Railways: **Jē Āru**
jelly fish: **kurage**
JIS: **Nihon Kōgyō Kikaku**
juvenile delinquent: **yankī**

Kamakura shogunate: **Kamakura period**
Kantō region: **Kantō chihō**
Keio Plaza Hotel: **Keio Puraza Hoteru**
kindergarten: **shūgakuzen kyōiku**
kiss: **kisu**
kitchen robe: **kappōgi**
kite flying: **tako-age**
Kiyomizu Temple: **Kiyomizudera**
knots, decorative: **mizuhiki**

lance: **naginata**
lantern festival: **Bon**
lantern, red: **aka-chōchin**
lantern, stone: **ishi-dōrō**
lanterns, hanging: **chōchin, tsuri-dōrō**

laver: **nori**
LDP: **Jiyū Minshutō**
legislature: **Kokkai**
Liberal Democratic Party: **Juyū Minshutō**
life force: **ki**
lightweight kimono: **yukata**
little finger: **jesuchā**
loanword: **gairaigo**
loincloth: **fundoshi**
Lolita complex: **rorikon**
lovers's suicide: **shinjū**
lunch box: **bentō, ekiben**
lute: **biwa**
lute priest: **biwa hōshi**

magic syllables: **kuji**
mah-jongg: **mājan**
mandarin orange: **mikan**
maple: **kaede to momiji**
Maritime Self Defense Force: **Jieitai**
marriage: **kon'in**
marriage ceremony: **shinzen kekkon**
martial art: **judō, jūjutsu, kendō, kyūdō, ninjutsu**
martial arts training hall: **dōjō**
mask: **okame, surgical masks worn in public**
massage parlor: **sōpurando**
master: **sensei**
mattress: **futon**
McDonald's: **Makudonarudo**
Meiji Shrine: **Meiji Jingū**
memorial altar, Buddhist: **butsudan**
men in black: **kurogo**
mermaid: **ningyo**
military art of the ninja: **ninjutsu**
miniature tree: **bonsai**
Ministry of Health and Welfare: **Kōseishō**
Ministry of International Trade and Industry: **Tsūshō Sangyō Shō**
mirror: **seidōkyō**
miso soup: **misoshiru**
Miyagi Prefecture: **Miyagi Ken**
money offering: **saisen**
monkey: **saru**

154

monkey show: **saru mawashi**
monk hat: **sando-gasa**
monster: **bakemono**
morning glory: **asagao**
motorcycle gang: **bōsōzoku**
mountain spirit: **tengu**
moxa treatment: **kyū**
moxibustion: **kyū**
Mt. Aso: **Asosan**
Mt. Fuji: **Fujisan**
Mt. Kōya: **Kōya-san**
Mt. Kurama: **Kuramayama**
mudra: **inzō**
musical instrument: **biwa, koto, mokugyo, shakuhachi, shamisen**
musician: **chindonya**

name card: **meishi**
name on funeral tablet: **kaimyō**
Narita Airport: **Shin Tōkyō Kokusai Kūkō**
neighborhood association: **chō-naikai**
new religions: **shinkō shūkyō**
New Tokyo International Airport: **Shin Tōkyō Kokusai Kūkō**
New Year's arrow: **hamaya**
New Year's bell ringing: **joya no kane**
New Year's card: **nengajō**
New Year's food: **osechi-ryōri**
New Year's ornament: **kadomatsu**
New Year's pine: **kadomatsu**
New Year's shrine or temple visit: **hatsumōde**
New Year's soup: **zōni**
New Year's temple bell: **joya no kane**
newspaper: **shinbun**
NHK: **Nippon Hōsō Kyōkai**
nine magic syllables: **kuji**
ninja: **ninjutsu**
Nippon Telegraph and Telephone Corporation: **Nippon Denshin Denwa**
noodles: **hiyamugi, sōmen; rāmen; yakisoba**
Northern Alps: **Hida Sanmyaku**

NRM: **shinkō shūkyō shinkō**
NTT: **Nippon Denshin Denwa**
nymph: **tennyo**

octopus: **tako**
octopus balls or dumplings: **takoyaki**
offering box at shrine or temple: **saisen**
office lady: **OL**
ogre: **oni**
oiled paper umbrella: **kasa**
on and *kun* readings: **kanji**
one-man orchestra: **chindonya**
orange: **mikan**
organizational crest: **mon**
organ transplant: **zōki ishioku**
origami: **senbazuru**
Osaka Tower: **Tsūtenkaku**
outdoor stall: **yatai**
"out with bad luck, in with good" (*oni wa soto, fuku wa uchi*): **setsubun**
ox-drawn carriage: **gissha**

pager: **poke-beru**
palanquin: **kago, koshi, mikoshi**
pancake: **okonomiyaki**
paper, umbrella: **kasa**
paper streamer: **gohei**
paper strip: **tanzaku**
Parliament: **kokkai**
party: **enkai**
pay phone: **denwa**
Peach Boy: **Momotarō**
Peach Festival: **hina matsuri**
period, historical: **jidai kubun**
pickle: **tsukemono, umeboshi**
pickled apricot: **umeboshi**
pickled plum: **umeboshi**
pilgrimage: **junrei**
pillow: **makura**
pinball: **pachinko**
pipe, tobacco: **kiseru**
pissing in public: **tachishōben**
pizza: **okonomiyaki**
plum: **ume, umeboshi**
poem card: **uta karuta**
pocket door: **tobukuro**

poetry card game: **uta karuta**
police, riot: **kidōtai**
Police, Tōkyō Metropolitan: **Keishichō**
police box: **kōban**
police truncheon, Edo period: **jitte**
pop singer: **aidoru**
porridge: **kayu**
portable shrine: **mikoshi**
posthumous Buddhist name: **kaimyō**
pot hook: **jizaikagi**
potstickers: **gyōza**
prayer beads: **juzu**
prayer: **inori, nenbutsu**
preschool education: **shūgakuzen kyōku**
priestess, Shintō: **miko**
prime minister: **Okada Keisuke**
Prize, Akutagawa: **Akutagawa shō**
puffer fish: **fugu**
puppet play: **bunraku**

rabu hoteru: **love hotels**
raccoon dog: **tanuki**
radish: **daikon**
rain charm: **teruteru bōzu**
raincoat made from reeds: **mino**
rain doors: **amado**
rainwear: **mino**
red and white: **aka to shiro**
red lantern: **aka-chōchin**
red sake cups at wedding: **sakazuki**
reed raincoat: **mino**
rice, cooked: **gohan**
rice ball: **nigirimeshi**
rice bowl: **chawan**
rice cake: **kashiwa mochi, mochi**
rice cooker: **denki-gama**
rice cracker: **senbei**
rice kami: **Inari**
rice porridge: **kayu**
rickshaw: **jinrikisha**
rifle: **teppō**
riot police: **kidōtai**
ritual suicide: **harakiri, kaishakunin, seppuku**
rope, sacred: **shimenawa**
rosary: **juzu**

round bell on rope at shrine: **suzu**
Russo-Japanese War: **Nichiro Sensō**

sacred rope: **shimenawa**
sacred tree: **shinboku**
sailor suit: **sailor fuku**
sake, spiced: **toso**
sake cup: **choko, masuzake,
  sakazuki**
sake flask: **tokkuri**
salaried man: **sararīman**
samurai, masterless: **rōnin**
sand shaped like stars: **hoshi-suna**
sandals: **geta, zōri**
sash: **obi**
satsuma orange: **mikan**
scattering soybeans: **setsubun**
school trip: **shūgaku ryokō**
school uniform, girl's: **sailor fuku**
scissors paper stone: **jan-ken**
scraper: **ichimonji**
scroll, hanging: **kakemono**
SDF: **Jieitai**
sea goddess: **Benten**
seal: **hanko**
seasonal symbol: **Awa Odori, Bon
  Odori, hotaru, kadomatsu, kiku,
  matsuri to nenchū gyōji**
seaweed: **nori**
Self Defense Forces: **jieitai**
seven deities of good fortune:
  Shichifuku-jin
7-5-3 Festival: **Shichi-go-san**
Seven Lucky Gods: **Shichifuku-jin**
shaking hands: **akushu-suru**
shaved ice: **kakigōri-ki**
shell-matching game: **kai-awase**
Shintō charm and talisman: **ofuda,
  omamori**
Shintō family altar: **kamidana**
Shintō heaven: **Takamagahara**
Shintō religious costume: **saifuku**
Shintō shrine handwashing area:
  temizuya
Shintō shrine: **jinja**
Shintō wedding: **shinzen kekkon**
shout: **ki-ai**
shrine card: **senja-fuda**

shrine gate: **torii**
shutter, box for storing: **tobukuro**
shuttlecock game: **hanetsuki**
signature: **hanko**
sitting cushion: **zabuton**
skiing: **sukī**
slips of paper pasted to temples and
  shrines: **senja-fuda**
sneeze: **kushami**
soapland: **sōpurando**
socks with split toe: **tabi**
sōmen: **hiyamugi, sōmen**
song style: **enka**
sorceress: **miko**
soup: **misoshiru, zōni**
souvenir: **miyage**
soybean paste: **miso**
soybean: **miso, nattō, Setsubun**
soy sauce: **shoyu**
sparkler: **senkō-hanabi**
spatula: **ichimonji**
spiced sake: **toso**
spirit lights: **hitodama**
spy: **ninjutsu**
square wooden box for sake: **masu**
squid: **ika**
stacked boxes used for holding food:
  jūbako
stage: **yagura**
stagehand: **kurogo**
stamina drink: **eiyō drink**
standards and banners: **fū-rin-ka-
  zan, koinobori, matoi**
standing under a waterfall: **mizugori**
statue of man and dog in park: **Saigō
  Takamori**
stickers in phone booth: **pinkku bira**
stickers pasted to temples and
  shrines: **senja-fuda**
stilts, "bamboo horse": **takeuma**
stone dogs: **koma-inu**
stone lantern: **ishi-dōrō**
stone lions: **koma-inu**
storm shutters: **amado, tobukuro**
straw raincoat: **mino**
straw rope: **shimenawa**
streamers on a stick: **gohei**
street vendor: **yatai**

suicide, group: **shinjū**
suicide: **seppuku, kaishakunin,
  shinjū**
sun goddess: **Amaterasu Ōmikami**
supernatural being: **bakemono,
  baku, oni, kappa, kami, kitsune,
  tanuki, tengu**
supernatural cat: **bakemononeko**
sweet potato: **satsumaimo**
syllabary: **kana**

table: **chabudai, kotatsu**
tag: **onigokko**
Takarazuka Opera Company:
  Takarazuka Kagekidan
taking off shoes: **genkan**
talisman, Shintō: **ofuda, omamori**
tangerine: **mikan**
Tango Festival: **Kodomo no Hi**
tapir: **baku**
tattoo: **irezumi**
taxi: **takushī**
tea: **cha**
tea bowl: **chawan**
tea ceremony: **cha-no-yu**
teacher: **sensei**
telephone: **denwa**
temple bell: **bonshō**
temple dogs: **koma-inu**
Temple of the Golden Pavilion:
  Kinkakuji
tennis: **tenisu**
Third Month Festival: **hina matsuri**
throwing soybeans: **setsubun**
TMPD: **Keishichō**
toilet, Japanese: **benjo**
Tokyo City Hall: **Tōkyō Tochōsha**
Tokyo Dome: **Tōkyō Dōmu**
Tokyo International Airport: **Tōkyō
  Kokusai Kūkō**
Tokyo Metropolitan Government Of-
  fices: **Tōkyō Tochōsha**
Tokyo Metropolitan Police:
  Keishichō
Tokyo Station: **Tōkyō Eki**
Tokyo Tower: **Tōkyō Tawā**
Tokyo University: **Tōkyō Daigaku**
tossing soybeans: **setsubun**

town committee or council: **chō-naikai**
toy: **kaishakunin,**
training hall: **dōjō**
train: **commuter trains, Shinkansen**
tree, sacred: **shinboku**
turkish bath: **sōpurando**
twelve guardians of yakushi-nyorai: **jūni-jinshō**
typhoon: **taifū**

Ueno Park: **Ueno Kōen**
Ueno Zoo: **Ueno Dōbutsuen**
umbrella: **kasa**
underwear: **fundoshi**
university: **Teikoku Daigaku**
urinating in the street: **tachishōben**

Vajra: **kongōshō**
Valentine's Day: **Sei Barentain no Shukujitsu**
vending machine: **jidō-hambaiki**

vengeful ghost: **goryō**
veranda: **engawa**
visiting grave: **meinichi, hakamairi**
visiting shrine: **hatsumōde**
vitamin drink: **eiyō drink**
volcano: **Asamayama, Aso-san**
votive card: **senja-fuda**

wallet: **inrō**
Warring States period: **Sengoku jidai**
Waseda University: **Waseda Daigaku**
water, used in purification: **misogi, mizugori**
watermelon smashing with a stick: **suika-wari**
waving: **jesuchā**
"Way of the Sword": **kendō**
weapon. See "Weaponry/War" in section "Entries Arranged by Category"

wearing surgical mask on the street: **surgical masks worn in public**
wedding ceremony: **shinzen kekkon**
white costume for religious ceremony: **saifuku**
willow: **yanagi**
wind bell: **fūrin**
wind, forest, fire, mountain: **fū-rin-ka-zan**
wooden paddle for game: **hagoita**
wooden plaques, hanging: **ema**
wooden sandals: **geta**
wooden stakes in graveyard: **sotoba**
wooden sword: **bokken**
word game: **shiritori**
wrapping cloth: **furoshiki**
wrestling: **sumō**
writing: **kanji, kana**

Yankee: **yankī**
year's end cleaning: **susu-harai**
yin-yang block: **sangi**

ENTRIES ARRANGED BY CATEGORY

Building/Structure/Landmark

Aoyama Reien
Asakusa Jinja
Budōkan
depāto (department store)
dōjō (training hall)
Hōryūji
Ise Jingū (Ise Shrine)
Izumo Taisha
jiin (Buddhist temple)
jinja (Shintō shrine)
Kaminarimon
Keio Puraza Hoteru (Keio Plaza Hotel)
Kinkakuji (Temple of the Golden Pavilion)
kissaten (coffeehouse)
Kiyomizudera
kōban (police box)
Meiji Jingū (Meiji shrine)

My City
Nihonbashi
rabu hoteru (love hotel)
ryokan (Japanese inn)
Sensōji
sentō (public bath)
Shin Tōkyō Kokusai Kūkō (New Tokyo International Airport)
shiro (castle)
Teikoku Daigaku (Imperial Universities)
Tōkyō Daigaku (Tokyo Unitversity)
Tōkyō Dōmu
Tōkyō Eki (Tokyo Station)
Tōkyō Kokusai Kūkō
Tōkyō Tawa (Tokyo Tower)
Tōkyō Tochōsha (Tokyo Metropolitan Government Offices)
Tsūtenkaku (Osaka Tower)
Ueno Dōbutsuen (Ueno Zoo)

Ueno Eki (Ueno Train Station)
Ueno Kōen (Ueno Park)
Waseda Daigaku (Waseda University)

Clothing

burūma (gym shorts worn by girls)
fundoshi (loincloth)
geta (wooden sandals)
hachimaki (headband)
hakama (trousers)
hana-kanzashi (hairpin)
haori (jacket)
happi (coat)
inrō
kappōgi (cooking apron)
kimono
kushi (comb)

mino (rainwear)
obi (sash, belt)
sailor fuku (sailor suit)
sando-gasa (hat)
tabi (split-toed sock)
tsunokakushi (headdress)
yukata (lightweight kimono)
zōri (thonged sandals)

Culture

aka to shiro (red and white)
akushu suru (shaking hands)
Akutagawa Shō
Awa Odori
bakemono (monster)
bakeneko (monster cat)
baku (dream eater)
banzai
biwa
cha-no-yu (tea ceremony)
Crane Wife
dogs and pregnant women
drinks, pouring for another
four things to fear in life
gairaigo (loanword)
goryō (vengeful ghost)
hanami (flower viewing)
hatsumōde
Hina Matsuri (Doll Festival)
kana (syllabary)
kanji (chinese character)
Kintarō
Kodomo no Hi (Children's Day)
koinobori (carp streamer)
kon'in (marriage)
koto
Kurisumasu (Christmas)
Man'yōshū
matsuri to nenchū gyōji (festivals
    and annual events)
mokugyo
Nebuta Matsuri (Nebuta Festival)
nengajō (New Year's card)
ningyo (mermaid)
ojigi(bow)
okuribi (ritual bonfire)
omiai
oni (demon)

Sei Barentain no Shukujitsu (Valen-
    tine's Day)
Setsubun
shakuhachi
shamisen
Shichi-go-san (7-5-3 Festival)
shinzen kekkon (Shintō wedding)
taiko (large drum)
Tanabata
tengu (mountain spirit)
White Day
yobikō (cram school)
yūrei (ghost)

Entertainment/Game

aidoru ("idol" singer)
bunraku
chindonya (music maker)
dōjinshi (fanzine)
enka (popular song)
enkai (party)
firecrackers in the sky
go
hagoita (paddle)
hanabi (fireworks)
hanafuda
jan-ken
kai-awase (shell-matching game)
karaoke
kendama (cup and ball toy)
kingyo-sukui (goldfish dipping)
Komiketto
kurogo (stagehand)
mājan (mah-jongg)
manga (Japanese comic)
okame
onigokko (tag)
Osero ("Othello")
pachinko
saikoro (dice)
saru mawashi (monkey show)
senkō-hanabi (sparkler)
shiritori (word game)
shōgi (Japanese "chess")
suika-wari (watermelon game)
Takarazuka Kagekidan (Takarazuka
    Opera Company)
takeuma (bamboo horse or stilts)

tako-age (kite flying)
uma-yaku
uta karuta (poem card)
yagura (stage)

Food and Drink

anmitsu
bentō (box lunch for one person)
bīru (beer)
Boss Coffee
Calpis
cha (tea)
chanpon
chazuke
choko (sake cup)
chōshoku (breakfast)
daikon (radish)
donburi (food bowl)
eiyō drink (nutritional supplement
    drink)
ekiben (station) lunch
fugu (puffer fish)
gohan (cooked rice)
gyōza (potsticker)
gyūdon (beef bowl)
hashi (chopsticks)
haze (goby)
hisago (gourd)
hiyamugi, sōmen (noodles)
ika (squid and cuttlefish)
kakigōri-ki (shaved ice)
karē raisu (curry rice)
kashiwa mochi
kayu (rice porridge)
konnyaku (devil's tongue root)
kyūri (cucumber)
manjū (bun, dumpling)
masu (box measure)
mikan
mismatched foods
miso (soy bean paste)
misoshiru (miso soup)
mochi (rice cake)
naruto
nasu (eggplant)
nattō
nigirimeshi (rice ball)
noodle slurping

nori (seaweed, laver)
oden
okonomiyaki
osechi-ryōri (New Year's food)
rāmen (noodles)
sakazuki (sake cup)
sake
satsumaimo (sweet potato)
senbei (rice cracker)
shabu-shabu
shichirin (ceramic brazier)
shiruko
shokuhin sanpuru (food model)
shōyu (soy sauce)
sukiyaki
sushi
tai-yaki
takenokawa (bamboo sheath)
tako (octopus)
takoyaki
tokkuri (sake flask)
toso
tsukemono (pickle)
UCC Coffee
ume
umeboshi (salted Japanese apricot)
umeshu (plum "wine")
unagi (eel)
yakisoba (noodles)
yakitori
zōni

General

aka-chōchin (red lantern)
atena (address)
benjo (toilet)
bōsōzoku (gang)
chalk marks and illegally parked
    cars
chōchin (hanging paper lantern)
commuter train
denwa (telephone)
hachikō
hankachi (handkerchief)
hanko (seal)
hara (stomach, belly)
hari (acupuncture)
he (fart)

headlights off
hiuchi-ishi (flint and steel)
homurūmu (homeroom)
irezumi (tattoo)
ishi-dōrō (stone lantern)
Jē Aru (JR)
jidō-hanbaiki (vending machine)
jinrikisha (rickshaw)
kago (sedan chair)
kaishakunin
kappa
kasa (umbrella)
kasō (cremation)
kasō (geomancy)
ketsueki-gata (blood type)
ki (spirit, life force)
ki-ai (shout)
kiseru (tobacco pipe)
kisu (kiss)
koshi (palanquin)
kushami (sneeze)
kyū (moxibustion)
magatama (beads)
Makudonarudo (McDonald's)
manekineko ("beckoning cat")
meishi (business card)
mimikaki (ear scoop)
miyage (souvenir)
mizuhiki (decorative cords)
mother-in-law
neko (cat)
Nippon Denshin Denwa (Nippon
    Telegraph and Telephone
    Corporation)
Nippon Hōsō Kyōkai (Japan Broad-
    casting Corporation)
noren (split curtains)
ōgi (folding fan)
otaku
pinkku bira ("pink leaflets")
poke-beru (beeper)
red triangle
renraku-sen (ferryboat)
rorikon ("lolita complex")
sangi (yin-yang divination block)
seidōkyō (bronze mirror)
senbazuru (origami paper cranes)
shiken jigoku (examination hell)
shinbun (newspaper)

shinjū (double or group suicide)
Shinkansen (New Trunk Line, Bullet
    Train)
shishiodoshi (deer scare)
shōyo (bonus)
shūgaku ryokō (school trip)
shūgakuzen kyōiku (preschool
    education)
sōpurando ("soapland")
students cleaning school
sumi (ink)
surgical masks worn in public
suzu (round bells)
tachishōben (peeing in the street)
takushi (taxi)
tanzaku
tsūkin (commuting)
tsuri-dōrō (hanging lantern)
uchiwa (non-folding fan)
water holding as punishment
yatai (outdoor stall)
yōshi (adoption)
yuinō (betrothal gift)
zōki ishioku (organ transplant)

Geographical Feature/Location

Aichi Ken
Akashi
Akihabara
Aoyama
Asakusa
Asamayama
Aso-san (Mt. Aso)
Atami
Azabu Jūban
Chiba Ken
Dotonbori
Enoshima
Fuji-san (Mt. Fuji)
Ginza
Gion
Hakone
Harajuku
Hayama
Hida Sanmyaku
Hiroshima
Hokkaido
Honshu

Ibaraki Ken
Iruma
Ise
Izumo
Kamakura
Kanagawa Ken
Kantō Chihō (Kantō region)
Kōya-san (Mt. Kōya)
Kuramayama
Kyoto
Kyushu
Miyagi Ken
Nagasaki
Okinawa Ken
Onomichi
Ōsaka
Roppongi
Sapporo
Shimane Ken
Shinjuku
Ueno

History/Society

chōnaikai (neighborhood association)
Edo Period
February 26, 1936
fū-rin-ka-zan
gissha (ox cart)
hata (ceremonial banner)
Heian Period
Heike Monogatari
Heisei Period
Jiyū Minshutō (Liberal Democratic Party)
Jukyō (Confucianism)
Kamakura Period
Keishichō (Tōkyō Metropolitan Police Department)
Keizai Kikaku Chō (Economic Planning Agency)
ken'etsu (censorship)
Kokkai (Diet)
Kōseishō (Ministry of Health and Welfare)
matoi (banner, standard)
Meiji Period
Minamoto

Minshatō (Democratic Socialist Party)
mon (family or organizational crest)
Muromachi Period
Nihon Kōgyō Kikaku (Japanese Industrial Standards)
Nihonkoku Kenpō (Constitution of Japan)
Nihon Kyōsantō (Japanese Communist Party)
ninjutsu
nobori (banner)
Sengoku Jidai
seppuku (ritual suicide)
taira
tenshō ken'ō shisetsu
Tokugawa
Tsūshō Sangyō Shō (Ministry of International Trade and Industry)

Home

amado (rain doors)
chabudai
chawan (small bowl)
denki-gama (electric rice cooker)
engawa (veranda)
fūrin (wind bell)
furo (bath)
furoshiki (carrying cloth)
fusuma
futon
genkan (entryway)
hataki
hibachi (charcoal heater)
ichimonji (spatula)
irori (sunken hearth)
jizaikagi (pot hook)
jūbako (stacking boxes)
kadomatsu (pine gate)
kakemono (hanging scroll)
kotatsu
makura (pillow)
ranma (transom)
renting
shachihoko (dolphin roof ornament)
shataku (company housing)
shōji
sudare (hanging blinds)

susu-harai (end-of-year-house-cleaning)
tatami
tobukuro (pocket door)
tokonoma (decorative alcove)
zabuton (floor cushion)

Nature

ajisai (Japanese hydrangea)
asagao (morning glory)
bonsai
ginkgo
heikegani
hoshi-suna ("star" sand)
hotaru (firefly)
jishin (earthquake)
kaede to momoji (maple tree)
karasu (crow)
kiku (chrysanthemum)
kingyo (goldfish)
kitsune (fox)
koi (carp)
kurage (jellyfish)
onsen (hot spring)
sakura (cherry blossom)
saru (monkey)
semi (cicada)
shika (deer)
taifū (typhoon)
tanuki
tsuru (crane)
yanagi (willow)

People

aging population
Ainu
Akagawa Jirō
Akutagawa Ryūnosuke
Bakin
Benkei
biwa hōshi ("lute priest")
Dōgen
En no Gyōja
Enomoto Ken'ichi
gaijin (foreigner)
geisha
Genji

Hayashi Fumiko
Hearn, Lafcadio
Higuchi Ichiyō
hosutesu ("hostess")
Ishihara Shintarō
Ishikawa Goemon
Izumi Kyōka
Kawabata Yasunari
kidōtai (riot police)
Kume Masao
Kurama Tengu
maiko (apprentice geisha)
miko (shrine maiden)
Minamoto no Yorimitsu
Minamoto no Yoshitsune
Miyamoto Musashi
Miyazawa Kenji
Momotarō (Peach Boy)
Mori Ōgai
Murasaki Shikubu
Mushanokōji Saneatsu
Natsume Sōseki
Okada Keisuke
OL ("office lady")
Ōtomo no Yakamochi
Ozaki Shirō
rōnin
Saigō Takamori
Saigyō
samurai
sarariman ("salaried man")
senpai (senior)
sensei (teacher, master)
Shinran
shōgun
Tanizaki Jun'ichirō
Toyotomi Hideyoshi
Urashima Tarō
yakuza (gangster)
yankī ("yankee," juvenile delin-
 quent)
yopparai (a drunk)

Religion/Mythology/Belief

Amaterasu Ōmikami
Benten
Bishamon
Bon

Bon Odori
bonshō
bosatsu (boddhisattva)
Bukkyō
butsudan (Buddhist altar)
daikokuten
daruma
ebisu
ema (votive tablet)
ennichi (feast day)
fudō-myōō
fukurokuju
gohei
hakamairi
hamaya
hitodama (spirit lights)
Hotei
inari
inori (prayer)
inzō
Jizō
Joya no kane
Jūni Jinshō
junrei (pilgrimage)
juzu (rosary)
kaimyō
kami
kamidana (Shintō altar)
kashiwade
kei (bell)
Kirisutokyō (Christianity)
koma-inu
kongōshō (vajra)
kuji
meinichi (death anniversary)
mikoshi (portable shrine)
mikuji (fortune stick)
misogi (purification)
mizugori (waterfall purification)
nenbutsu
ofuda
okiku
omamori (amulet)
Raijin (god of thunder)
saifuku
saisen (money offering)
senja-fuda (shrine card)
Shichifuku-jin (seven deities of good
 fortune)

shimenawa (sacred rope)
shinboku (sacred tree)
shinkō shūkyō (new religion)
shintai ("kami-body")
Shintō
shugendō
sotoba
Susanoo-no-mikoto
tachimono (something abstained
 from)
Takamagahara (plain of high heav-
 en)
temizuya
tennyo (heavenly maiden, nymph,
 angel)
teruteru bōzu (rain doll)
torii (shrine gate)
tsukimono otoshi (exorcism)
yamabushi (mountain ascetic)
Zashiki Warashi
Zenki

Sport/Activity

hanetsuki
jūdō
jūjutsu
kata (form or sequence)
kemari (Japanese football)
kendō ("way of the sword")
kōkō yakyū (high school baseball)
kyūdō (Japanese archery)
sukī (skiing)
sumō
tenisu (tennis)

Weaponry/War

bokken (wooden sword)
Dannoura no Tatakai
Jieitai (Self Defense Forces; SDF)
jitte (truncheon)
naginata (halberd)
Nichiro Sensō (Russo-Japanese War)
nihontō (Japanese sword)
shinai (bamboo sword)
teppō (firearm)

SELECTED REFERENCES

Arai, Yūsei. *Shingon Esoteric Buddhism: A Handbook for Followers*. Translated by Dr. George Tanabe, Rev. Seichō Asahi, and Rev. Shoken (Ana) Harada. Edited and adapted by Rev. Eijun (Bill) Edison. Fresno, Calif.: Shingon Buddhist International Institute, 1997.

Bisignani, J. D. *Japan Handbook*. 2nd ed. Chico, Calif.: Moon Publications, 1993.

Blacker, Carmen. *The Catalpa Bow: A Study of Shamanistic Practices in Japan*. 2nd ed. London and Boston: G. Allen & Unwin, 1986.

Bocking, Brian. *A Popular Dictionary of Shinto*. Richmond, Surrey: Curzon Books, 1996.

Bornoff, Nicholas. *Pink Samurai: Love, Marriage, and Sex in Contemporary Japan*. New York: Pocket Books, 1991.

Carroll, John. *Trails of Two Cities: A Walker's Guide to Yokohama and Kamakura*. Tokyo and New York: Kodansha International, 1994.

Clements, Jonathan. "Japan Rocks." *Anime UK New Series*, vol. 1, no. 3 (New Series, issue 3, May 1995), pp. 12–13.

Condon, Jack, and Camy Condon. *The Simple Pleasures of Japan*. Tokyo: Shufunotomo, 1975.

Condon, John, and Keisuke Kurata. *In Search of What's Japanese about Japan*. Tokyo: Shufunotomo, 1974.

De Mente, Boye. *Bachelor's Japan*. Tokyo: Yenbooks, 1991.

———. *Behind the Japanese Bow*. Lincolnwood, Ill.: Passport Books, 1993.

———. *Etiquette Guide to Japan: Know the Rules That Make the Difference*. Tokyo: Yenbooks, 1990.

Discover Japan. Previously published as *A Hundred Things Japanese* and *A Hundred More Things Japanese*. Tokyo and New York: Kodansha International, vol. 1, 1982; vol. 2, 1983.

Draeger, Donn F. *Classical Budo*. New York: Weatherhill, 1990.

———. *Classical Bujutsu*. New York: Weatherhill, 1990.

Earhart, H. Byron. *A Religious Study of the Mount Haguro Sect of Shugendo: An Example of Japanese Mountain Religion*. Tokyo: Sophia University, 1970.

Eating in Japan. Edited by Japan Travel Bureau. Tokyo: Nihon Kōtsū Kōsha Shuppan Jigyōkyoku, 1995.

Enbutsu, Sumiko. *Old Tokyo: Walks in the City of the Shogun*. Tokyo and Rutland, Vt.: Charles E. Tuttle, 1993.

Festivals of Japan. Edited by Japan Travel Bureau. Tokyo: Nihon Kōtsū Kōsha Shuppan Jigyōkyoku, 1993.

Frederic, Louis. *Dictionary of the Martial Arts*. Translation of *Dictionnaire des arts martiaux*. Translated and edited by Paul Crompton. Tokyo and Rutland, Vt.: Charles E. Tuttle, 1995.

Gluck, Jay; Sumi Gluck; and Garet Gluck. *Japan Inside Out*. Revised edition. New York: Weatherhill, 1989.

Hosking, Richard. *A Dictionary of Japanese Food: Ingredients and Culture*. Tokyo and Rutland, Vt.: Charles E. Tuttle, 1996.

Huddleston, Daniel. "Kenji Miyazawa." *Animerica*, vol. 6, no. 1, pp. 8–9, 26–29.

"Idol Chatter." *Animerica*, vol. 5, no. 2, pp. 8–9.

Inagaki, Hisao. *A Dictionary of Japanese Buddhist Terms: Based on References in Japanese Literature* [Nichi-Ei Bukkyōgo Jiten]. Kyoto: Nagata Bunshōdō, 1984.

International Congress for the History of Religions. *Basic Terms of Shinto*. Tokyo: Jinja Honchō (Association of Shintō Shrines), 1958.

Japan: An Illustrated Encyclopedia. Tokyo and New York: Kodansha, 1993.

Japanese Family and Culture. Edited by Japan Travel Bureau. Tokyo: Nihon Kōtsū Kōsha Shuppan Jigyōkyoku, 1995.

Japanese Inn and Travel. Edited by Japan Travel Bureau. Tokyo: Nihon Kōtsū Kōsha Shuppan Jigyōkyoku, 1990.

Joya, Mock. *Japanese Customs and Manners*. Tokyo: Sakurai Shoten, 1953.

———. *Mock Joya's Things Japanese*. 3rd ed. Tokyo: Tokyo News Service, 1961.

KEK Kokusai Koryūkai. *Taiken Shiyō: Nihon no Bunka* (Experiencing Japanese Culture: An Activity and Q-A Approach). Tokyo: Apricot, 1989.

Living in Japan. 11th ed. Tokyo: American Chamber of Commerce in Japan, 1993.

Living Japanese Style. 13th ed. Edited by Japan Travel Bureau. Tokyo: Nihon Kōtsū Kōsha Shuppan Jigyōkyoku, 1994.

Look into Japan, A. Edited by Japan Travel Bureau. Tokyo: Nihon Kōtsū Kōsha Shuppan Jigyōkyoku, 1986.

Look into Tokyo, A. 6th ed. Edited by Japan Travel Bureau. Tokyo: Nihon Kōtsū Kōsha Shuppan Jigyōkyoku, 1991.

Martial Arts and Sports in Japan. Edited by Japan Travel Bureau. Tokyo: Nihon Kōtsū Kōsha Shuppan Jigyōkyoku, 1993.

Morse, Edward S. *Japanese Homes and Their Surroundings.* Reprint of 1886 edition. New York: Dover Publications, 1961.

Must-See in Kyoto. 7th ed. Edited by Japan Travel Bureau. Tokyo: Nihon Kōtsū Kōsha Shuppan Jigyōkyoku, 1991.

Must-See in Nikko. 3rd ed. Edited by Japan Travel Bureau. Tokyo: Nihon Kōtsū Kōsha Shuppan Jigyōkyoku, 1991.

Oshiguchi, Takashi. "On Idols and Anime." *Animerica,* vol. 5, no. 2, p. 61.

Outlook on Japan. Edited by Japan Travel Bureau. Tokyo: Nihon Kōtsū Kōsha Shuppan Jigyōkyoku, 1987.

Palter, D. C. "Tonic Eiyo Drinks." *Mangajin,* no. 21 (October 1992), pp. 12–17.

Parker, L. Craig. *The Japanese Police System Today: An American Perspective.* Tokyo and New York: Kodansha International, 1987.

Pictorial Encyclopedia of Japanese Life and Events. Tokyo: Gakken, 1993.

Piggott, Juliet. *Japanese Mythology.* New York: Peter Bedrick Books, 1983.

Richie, Donald. *A Taste of Japan: Food Fact and Fable: What the People Eat, Customs and Etiquette.* Tokyo and New York: Kodansha International, 1985.

Rohlen, Thomas P. *Japan's High Schools.* Berkeley: University of California Press, 1983.

"Salaryman" in Japan. Edited by Japan Travel Bureau. Tokyo: Nihon Kōtsū Kōsha Shuppan Jigyōkyoku, 1991.

Saphir, Ann. "Ketsueki-gata: Japan's Answer to 'What's Your Sign?'" *Mangajin,* no. 41 (December 1994), pp. 14–19, 50, 87.

Sato, Ikuya. *Kamikaze Biker: Parody and Anomy in Affluent Japan.* Chicago: University of Chicago Press, 1991.

Schodt, Frederik L. *America and the Four Japans: Friend, Foe, Model, Mirror.* Berkeley: Stone Bridge Press, 1994.

———. *Dreamland Japan: Writings on Modern Manga.* Berkeley: Stone Bridge Press, 1996.

———. *Inside the Robot Kingdom: Japan, Mechatronics, and the Coming Robotopia.* Tokyo and New York: Kodansha International, 1988.

———. *Manga! Manga! The World of Japanese Comics.* Tokyo and New York: Kodansha International, 1983.

Schuhmacher, Stephan, and Gert Woerner, eds. *The Encyclopedia of Eastern Philosophy and Religion: Buddhism, Hinduism, Taoism, Zen.* Translated by Michael H. Kohn, Karen Ready, and Werner Wünsche. Boston: Shambhala, 1989.

Silverman, Laura K., ed. *Bringing Home the Sushi.* Atlanta: Mangajin, 1995.

Today's Japan. Edited by Japan Travel Bureau. Tokyo: Nihon Kōtsū Kōsha Shuppan Jigyōkyoku, 1991.

Tuttle, Charles E. *Incredible Japan.* Tokyo and Rutland, Vt.: Charles E. Tuttle, 1975.

Vardaman, James M., and Michiko Sakaki Vardaman. *Japanese Etiquette Today: A Guide to Business and Social Customs.* Tokyo and Rutland, Vt.: Charles E. Tuttle, 1994.

———. *Japan from A to Z: Mysteries of Everyday Life Explained.* Tokyo: Yenbooks, 1995.

Waterhouse, David. "Notes on the Kuji." In *Religion in Japan,* edited by P. F. Kornicki and I. J. McMullen, pp. 1–38. Cambridge: Cambridge University Press, 1996.

Who's Who of Japan. Edited by Japan Travel Bureau. Tokyo: Nihon Kōtsū Kōsha Shuppan Jigyōkyoku, 1991.

Young Women's Christian Association, Tokyo, World Fellowship Committee. *Japanese Etiquette: An Introduction.* Tokyo and Rutland, Vt.: Charles E. Tuttle, 1955.

REMEMBER!

For the latest Anime Companion news and updates, check out the Anime Companion Web Supplement at **http://www.sirius.com/~cowpunk/**.

ALSO OF INTEREST